W9-BVR-905

SWAIN SC
Harry Furniss

Sylvie and Bruno

by Lewis Carroll

With the 46 Original Illustrations
by Harry Furniss
and a New Introduction
by Martin Gardner

DOVER PUBLICATIONS, INC.
New York

Published in Canada by General Publishing Company, Ltd., 30 Lesmill Road, Don Mills, Toronto, Ontario.

Published in the United Kingdom by Constable and Company, Ltd.

This Dover edition, first published in 1988, is an unabridged, unaltered republication of the first edition as published by Macmillan and Co., London, 1889 (dated 1890). A new Introduction has been specially written for the Dover edition by Martin Gardner.

Manufactured in the United States of America
Dover Publications, Inc.
31 East 2nd Street
Mineola, N.Y. 11501

Library of Congress Cataloging-in-Publication Data

Carroll, Lewis, 1832–1898.
Sylvie and Bruno / by Lewis Carroll ; with the 46 original illustrations by Harry Furniss ; and a new introduction by Martin Gardner.
p. cm.
Includes index.
Summary: Two little children meet adventure in such places as Dogland, Outland, and Elfland.
ISBN 0-486-25588-3 (pbk.)
[1. Fantasy.] I. Furniss, Harry, 1854–1925, ill. II. Title.
PR4611.S9 1988
823′.8 [Fic]—dc19 87-31870
CIP
AC

INTRODUCTION TO THE DOVER EDITION.

Ever drifting down the stream—
Lingering in the golden gleam—
Life, what is it but a dream?

THE lines above are the final stanza of the poem that closes the second *Alice* book, *Through the Looking-Glass.* The first letters of each line of the poem spell the name of Alice Pleasance Liddell, Lewis Carroll's most-loved child-friend. Turn now to the prefatory poem of *Sylvie and Bruno*, the book you now hold. It has the same meter and rhyme scheme, and the last words of its first stanza—"dream," "gleam," "stream"—are the same as the last words of the above lines except that their order is reversed.[1]

Carroll's prefatory poem to *Sylvie and Bruno* is even more remarkable as an acrostic than the earlier poem. Not only do its first letters spell Isa Bowman, perhaps Carroll's second-favorite child, but the first three letters of each stanza are "Isa," "Bow," and "Man." Isa played Alice on the stage, and later wrote a delightful book, *Lewis Carroll as I Knew Him.* When her "uncle" (as she called Carroll) sent her an inscribed copy of *Sylvie and Bruno*, Isa did not realize it was dedicated to her. "She was so long, without finding it out," Carroll wrote to a friend, "that I've had to give her a hint: and I don't *yet* know whether she has found out that it comes in *two* different ways."

Although Carroll clearly intended to link *Sylvie and Bruno*

[1]For this observation of how cleverly Carroll attached *Sylvie and Bruno* to the second *Alice* book I am indebted to Brian Sibley's informative essay "The Poems in *Sylvie and Bruno*," in *Jabberwocky* (the periodical of England's Lewis Carroll Society), Summer 1975, pp. 51–58. It is the first full discussion of all the poems in the novel. The same issue also features a splendid article by Denis Crutch, "*Sylvie and Bruno*: An Introduction," and a detailed "Bibliography of *Sylvie and Bruno*," by Selwyn Goodacre.

to his earlier masterwork, he also wanted it to be entirely different. The *Alice* volumes were pure fun, Carrollian nonsense without morals. Devout Anglican that he was, Carroll longed to write a more serious book in which he could combine humor with his deepest beliefs, both sacred and secular. Here is how he put it in a memorable letter:[2]

> In *Sylvie and Bruno* I took courage to introduce, what I had entirely avoided in the two *Alice* books, some reference to subjects which are after all the *only* subjects of real interest in life; subjects which are so intimately bound up with every topic of human interest, that it needs more effort to avoid them than to touch on them. And I felt that such a book was more suitable to a clerical writer than one of mere fun.
>
> I hope I have not offended many (evidently I have not offended *you*) by putting scenes of mere fun, and talk about God, into the same book.
>
> Only *one* of all my correspondents ever guessed there was more to come of the book. She was a child, personally unknown to me, who wrote to "Lewis Carroll" a sweet letter about the book, in which she said "I'm so glad it hasn't got a regular wind-up, as it shows there is more to come!"
>
> There is indeed "more to come." When I came to piece together the mass of accumulated material, I found it was quite *double* what could be put into one volume. So I divided it in the middle: and I *hope* to bring out *Sylvie and Bruno Concluded* next Christmas—if, that is, my heavenly Master gives me the time, and the strength, for the task: but I am nearly 60, and have no right to count on years to come.

The two volumes of *Sylvie and Bruno*, together running to some 850 pages, was Carroll's last major work. "Whether it is better, or worse, than the *Alice* books," he wrote in another letter, "I have no idea: but I take a far deeper interest in it, as having tried to put more real *thought* into it."

Carroll's great nonsense ballad *The Hunting of the Snark* was written in a bizarre backward way. After its last line, "For the Snark *was* a Boojum, you see," occurred to him suddenly during a walk, he composed over the next two years a ballad to lead up to it. *Sylvie and Bruno*, we learn from his

[2]The full text of this letter, written in 1892 to the Reverend Charles Alfred Goodhart, can be found in *The Letters of Lewis Carroll*, edited by Morton N. Cohen and Roger Lancelyn Green (New York: Oxford University Press, 1979), vol. 2, p. 885.

idiosyncratic preface, was also written in a reverse manner. Instead of inventing a plot, then fitting scraps of his experience into it, he did just the opposite. He took odds and ends of his life—remembered incidents, remarks of children, old letters, half-forgotten poems he had written, even two ideas that came to him in dreams—then over many years worked out a plot that would weave together this "huge unwieldy mass of litterature" (the extra "t" was of course intended).

In keeping with his fondness for puzzles, Carroll posed two problems in his preface: to identify spots where he "padded" his narrative to bind fragments together, and to determine which stanzas of the mad Gardener's song were adapted to the plot, and which suggested aspects of the plot. Both questions were answered in the preface to *Sylvie and Bruno Concluded*, where Carroll introduced more puzzles about his novel, promising to answer them in a book of original puzzles and games that he never got around to writing. As Florence Becker Lennon says in her *Life of Lewis Carroll*, the main unity behind his patchwork story is Carroll himself, with his unique blend of interests and beliefs.

Sylvie and Bruno had its origin in Carroll's short story "Bruno's Revenge," published in 1867 in *Aunt Judy's Magazine*. (With many changes, the story became Chapters XIV and XV of this book.) For a while his working title was "Four Seasons," presumably because the plot covers one year. The first volume, *Sylvie and Bruno*, was published by Macmillan in England a few days before Christmas 1889 and by the same company in the United States the following year. That Carroll thought of the book as partly nonfiction is indicated by his playful index. Volume two, *Sylvie and Bruno Concluded*, issued shortly after Christmas in 1893 by Macmillan (in the United States in 1894), had a combined index for both volumes.

Although Carroll occasionally addressed his readers as children (for instance, "dear Child who reads this!" in Chapter XIV), he realized that much of his book could be understood only by adults. "It is a book intended for *all* ages—not for children only, as *Alice* was," he said in a letter. Two attempts were made by others to omit the adult episodes and limit the novel to scenes involving only Sylvie and Bruno. Carroll's youngest brother Edwin edited the first abridgement, *The Story of Sylvie and Bruno* (Macmillan, 1904). Philip Blackburn and Lionel White made the second abridgement for their anthology *Logical Nonsense: The Works of Lewis Carroll* (Putnam, 1934). The story has twice been dramatized for children, by Miss H. B. Griffiths in 1896 and by Roger Lancelyn Green in 1945, though neither play has been printed or acted.

John Ruskin once asked Carroll to write a novel that would not be a dream, but whether *Sylvie and Bruno* fulfilled this hope is debatable. Although the elderly narrator frequently falls asleep, Carroll makes clear that he is not dreaming in the conventional way. In the Preface to the second volume, he distinguishes between two "psychical states": an "eerie" state in which the narrator is conscious of actual surroundings, but also conscious of fairies, and a "trance state" in which his soul "migrates to other scenes, in the actual world, or in Fairyland." Using today's parlance, the second state is an OBE or "out-of-body experience." Such experiences were stressed by the theosophists of Carroll's time; indeed, he notes in his Preface that the trance state is similar to "such as we meet with in 'Esoteric Buddhism,' " the title of a book by theosophist A. P. Sinnett.

The narrator, though never named, is obviously Carroll. At age 55, when he was working on the novel, he speaks in a letter of "passing into the sere and yellow leaf" of his dotage, and throughout his adult life he was painfully aware of the age gap between himself and his child-friends. In *Sylvie and Bruno* he imagines himself to be 70, a weary, lonely, bespectacled old man who periodically dozes on trains or when gazing into a fire. In the story "Bruno's Revenge" the narrator actually says to Bruno, "My name's Lewis Carroll," but in *Sylvie and Bruno* he keeps himself vague and anonymous. We are not told his profession, though we do learn that he knows a lot about mathematics and likes to sketch. He suffers from a heart ailment, perhaps symbolic of Carroll's sadness over the loss of child-friends, like Isa Bowman, who grow up, marry, and stop writing to him. In a letter to a child-friend just married, written between the publication dates of the two volumes of *Sylvie and Bruno,* he calls himself "a solitary, broken-hearted hopeless old bachelor." Harry Furniss, who illustrated *Sylvie and Bruno,* was instructed not to show the narrator in any of the pictures.

The book has three main settings: England, Fairyland, and Outland.

The nameless narrator is a Londoner. His doctor friend, Arthur Forester, lives in Elveston (note the "elves"), an imaginary town said to be modeled on Hatfield, where Carroll often stayed. It is reached by train, by way of Fayfield (note the "fay") Junction.

Fairyland, of which Elfland and Dogland are provinces, is to a large extent modeled on the fairyland of Shakespeare's *Midsummer Night's Dream.* Bruno, we are told, had been a servant of King Oberon, and Queen Titania is also mentioned (Chapter XXIV).

Outland is an outlandish parody of Oxford, with its wardens, subwardens, and learned professors. As we learn in Chapter VI, it is a thousand miles from Elfland. Dogland, some fifty miles from Outland, has its own language, Doggee, which all fairies understand. Raymond Queneau, a noted French novelist, wrote an entire article (translated in *Jabberwocky,* Winter 1977) on Doggee syntax. *Wow* means "What do you want?" *Hooyah wah* is "Come in." There is even a word for "not to be"—*wooh.* In the second volume we meet the dog king again and learn a new Doggee word, *bosh.* It means the same thing as in English, and is pronounced with half a cough and half a bark.

Sylvie (from the Latin name *Sylvia,* "female forest dweller") is nine or ten, with long curly brown tresses and big brown eyes. Like her brother Bruno, after she becomes a fairy her normal height is only a few inches, small enough to sit on a mushroom and produce "teeny-tiny" music by stroking a daisy's petals. Her main task seems to be taking care of Bruno—making him study his lessons, correcting his speech and behavior, and trying to keep him out of mischief. She is, of course, Carroll's ideal child—beautiful, loving, innocent, pure in heart. At the close of the second book she becomes an angel.

Bruno (from the Old High German word for "brown") is about five, with brown hair and eyes like his sister. He is extremely clever, as merry, mischievous, and hyperactive as Robin Goodfellow (alias Puck), and smart enough to know something about Shakespeare, as we learn from the amateur theatrical he performs (Chapter XXIV) for an audience of frogs. I suppose it's a coincidence, but change

"Robin" to "Robun," and the name is an anagram of "Bruno."

Bruno's adult knowledge contrasts sharply with his babyishness. He frequently sucks his thumb, and speaks in a baby talk that Carroll thought he based on the actual talk of children, but surely no English child ever talked like Bruno. Although baby talk was a convention in Victorian fiction, Bruno's "oo's" and "welly's" must have been almost as hard to take by Carroll's readers as they are tody. Evelyn Waugh (reviewing *The Complete Works of Lewis Carroll* in *The Spectator*, October 13, 1939) calls Bruno "a creation of unique horror, who babbles throughout in baby-talk, like the 'control' of a 'medium.' " Happily, he drops his infantile accents when he sings. *Sylvie and Bruno*, many critics have noted, is the only work of Carroll's in which a boy is likable.

Critics have also observed that Bruno is a common name for both bears and dogs; also that it begins with the famous "B" of Carroll's *Snark.* Cats dominate the *Alice* books, but in this book the dog is dominant. Did Carroll associate cats with girls, dogs with boys?

More unbearable than Bruno's baby talk is the incessant hugging and kissing that goes on between the two siblings. It is, of course, as innocent as Carroll's constant kissing of little girls, but it occurs so often that it is as hard to avoid speculating about unconscious sexual emotion as it is to avoid similar speculation about such emotions in Carroll's fondness for photographing attractive little girls in the nude.

His Imperial Fatness, Prince Uggug (note the "ugh" and "ugly" in his name), is everything Carroll hated in boys. He is the same age as his cousin Sylvie, but stupid, fat, and cruel. In *Alice in Wonderland* the Ugly Duchess's baby boy turns into a pig. In *Sylvie and Bruno Concluded*, Uggug's "prickly" nature turns him into a porcupine.

The benevolent Warden of Outland, father of Sylvie and Bruno, is for a time disguised as a beggar. Eventually he becomes King of Elfland. His evil younger brother Sibimet is the Sub-Warden and father of Uggug. In the Preface to the second volume Carroll writes: "May I take this opportunity of calling attention to what I flatter myself was a successful piece of name-coining. . . . Does not the name 'Sibimet' fairly embody the character of the Sub-Warden? The gentle Reader has no doubt observed what a singularly useless article in a house a brazen trumpet is, if you simply leave it lying about, and never blow it!"

The remark about the brazen trumpet is clear: Carroll is defending his right to blow his own horn. But what in the world does "Sibimet" mean? After some inquiries, the mystery was finally resolved by two correspondents of mine: Denis Crutch in England (whose interpretation came by way of Dr. Selwyn Goodacre) and Everett Bleiler, an erudite friend in New Jersey. *Sibi* is a Latin third person reflexive pronoun, in the dative case, with its use as a name in this instance implying a person concerned mainly with himself. The suffix *-met* intensifies the pronoun. A rough English equivalent would be "his very self," with implications of selfishness. Ruth Berman suggests that Carroll may have also had in mind the word "sibilant," suggesting the sound of a snake. (My wife noticed that the first two consonants of Sibimet are "S" and "B," the initials of Sylvie and Bruno, but this may be sheer coincidence.) I assume that Tabikat, the name of Sibimet's evil wife, is a play on "tabby cat," but because *tabes* is Latin for disease and moral decay, Carroll may have intended a portmanteau word meaning a morally depraved cat.

Roger Lancelyn Green believes, and Morton Cohen concurs, that Sibimet and Tabikat are caricatures of Alice Liddell's father and mother. Carroll had little admiration for either. After all, it was Mrs. Liddell who stopped Alice from seeing him and who burned all his letters to Alice. Mrs. Liddell had a reputation for being "catty." Professor Cohen called my attention to Tabby's remark in Chapter V, "And am I Vice-Wardeness?" and reminded me of the anonymously written epigram that made its rounds at Oxford:

I am the Dean and this is Mrs. Liddell.
She plays the first, and I the second fiddle.
She is the Broad: I am the High:
And we are the University.

Sibimet's attitude toward his son is one of constant disrespect. In one episode he hangs his hat on Uggug as if he were no more than a hatrack. In another, he beats him over the head with an umbrella as if driving a loose nail into the floor. In her biography of Carroll, Anne Clark calls attention to the prototypes of Sibimet and Tabikat in a story Carroll wrote in his youth for his *Rectory Magazine.*

The Professor, a caricature of an absent-minded Oxford scholar, is (as we learn in the second book) probably an extraterrestrial, perhaps from the Moon. His colleague, the Other Professor, keeps his nose buried in books when he's not tripping over furniture.

The mad Gardener, whose song is the best nonsense poem of the story, could have strayed from Wonderland. He does frantic jigs while he sings, likes to stand on one leg when silent, and likes to water plants with an empty can because it's lighter to hold. Furniss has drawn him with wisps of straw sticking out from his hair and clothes. It was a Victorian convention to depict lunatics this way. You'll see similar straw in John Tenniel's drawings of the mad March Hare.

Arthur Forester (note the "forest") is an adult version of Bruno—handsome, wise, good, and devout. In a letter to Furniss, Carroll says he is "forty at least," and suggests he be drawn with a likeness to King Arthur. The doctor's whimsical ideas show that he has as much in common with the narrator as he has with Bruno.

Lady Muriel Orme (*orme* is French for "elm") is a grown-up Sylvie. Her age is about 21, almost exactly as much younger than Arthur as Alice Liddell was younger than Carroll. She is as witty as Arthur and the narrator. Her father, the Earl of Ainslee, is said to be based on Carroll's friend Lord Salisbury of Hatfield.

Captain Eric Lindon (did Carroll have in mind a similarity to "linden," the name of a tree?)[3] is only a few years older than his cousin Muriel. Carroll portrays him as a religious skeptic who nevertheless is brave and good. In Chapter XXII Lindon rescues Bruno from an onrushing express train, and in the second volume he saves the life of his rival Arthur. Carroll transforms him into a theist at the end of the second book, intimating that he is on his way to becoming a Christian.

There is lots of magic in the story. Bruno is capable of making what he calls "phlizzes"—objects and even people

[3]The suggestion that Eric Lindon and Muriel Orme have last names based on trees was made by Alfreda Blanchard in her entertaining article "Sylvie and Bruno Re-opened," *Jabberwocky,* Winter 1983/84, pp. 14–17.

that he conjures "out of air." In Chapter XXIX he materializes an entire nursemaid, using ventriloquism to make her talk! In the same chapter he creates a nosegay of rare flowers from India. We are told in volume two that he performs "conjuring tricks," presumably of the sort ordinary magicians do.

Sylvie's Magic Locket, given to her by her father, is the novel's central symbol. We are told originally that there are two lockets, both heart-shaped, one red, one blue. When Sylvie chooses the red one, with the inscription "Sylvie will love all," rather than the blue one, with "All will love Sylvie," her father weeps with joy. (Characters weep as often in this novel as Sylvie and Bruno hug and kiss.) In the concluding book we learn that the locket is really a single one that can be viewed two ways. "When you look *at* it, it's red and fierce like the sun—and, when you look *through* it, it's gentle and blue like the sky!" It has marvelous powers. In Chapter VIII Sylvie uses it to make trees, and to turn a mouse into a lion on which Bruno rides.

The Professor's crazy inventions (and the inventions of his real-life counterpart, the German Professor Mein Herr in the sequel) provide the story's most delicious nonsense. We learn here about the Professor's boots with umbrellas to ward off horizontal rain, his portable plunge bath, his machine for shortening and stretching animals, above all his Outlandish Watch. The episodes created by the watch are the second earliest known instances in fiction of time-travel made possible by a machine. (H. G. Wells's *The Time Machine* had appeared a year earlier in a magazine.) Unlike so many later science-fiction writers, Carroll was well aware that travel into the past could generate logical contradictions. Going back in time, the narrator prevents a tragic accident, but when he returns to the present, the accident happens again just the way it did before. You can enter the past and think you are altering it, but the changes are unreal. The backward events that occur when the watch's Reversal Peg is turned are the first scenes in fiction in which time goes the wrong way. Note that although the events run backward, like a reversed motion-picture film, each sentence of the dialogue remains forward—Carroll's concession to readability. It is much harder to read backward spelling than to read a mirror-reversed poem like "Jabberwocky" by holding it up to a mirror.

Arthur doesn't build devices, but his "thought experiments" are as fantastic as the Professor's mad inventions. His elevator ideas in Chapter VIII are striking anticipations of a famous thought experiment used by Einstein to explain the equivalence of gravity and inertia. Zero gravity prevails in a free-falling elevator, and objects inside would rise as though attracted by gravity from above if the elevator moved downward at a faster rate of acceleration than the objects inside. Later in the book Arthur suggests that the reason we don't see the images on our retinas as inverted (which they are) is because our brain is also upside down. A Sillygism, he explains in an often quoted passage, consists of combining two prim Misses to produce a Delusion.

We have already mentioned the Gardener's song as one of Carroll's finest nonsense poems. Its great last stanza, in *Sylvie and Bruno Concluded*, is:

He thought he saw an Argument
That proved he was the Pope:
He looked again, and found it was
A Bar of Mottled Soap.
"A fact so dread," he faintly said,
"Extinguishes all hope!"

After finishing, the Gardener chokes up with sobs. "That song is his own history, you know," explains the Professor. Tears glitter in Bruno's eyes when he remarks, "I's *welly* sorry he isn't the Pope! Aren't *you* sorry, Sylvie?"

"Well—I hardly know," his sister answers. "Would it make him any happier?"

"It wouldn't make the *Pope* any happier," says the Professor.

All this banter is Carroll at his Carrollian best. In contrast, consider the long ballad recited by the Other Professor in Chapter XI that tells about a cruel April Fool joke. Exploiting the ancient phrase about robbing Peter to pay Paul, a phrase originally applied to St. Peter and St. Paul, the ballad has nothing to do with the story. It struck me as one of Carroll's longest, most boring poems until I came across Roger Lancelyn Green's note in his edition of Carroll's *Diaries* (New York, 1954, p. 404) stating that the ballad is a parody of a famous 1785 speech to Parliament by Edmund

Burke. Titled "On a Motion Made for the Papers Relative to the Nabob of Arcot's Debts," the speech was a savage indictment of England's cruel, avaricious policy toward India.

Arcot was a district in India's Carnatic region. The East India Company had installed a Moslem prince as the region's nabob (governor) and furnished him mercenaries for expanding his domain. But the nabob proved to be so inept that he allowed the Carnatic region to be devastated and plundered by an invading army. The British moved in troops to take over the region, but instead of providing funds to feed the starving, and helping the region recover, they imposed a heavy burden of debt that the impoverished region could not pay. When the debt reached about two million pounds, the British "generously" provided more loans at usurious rates that soon doubled the debt to four million. The debts were in the form of fraudulent mortages provided by unscrupulous private moneylenders of whom one Paul Benfield was chief. In Carroll's poem, Peter is India, kept "sweetly picturesque in rags" by the cruel "loans" of Paul, who represents England's moneylenders. In Burke's strong words, the nabob of Arcot's debts were a "foul, putrid mucus" imposed by "tape-worms, which devour the nutriment, and eat up the bowels of India."[4]

Note that Alice's birthday of May 4 appears in the poem's second stanza. Peter, tearing out his yellow curls and later acquiring a wig, calls to mind the youthful yellow ringlets of the wasp in a wig, in the famous lost episode of *Through the Looking-Glass.*

Like the *Alice* books, *Sylvie and Bruno* is laced with wordplay. There are hundreds of puns, most of them not memorable, and the narrator has an annoying habit of explaining lots of them by making comments or italicizing the relevant words. The constant quibbling by Bruno and others is much funnier. Like so many characters in Wonderland and behind the mirror, Bruno is fond of taking statements so literally that their meanings become absurd.

[4]Burke's complete speech is given in *The Speeches of the Right Honourable Edmund Burke* (London, 1816). An abridged version appears in *Irish Orators*, edited by Thomas Kettle (London, 1915). I wish to thank Ruth Berman and Russell Barnhart for their help in obtaining copies of Burke's speech.

Uggug is too fat to go through a hole in a target, Bruno remarks, after being told that Uggug "went in right *here.*" When Tabikat asks her husband what he got a dagger for, he says he got it for eightpence. As in *Alice*, there are numerous instances of amusing logical contradictions. The distance between Outland and Fairyland is five times longer in one direction than the other. A crocodile crawls along its tail, up its back, and down its own head to its nose. The Professor tells Sylvie that the Other Professor, on three occasions, started reciting a poem and never stopped.

When Carroll chose Harry Furniss to illustrate his novel, Tenniel warned Furniss that he would soon be in serious trouble with Carroll over the pictures. The warning was accurate. Their relationship became so strained that at one point Furniss refused to continue. (See the Appendix to this Introduction for Furniss's revealing memories of Carroll.) Carroll was constantly sending him sketches to show how he wanted his characters to look (fifteen are reproduced by Edward Guiliano in a book he edited, *Lewis Carroll Observed*), recommending various little girls as models, and debating with Furniss about how Sylvie and Bruno should be clothed. In one letter Carroll wrote: "I *wish* I dared dispense with *all* costume; naked children are so perfectly pure and lovely, but Mrs. Grundy would be furious—it would never do." Carroll proposed a transparent dress for Sylvie, but Furniss decided it would be best to make it opaque, though filmy and clinging. No wings on the pair, and no high heels on Sylvie, were two of Carroll's firmest injunctions.

The novel's two plots, which interlock as the narrator shuttles back and forth between England and Outland or Fairyland, are so hard to follow on a first reading that perhaps brief summaries (including the action of *Sylvie and Bruno Concluded*) will be helpful.

Like *Finnegans Wake*, the story opens in the middle of a sentence. I take this to indicate that the narrator has abruptly experienced his first OBE. He finds himself in Outland, invisible, though capable of seeing and hearing everything. The Warden of Outland is about to leave for Elfland. His crafty brother, Sibimet, the Sub-Warden, tricks him into signing a document that makes the brother and his simple-minded wife the equivalent of king and queen, and their disgusting son Uggug heir to the throne.

The Warden's children, Sylvie and Bruno, aided by the court Professor, run off to Elfland, with a stopover in Dogland. Their father is made King of Elfland, and Sylvie and Bruno become tiny fairies. The Professor later takes them back to Outland to help block the Sub-Warden's power grab. To delay the Coronation Banquet, the Professor begins a lengthy lecture. It is interrupted by a brief, mysterious hurricane which I believe Carroll intended to be a whirlwind from heaven, like the wind that rescued and transformed Coleridge's Ancient Mariner. When the King of Elfland returns, his brother, cleansed by God's whirlwind, instantly repents. The King of Elfland forgives him, and allows him to remain the ruler. Uggug turns into a porcupine. Everybody except Uggug is happy. As the sun sets, Sylvie becomes an angel who whispers, from a "darling blue" sky, "It is love."

The other plot, taking place in the real world of England, begins with the narrator's journey by train to Elveston to see his old friend Dr. Arthur Forester. Arthur, a country doctor, has long been in love with Lady Muriel, but because he is too poor to marry, and perhaps too old for Muriel, he has concealed his feeling. Lady Muriel loves Arthur, but not knowing how he feels about her, and supposing herself bound to her cousin Captain Eric Lindon, she also keeps her distance from Arthur. Muriel has mixed emotions about Eric. She is fond of him, though dismayed by his unshakable atheism.

Arthur inherits a fortune, but believing Lady Muriel to be in love with Eric, he still does not tell her how he feels. After an Army promotion, Eric proposes to Muriel and she accepts. Heartbroken, Arthur heads for India.

When Lady Muriel tells Eric about her fears that she would be unhappy married to a non-Christian, he gallantly releases her from their engagement. Arthur returns to Elveston to propose to Muriel. No sooner are they betrothed than Arthur is compelled to leave to help the residents of a nearby town battle an epidemic. After a false report of his death, Eric finds him and brings him home in a crippled, debilitated state. Presumably Muriel will nurse him back to health and they will live happily ever after.

Compared with the flood of literature about *Alice*, surprisingly little has been written about *Sylvie and Bruno*, though in recent years critical interest in the novel may have been slowly rising. Carroll was not, as he himself realized, a skillful writer of fiction. The consensus on *Sylvie and Bruno* is that, aside from its word play and nonsense, it is a flawed, embarrassing work, produced at a time when Carroll correctly perceived that his creative powers were waning. It is difficult for modern readers to be impressed by the book's pious exhortations. In the first volume's preface Carroll sounds exactly like one of today's television evangelists when he urges his readers to get right with God because at any moment they may die. His rule for those who attend the theater, as he himself loved to do, is to ask whether they would like to be enjoying the play if death suddenly struck. "The safest rule is that we should not dare to *live* in any scene in which we dare not *die.*" Carroll was so incensed by sex on stage and by what he considered blasphemy that he wanted to Bowdlerize Bowdler. A new edition of Shakespeare should be written for girls, he maintained, because Bowdler's version was insufficiently expurgated!

Death and the mystery of evil pervade the novel, from such playful scenes as Bruno using a dead mouse for a ruler or a pillow, to one in which Sylvie lies on the grass, sobbing uncontrollably over a dead rabbit. "And God meant your life to be so beautiful!" she cries. One need not be a Christian to take an interest in Arthur's opinions about good and evil, free will, prayer, and other theological topics, but readers with no faith in a personal God and an afterlife will be singularly unimpressed.

In *Sylvie and Bruno Concluded* Arthur strongly opposes the notion that eternity in heaven will be dull. On the contrary, there will be an infinity of new things to be learned, even in mathematics, and new experiences to undergo. His greatest departure from conservative Anglican theology is an impassioned conjecture that because of the enormous influence of bad environment on behavior there will be far fewer lost souls than we imagine. Carroll, by the way, did not believe that the Christian hell meant an eternity of suffering. He even published a pamphlet on the topic, and said that if he believed Jesus had taught such a doctrine he would stop calling himself a Christian!

On the deepest metaphorical level Carroll surely intended the contrast between England and Fairyland to reflect a Platonic dichotomy between the world we know and the transcendent world of God. Like the narrator, we lead double lives. Our bodies are trapped for a brief time in the fallen world, the lost Paradise, but our true home is the Paradise we will enter when we have our last and greatest OBE. Arthur's cry of "Look Eastward!" as he views a rising sun on the last pages of this book, suggests the Easter hope of the Resurrection. Compared to the new dimensions we are destined to enter, our life here among the shadows on the wall of Plato's cave is indeed a kind of dream. The *Alice* books end with Alice wondering if she dreamed her adventures or if she herself is no more than a phantom in the mind of the dreaming Red King. As Ruth Berman observes in her valuable essay "Patterns and Unification in *Sylvie and Bruno*," each Alice volume starts and ends in the real world, but *Sylvie and Bruno* starts in Outland, and in the sequel ends in either Outland or Fairyland.

How should we finally assess this long, complicated, curious "novel of ideas," so rich in nonsense, linguistic play, and philosophical reflection? Victorian popular fiction often combined religious piety with sentimentality—the prolonged death of Dickens's Little Nell is a frequently cited example—but there is no use denying that *Sylvie and Bruno*, more than most, oozes with sentimentalism, mawkish moralizing, and a cloying sweetness "as unpalatable," in Miss Berman's words, "as too much cotton candy." Miss Lennon called it Carroll's "biggest doodle," a "dreadful book," a book of "infernal dullness." Yet she could also exclaim, "What a book! What a noble ruin!"

Derek Hudson, in his *Lewis Carroll: An Illustrated Biography* (1977), said it best. *Sylvie and Bruno* is "one of the most interesting failures in English literature. It is certainly unique; no one but Dodgson could have written it; nothing like it will be produced again."

MARTIN GARDNER

Hendersonville, North Carolina

Appendix

Harry Furniss's two-volume autobiography, *The Confessions of a Caricaturist*, was published in 1902 (dated December 1901 on copyright page) by Harper and Brothers, New York and London. The following excerpt, with its illustrations, is from Chapter IV.

he name of Charles Lutwidge Dodgson is practically unknown outside of Oxford University, where he was mathematical lecturer of Christ Church; but the name and fame of "Lewis Carroll," author of those inimitable books for children, both young and old, "Alice's Adventures in Wonderland" and "Through the Looking-glass and what Alice found there," are known and beloved all over the world. His first book for children, "Alice's Adventures," was published at a time exactly to suit me. I was just eleven—*the* age to be first impressed by the pen of Carroll and the pencil of Tenniel.

When I, a little, a very little boy in knickerbockers, first enjoyed the adventures of Alice and worshipped the pen and the pencil which recorded them, I little thought I would some day work hand in hand with the author, and when that day did arrive I regretted that I had not been born twenty-two years before I had, for for me to follow Tenniel was quite as difficult and unsatisfactory a task as for Carroll to follow Carroll. The worst of it was that I was conscious of this, and Lewis Carroll was not. Fortunately for me Sylvie was not like her prototype Alice; the illustrations for Sylvie would not have suited Tenniel as Alice did. I therefore did not fear comparison, but what I did fear was that Carroll would not be Carroll, and Carroll wasn't—he was Dodgson. I wish I had illustrated him when he was Carroll; that he was not the Carroll of "Alice" is plainly indicated in his life in the following passage:* "The publication of 'Sylvie and Bruno' marks an epoch in its author's life, for it was the publication of all

*"The Life and Letters of Lewis Carroll," by Stuart Dodgson Collingwood (Fisher Unwin).

the ideals and sentiments which he held most dear. It was a book with a definite purpose; it would be more true to say with several definite purposes. For this very reason it is not an artistic triumph as the two 'Alice' books undoubtedly are; it is on a lower literary level, there is no unity in the story. But from a higher standpoint, that of the Christian and the philanthropist, the book is the best thing he ever wrote. It is a noble effort to uphold the right, or what he thought to be the right, without fear of contempt or unpopularity. The influence which his earlier books had given him he was determined to use in asserting neglected truths.

"Of course the story has other features—delightful nonsense not surpassed by anything in 'Wonderland,' childish prattle with all the charm of reality about it, and pictures which may

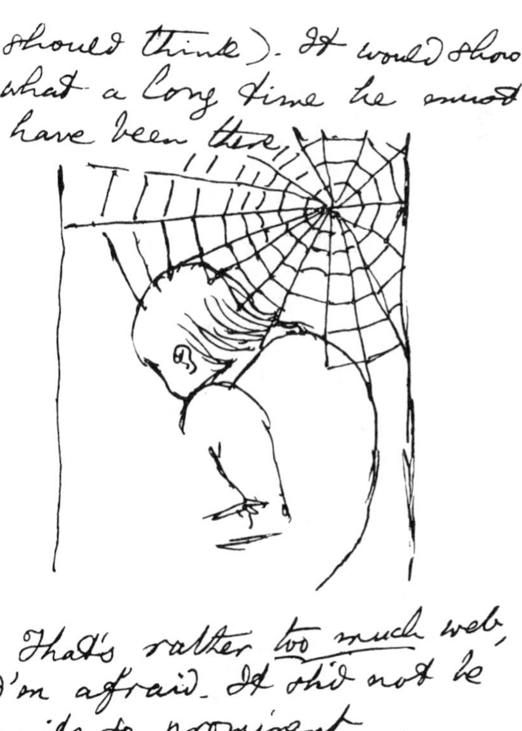

INSTRUCTIONS IN A LETTER FROM LEWIS CARROLL.

fairly be said to rival those of Sir John Tenniel. Had these been all, the book would have been a great success. As things are, there are probably hundreds of readers who have been scared by the religious arguments and political discussions which make up a large part of it, and who have never discovered that Sylvie is just as entrancing a personage as Alice when you get to know her."

The character of the book was a bitter disappointment to me. I did not want to illustrate a book of his with any "purpose" other than the purpose of delightful amusement, as "Alice" was. Tenniel had point-blank refused to illustrate another story for Carroll—he was, Tenniel told me, "impossible"—and Carroll evidently was not satisfied with other artists he had tried, as he wrote me: "I have a considerable mass of chaotic materials for a story, but have never had the heart to go to work to construct the story as a whole, owing to its seeming so hopeless that I should ever find a suitable artist. Now that *you* are found," etc. That was in 1885, and we worked together for seven years. Tenniel and other artists declared I would not work with Carroll for seven weeks! I accepted the challenge, but I, for that purpose, adopted quite a new method. No artist is more matter-of-fact or business-like than myself: to Carroll I was not Hy. F., but someone else, as *he* was someone else. I was wilful and erratic, bordering on insanity. We therefore got on splendidly.

Of course it was most interesting to me to study such a genius at such a time, and in recording my experiences and impressions of Lewis Carroll my object is not so much to deal with the actual illustration to those ill-conceived books "Sylvie and Bruno," but to deal with my impressions of the man obtained by working with him for so long, for to have known the man was even as great a treat as to read his books. Lewis Carroll was as unlike any other man as his books were unlike any other author's books. It was a relief to meet the pure simple, innocent dreamer of children, after the selfish commercial mind of most authors. Carroll was a wit, a gentleman, a bore and an egotist—and, like Hans Andersen, a spoilt child. It is recorded of Andersen that he actually shed tears, even in late life, should the cake at tea be handed to anyone before he chose the largest slice. Carroll was not selfish, but a liberal-minded, liberal-handed philanthropist, but his egotism was all but second childhood.

He informed my wife that she was the most privileged woman in the world, for she knew the man who knew his (Lewis Carroll's) ideas—that ought to content her. She must not *see* a picture or read a line of the MS.; it was sufficient for her to gaze at me outside of my studio with admiration and respect, as the only man besides Lewis Carroll himself with a knowledge of Lewis Carroll's forthcoming work. Furthermore he sent me an elaborate document to sign committing myself to secrecy. This I indignantly declined to sign. "My word was as good as my bond," I said, and, striking an attitude, I hinted that I would "strike," inasmuch as I would not work for years isolated from my wife and friends. I was therefore no doubt looked upon by him as a lunatic. That was what I wanted. I was allowed to show my wife the drawings, and he wrote: "For my own part I have shown *none* of the MS. to anybody; and, though I have let some special friends see the pictures, I have uniformly declined to *explain* them. 'May I ask so-and-so?' they enquire. 'Certainly!' I reply; 'you may *ask* as many questions as you like!' That is all they get out of me."

But his egotism carried him still further. He was determined no one should read his MS. but he and I; so in the dead of night (he sometimes wrote up to 4 a.m.) he cut his MS. into horizontal strips of four or five lines, then placed the whole of it in a sack and shook it up; taking out piece by piece, he pasted the strips down as they happened to come. The result, in such an MS., dealing with nonsense on one page and theology on another, was audacious in the extreme, if not absolutely profane—for example:

> "And I found myself repeating, as I left the Church, the words of Jacob, when he '*awaked out of his sleep*,' surely the Lord is in this.
>
> "And once more those shrill discordant tones rang out:—
>
> " ' He thought he saw a Banker's Clerk
> Descending from a bus;
> He looked again, and found it was—
> A Hippopotamus.' "

These incongruous strips were elaborately and mysteriously marked with numbers and letters and various hieroglyphics, to decipher which would really have turned my assumed eccentricity into positive madness. I therefore sent the whole MS. back to him, and again threatened to strike! This had the desired effect. I then received MS. I could read, although frequently puzzled by its being mixed up with Euclid and problems in abstruse mathematics.

I soon discovered that I had undertaken a far more difficult task than I anticipated, for in the first letter of instructions I received from the author he frankly acknowledged I had my work "cut out." "Cut out" suggests dressmaking, the very subject first chosen for discussion and correspondence.

The extraordinary workings of this unique mind are shown by quotations from his letters to me:

"I think I had better explain part of the plot, as to these two—Sylvie and Bruno. They are not fairies right through the book—but *children.* All these conditions make their *dress* rather a puzzle. They mustn't have *wings*; that is clear. And it must be *quite* the common dress of London life. It should be as fanciful as possible, so as *just* to be presentable in Society. The friends might be able to say 'What oddly-dressed children!' but they oughtn't to say 'They are not human!'

"Now I think you'll say you have 'got your work cut out for you,' to invent a suitable dress!"

How I wish I had had those dresses cut out for me! The above instructions were quickly followed by other suggestions which added to my already scanty idea of a costume suitable to Kensington Gardens and to fairyland! I was thinking this

Now as to that picture
itself - I think it's simply
lovely. And I can hardly
leave off looking at Sylvie:
face, figure, everything, is
the Sylvie I want for my

SPECIMEN OF LEWIS CARROLL'S DRAWING AND WRITING.

difficulty would be lessened if the story took place in winter, when I received another letter, which I must frankly confess rather alarmed me:

> "As to the dresses of these children in their fairy state (we shall sometimes have them mixing in Society, and supposed to be real children; and for *that* they must, I suppose, be dressed as in ordinary life, but *eccentrically*, so as to make a little distinction). I *wish* I dared dispense with *all* costume; naked children are so perfectly pure and lovely, but Mrs Grundy would be furious—it would never do. Then the question is, how little dress will content her? Bare legs and feet we *must* have, at any rate. I so entirely detest that monstrous fashion *high heels* (and in fact have planned an attack on it in this very book), that I cannot possibly allow my sweet little heroine to be victimised by it."

Another monstrous fashion he condemns refers to a picture of his grown-up heroine in London Society:

> "Could you cut off those high shoulders from her sleeves? Why should we pay any deference to a hideous fashion that will be extinct a year hence? Next to the unapproachable ugliness of 'crinoline,' I think these high-shouldered sleeves are the worst things invented for ladies in our time. Imagine how horrified they would be if one of their daughters were *really* shaped like that!"

ORIGINAL SKETCH BY LEWIS CARROLL OF HIS CHARMING HERO AND HEROINE.

I did make a note of a horrified mother with a nineteenth century malformation, but I did not send it to the author, as it struck me, when re-reading his letter, he was possibly serious. Still we had Sylvie's dress, Mrs. Grundy, crinolines, and high heels to discuss:

> "As to your Sylvie I am charmed with your idea of dressing her in *white*; it exactly fits my own idea of her; I want her to be a sort of embodiment of Purity. So I think that, in Society, she should be wholly in white—white frock ('clinging' certainly; I *hate* crinoline fashion): also I *think* we might venture on making her *fairy* dress transparent. Don't you think we might face Mrs. Grundy to *that* extent? In fact I think Mrs. G. would be fairly content at finding her *dressed*, and would not mind whether the material was silk, or muslin, or even gauze. One thing more. *Please* don't give Sylvie high heels! They are an abomination to me."

Then for months we corresponded about the face of the Heroine alone. My difficulty was increased by the fact that the fairy child Sylvie and the Society grown-up Lady Muriel were one and the same person! So I received reams of written descriptions and piles of useless photographs intended to inspire me to draw with a few lines a face embodying his ideal in a space not larger than a threepenny-piece. By one post I would receive a batch of photographs of some young lady Lewis Carroll fancied had one feature, or half a feature, of that ideal he had conjured up in his own mind as his heroine.

He invited me to visit friends of his, and strangers too, from John o'Groats to Land's End, so as to collect fragments of faces. *A propos* of this I wrote in an artists' magazine a brief account of artists' difficulties with the too exacting author. (It is quite safe to write anything about Judges and Dons: they never read any-

LEWIS CARROLL'S NOTE TO ME FOR A PATHETIC PICTURE.

thing.) I described how I received the author's recipe for constructing the ideal heroine. I am not to take *one* model for the lady-child or child-lady. I am to take *several*; for all know no face—at least, no face with expression, or with plenty of life or good abilities, or when showing depth of religious thought—is perfect. I am therefore to go to Eastbourne to see and study the face of Miss Matilda Smith, in a pastry-cook's shop, for the eyes. I am to visit Eastbourne and eat buns and cakes, gazing the while into the beauteous eyes of Miss Smith. Then in Glasgow there is a Miss O'Grady, "with oh, such a perfect nose! Could I run up to Scotland to make a sketch of it?" A letter of introduction is enclosed, and, as a precaution, I am enjoined that I "must not mind her squint." But I *do* mind, and I am sure the blemish would sadly mar my proper judgment of the lovely feature for gazing on which those eyes have lost their rectitude. For the ears a journey to Brighton to see Miss Robinson, the Vicar's daughter, is recommended. No, she may listen, think I, to the "sad sea-waves," or to her father's sermons, but never to any flattery from me. The mouth I shall find in Cardiff—not an English or Welsh mouth, but a sweet Spaniard's Señora Niccolomino, the daughter of a merchant there. In imagination I picture that cigarette held so lovingly in those perfect lips. But I am to draw an English heroine of fifteen innocent summers—how those curly wreaths of pearly smoke would disenchant my mind of the spell of youth and innocence! For the hair I must go to Brighton; for the figure to a number of different places. In fact, my author had mapped out a complete tour for me. Had he never heard the old story of the artist who was determined to paint a perfectly correct figure, strictly in accordance with the orthodox rules of art? As he painted a portion he covered it up, and so went on until the figure was complete. When it was finished he tore off the covering. The result was hideous! He went mad! I feel sure that fate would have been mine had I attempted to carry out Lewis Carroll's instructions. I therefore worked on my own lines with success. As his biographer states: "Meanwhile, with much interchange of correspondence between author and artist, the pictures for the new fairy tale, 'Sylvie and Bruno,' were being gradually evolved. Each of them was subjected by Lewis Carroll to the most minute criticism—hypercriticism, perhaps, occasionally." Still he was enthusiastic in his praise, and absurdly generous in his thanks. He was jealous that I would not disclose to him who my model was for Sylvie. When dining with us many a smile played over the features of my children when he cross-questioned me on this point. Repeatedly he wrote to me: "How old is your model for Sylvie? And may I have her name and address?" "My friend

Miss E. G. Thomson, an artist great in 'fairies,' would be glad to know of her, I'm sure," and so on.

The fairy Sylvie was my own daughter! All the children in his books I illustrated were my own children; yet this fact never struck him! He visited us in the country when I was at work, and I soon afterwards received the following letter:

> "Thanks. I was not aware that the boy, whose photo I sent you, had far-apart eyes. If you think (and you are *quite* the best judge of the point) that these eyes are needed in order to give to the face the fun and roguery I want expressed, by all means retain them.
>
> "It had occurred to me to write and beg that, if Arundel did not furnish all requisite models for drawing from life, you would let all portions of pictures which would have to be done without models or wait till you return to town, *wait.*

SYLVIE AND BRUNO. MY ORIGINAL DRAWING FOR LEWIS CARROLL.
(Never published.)

But as I think you definitely told me that you never do the finished pictures *except* from life, I presume the petition to be superfluous."

When I received this letter at Arundel my second boy was sitting in his bathing costume on a garden-roller on the lawn for a picture of Bruno sitting on a dead mouse. I was chaffing my model about flirting with a young lady he met at a children's garden party, and threatened to inform his sweetheart in London, when he assured me with knowingness, "Fact is, papa, the young lady here is all right for the country, you know—but she would *never* do in town!"

It was the same idea as Lewis Carroll's about models.

As I have brought my family into this, I may mention that there is one picture in "Sylvie and Bruno" (vol. i., p. 134) which brings back to me the only sorrowful hour I had in connection with the otherwise enjoyable work. My wife was very ill—so ill it was a question of life and death. Expert opinion was called in, and the afternoon I had to make that drawing—with my own children as models—the "consultation" was being held in my wife's room. Carroll was on his way from Oxford to see the work, and I was drawing against time. It's the old story of the clown with the sick wife. Caricaturists are after all but clowns of the pencil. They must raise a laugh whatever their state of mind may be. For a long time I never would show Lewis Carroll my work, for the simple reason I did not do it. He thought I was at work, but I was not. That's where my acting eccentricity came in. I knew that I would have to draw the subjects "right off," not one a month or one in

I GO MAD!

six months. Correspondence for three months, as a rule, led to work for one week. Isolated verse I did let him have the illustrations for, but not the body of the book. This was my only chance, and I arrived at this secrecy by the following bold stroke.

Lewis Carroll came from Oxford one evening, early in the history of the work, to dine, and afterwards to see a batch of work. He ate little, drank little, but enjoyed a few glasses of sherry, his favourite wine. "Now," he said, "for the studio!" I rose and led the way. My wife sat in astonishment. She knew I had nothing to show. Through the drawing-room, down the steps of the conservatory to the door of my studio. My hand is on the handle. Through excitement Lewis Carroll stammers worse than ever. Now to see the work for his great book! I pause, turn my back to the closed door, and thus address the astonished Don: "Mr. Dodgson, I am *very* eccentric—I cannot help it! Let me explain to you clearly, before you enter my studio, that my eccentricity sometimes takes a violent form. If I, in showing my work, discover in your face the slightest sign that you are not *absolutely* satisfied with any particle of this work in progress, the *whole* of it goes into the fire! It is a risk: will you accept it, or will you wait till I have the drawings *quite* finished and send them to Oxford?"

"I—I—I ap—appreciate your feelings—I—I—should feel the same myself. I am off to Oxford!" and he went.

I sent him drawings as they were finished, and each parcel

(5) 49874

climax, to draw the last picture first, & work backwards (as Poe tells us he wrote "The Raven".)

brought back a budget of letter-writing, each page being carefully numbered. This is the top of page 5 in his 49,874th letter. I am not sure if I received all the remaining 49,873 letters in the seven years. To meet him and to work for him was to me a great treat. I put up with his eccentricities—real ones, not sham like mine.—I put up with a great deal of boredom, for he was a bore at times, and I worked over seven years with his illustrations, in which the actual working hours would not have occupied me more than seven weeks, purely out of respect for his genius. I treated him as a problem, and I solved him, and had he lived I would probably have still worked with him. He remunerated me liberally for my work; still, he actually proposed that in addition I should partake of the profits; his gratitude was overwhelming. "I am grateful; and I feel sure that if *pictures* could sell a book 'Sylvie and Bruno' would sell like wildfire."

Is all our Life, then, but a dream
Seen faintly in the golden gleam
Athwart Time's dark resistless stream?

Bowed to the earth with bitter woe,
Or laughing at some raree-show,
We flutter idly to and fro.

Man's little Day in haste we spend,
And, from its merry noontide, send
No glance to meet the silent end.

PREFACE.

ONE little picture in this book, the Magic Locket, at p. 77, was drawn by 'Miss Alice Havers.' I did not state this on the title-page, since it seemed only due, to the artist of all these (to my mind) *wonderful* pictures, that his name should stand there alone.

The descriptions, at pp. 386, 387, of Sunday as spent by children of the last generation, are quoted *verbatim* from a speech made to me by a child-friend and a letter written to me by a lady-friend.

The Chapters, headed 'Fairy Sylvie' and 'Bruno's Revenge,' are a reprint, with a few alterations, of a little fairy-tale which I wrote in the year 1867, at the request of the late Mrs. Gatty, for 'Aunt Judy's Magazine,' which she was then editing.

It was in 1874, I believe, that the idea first occurred to me of making it the nucleus of a longer story. As the years went on, I jotted down, at odd moments, all sorts of odd ideas, and fragments of dialogue, that occurred to me——who knows how?——with a transitory suddenness that left me no choice but either to record them then and there, or to abandon them to oblivion. Sometimes one could trace to their source these random flashes of thought—as being suggested by the book one was reading, or struck out from the 'flint' of one's own mind by the 'steel' of a friend's chance remark—but they had also a way of their own, of occurring, *à propos* of nothing—specimens of that hopelessly illogical phenomenon, 'an effect without a cause.' Such, for example, was the last line of 'The Hunting of the Snark,' which came into my head (as I have already related in 'The Theatre' for April, 1887) quite suddenly, during a solitary walk: and such, again, have been passages which occurred in *dreams*, and which I cannot trace to any antecedent cause whatever. There are at least *two* instances of such dream-suggestions in this book—one, my Lady's remark, 'it often runs in families, just as a love for pastry does', at p. 88; the other, Eric Lindon's *badinage* about having been in domestic service, at p. 332.

And thus it came to pass that I found myself at last in possession of a huge unwieldy mass of litterature—if the reader will kindly excuse the spelling—which only needed stringing together, upon the thread of a consecutive story, to constitute the book I hoped to write. Only! The task, at first, seemed absolutely hopeless, and gave me a far clearer idea, than I ever had before, of the meaning of the word 'chaos': and I think it must have been ten years, or more, before I had succeeded in classifying these odds-and-ends sufficiently to see what sort of a story they indicated: for the story had to grow out of the incidents, not the incidents out of the story.

I am telling all this, in no spirit of egoism, but because I really believe that some of my readers will be interested in these details of the 'genesis' of a book, which looks so simple and straight-forward a matter, when completed, that they might suppose it to have been written straight off, page by page, as one would write a letter, beginning at the beginning and ending at the end.

It is, no doubt, *possible* to write a story in that way: and, if it be not vanity to say so, I believe that I could, myself,—if I were in the unfortunate position (for I do hold it to be a real misfortune) of being obliged to produce a given amount of fiction in a given time,—that I could 'fulfil my task,' and produce my 'tale of bricks,' as other slaves have done. One thing, at any rate, I could guarantee as to the story so produced—that it should be utterly commonplace, should contain no new ideas whatever, and should be very very weary reading!

This species of literature has received the very appropriate name of 'padding'—which might fitly be defined as 'that which all can write and none can read.' That the present volume contains *no* such writing I dare not avow: sometimes, in order to bring a picture into its proper place, it has been necessary to eke out a page with two or three extra lines: but I can honestly say I have put in no more than I was absolutely compelled to do.

My readers may perhaps like to amuse themselves by trying to detect, in a given passage, the one piece of 'padding' it contains. While arranging the 'slips' into pages, I found that the passage, which now extends from the top of p. 35 to the middle of p. 38, was 3 lines too short. I supplied the deficiency, not by interpolating a word here and a word there, but by writing in 3 consecutive lines. Now can my readers guess *which* they are ?

A harder puzzle——if a harder be desired——would be to determine, as to the Gardener's Song, in *which* cases (if any) the stanza was adapted to the surrounding text, and in *which* (if any) the text was adapted to the stanza.

Perhaps the hardest thing in all literature——at least *I* have found it so : by no voluntary effort can I accomplish it : I have to take it as it comes——is to write anything *original*. And perhaps the easiest is, when once an original line has been struck out, to follow it up, and to write any amount more to the same tune. I do not know if 'Alice in Wonderland' was an *original* story——I was, at least, no *conscious* imitator in writing it——but I do know that, since it came out, something like a dozen story-books have appeared, on identically the same pattern. The path I timidly explored——believing myself to be 'the first that ever burst into that silent sea'——is now a beaten high-road : all the way-side flowers have long ago been trampled into the dust : and it would be courting disaster for me to attempt that style again.

Hence it is that, in 'Sylvie and Bruno,' I have striven——with I know not what success——to strike out yet another new path : be it bad or good, it is the best I can do. It is written, not for money, and not for fame, but in the hope of supplying, for the children whom I love, some thoughts that may suit those hours of innocent merriment which are the very life of Childhood ; and also in the hope of suggesting, to them and to others, some thoughts that may prove, I would fain hope, not wholly out of harmony with the graver cadences of Life.

If I have not already exhausted the patience of my readers, I would like to seize this opportunity—perhaps the last I shall have of addressing so many friends at once—of putting on record some ideas that have occurred to me, as to books desirable to be written—which I should much like to *attempt*, but may not ever have the time or power to carry through—in the hope that, if *I* should fail (and the years are gliding away *very* fast) to finish the task I have set myself, other hands may take it up.

First, a Child's Bible. The only real *essentials* of this would be, carefully selected passages, suitable for a child's reading, and pictures. One principle of selection, which I would adopt, would be that Religion should be put before a child as a revelation of *love*—no need to pain and puzzle the young mind with the history of crime and punishment. (On such a principle I should, for example, omit the history of the Flood.) The supplying of the pictures would involve no great difficulty: no new ones would be needed : hundreds of excellent pictures already exist, the copyright of which has long ago expired, and which simply need photo-zincography, or some similar process, for their successful reproduction. The book should be handy in size——with a pretty attractive-looking cover——in a clear legible type——and, above all, with abundance of pictures, pictures, pictures!

Secondly, a book of pieces selected from the Bible ——not single texts, but passages of from 10 to 20 verses each——to be committed to memory. Such passages would be found useful, to repeat to one's-self and to ponder over, on many occasions when reading is difficult, if not impossible: for instance, when lying awake at night——on a railway-journey ——when taking a solitary walk——in old age, when eye-sight is failing or wholly lost——and, best of all, when illness, while incapacitating us for reading or any other occupation, condemns us to lie awake through many weary silent hours: at such a time how keenly one may realise the truth of David's rapturous cry '*O how sweet are thy words unto my throat: yea, sweeter than honey unto my mouth!*'

I have said 'passages,' rather than single texts, because we have no means of *recalling* single texts: memory needs *links*, and here are none: one may have a hundred texts stored in the memory, and not be able to recall, at will, more than half-a-dozen—— and those by mere chance: whereas, once get hold of any portion of a *chapter* that has been committed to memory, and the whole can be recovered: all hangs together.

Thirdly, a collection of passages, both prose and verse, from books other than the Bible. There is not perhaps much, in what is called 'un-inspired' literature (a misnomer, I hold: if Shakespeare was not inspired, one may well doubt if any man ever was), that will bear the process of being pondered over, a hundred times: still there *are* such passages——enough, I think, to make a goodly store for the memory.

These two books——of sacred, and secular, passages for memory——will serve other good purposes besides merely occupying vacant hours: they will help to keep at bay many anxious thoughts, worrying thoughts, uncharitable thoughts, unholy thoughts. Let me say this, in better words than my own, by copying a passage from that most interesting book, Robertson's Lectures on the Epistles to the Corinthians, Lecture XLIX. "If a man finds himself haunted by evil desires and unholy images, which will generally be at periodical hours, let him commit to memory passages of Scripture, or passages from the best writers in verse or prose. Let him store his mind with these, as safeguards to repeat when he lies awake in some restless night, or when despairing imaginations, or gloomy, suicidal thoughts, beset him. Let these be to him the sword, turning everywhere to keep the way of the Garden of Life from the intrusion of profaner footsteps."

Fourthly, a "Shakespeare" for girls: that is, an edition in which everything, not suitable for the perusal of girls of (say) from 10 to 17, should be omitted. Few children under 10 would be likely to understand or enjoy the greatest of poets: and those, who have passed out of girlhood, may safely be left to read Shakespeare, in any edition, 'expurgated' or not, that they may prefer: but it seems a pity that so many children, in the intermediate stage, should be debarred from a great pleasure for want of an edition suitable to them. Neither Bowdler's, Chambers's, Brandram's, nor Cundell's 'Boudoir' Shakespeare, seems to me to meet the want: they are not sufficiently 'expurgated.' Bowdler's is the most extraordinary of all: looking through it, I am filled with a deep sense of wonder, considering what he has left in, that he should have cut *anything* out! Besides relentlessly erasing all that is unsuitable on the score of reverence or decency, I should be inclined to omit also all that seems too difficult, or not likely to interest young readers. The resulting book might be slightly fragmentary: but it would be a real treasure to all British maidens who have any taste for poetry.

If it be needful to apologize to any one for the new departure I have taken in this story—by introducing, along with what will, I hope, prove to be acceptable nonsense for children, some of the graver thoughts of human life—it must be to one who has learned the Art of keeping such thoughts wholly at a distance in hours of mirth and careless ease. To him such a mixture will seem, no doubt, ill-judged and repulsive. And that such an Art *exists* I do not dispute: with youth, good health, and sufficient money, it seems quite possible to lead, for years together, a life of unmixed gaiety——with the exception of one solemn fact, with which we are liable to be confronted at *any* moment, even in the midst of the most brilliant company or the most sparkling entertainment. A man may fix his own times for admitting serious thought, for attending public worship, for prayer, for reading the Bible: all such matters he can defer to that 'convenient season', which is so apt never to occur at all: but he cannot defer, for one single moment, the necessity of attending to a message, which may come before he has finished reading this page, '*this night shall thy soul be required of thee.*'

The ever-present sense of this grim possibility has been, in all ages,[1] an incubus that men have striven to shake off. Few more interesting subjects of enquiry could be found, by a student of history, than the various weapons that have been used against this shadowy foe. Saddest of all must have been the thoughts of those who saw indeed an *existence* beyond the grave, but an existence far more terrible than annihilation——an existence as filmy, impalpable, all but invisible spectres, drifting about, through endless ages, in a world of shadows, with nothing to do, nothing to hope for, nothing to love! In the midst of the gay verses of that genial 'bon vivant' Horace, there stands one dreary word whose utter sadness goes to

[1] At the moment, when I had written these words, there was a knock at the door, and a telegram was brought me, announcing the sudden death of a dear friend.

one's heart. It is the word '*exilium*' in the well-known passage

> *Omnes eodem cogimur, omnium*
> *Versatur urnâ serius ocius*
> *Sors exitura et nos in æternum*
> *Exilium impositura cymbæ.*

Yes, to him this present life—spite of all its weariness and all its sorrow—was the only life worth having: all else was 'exile'! Does it not seem almost incredible that one, holding such a creed, should ever have smiled?

And many in this day, I fear, even though believing in an existence beyond the grave far more real than Horace ever dreamed of, yet regard it as a sort of 'exile' from all the joys of life, and so adopt Horace's theory, and say 'let us eat and drink, for to-morrow we die.'

We go to entertainments, such as the theatre—I say 'we', for *I* also go to the play, whenever I get a chance of seeing a really good one—and keep at arm's length, if possible, the thought that we may not return alive. Yet how do you know—dear friend, whose patience has carried you through this garrulous preface—that it may not be *your* lot, when mirth is fastest and most furious, to feel the sharp pang, or the deadly faintness, which heralds the final crisis—to see, with vague wonder, anxious friends bending over you—to hear their troubled whispers—perhaps yourself to shape the question, with trembling lips, "Is it serious?", and to be told "Yes: the end is near" (and oh, how different all Life will look when those words are said!)——how do you know, I say, that all this may not happen to *you*, this night?

And *dare* you, knowing this, say to yourself "Well, perhaps it *is* an immoral play: perhaps the situations *are* a little too 'risky', the dialogue a little too strong, the 'business' a little too suggestive. I don't say that conscience is *quite* easy: but the piece is so clever, I must see it this once! I'll begin a stricter life to-morrow." *To-morrow, and to-morrow, and to-morrow!*

> "*Who sins in hope, who, sinning, says,*
> *'Sorrow for sin God's judgement stays!'*
> *Against God's Spirit he lies; quite stops*
> *Mercy with insult; dares, and drops,*
> *Like a scorch'd fly, that spins in vain*
> *Upon the axis of its pain,*
> *Then takes its doom, to limp and crawl,*
> *Blind and forgot, from fall to fall.*"

Let me pause for a moment to say that I believe this thought, of the possibility of death——if calmly realised, and steadily faced——would be one of the best possible tests as to our going to any scene of amusement being right or wrong. If the thought of sudden death acquires, for *you*, a special horror when imagined as happening in a *theatre*, then be very sure the theatre is harmful for *you*, however harmless it may be for others; and that *you* are incurring a deadly peril in going. Be sure the safest rule is that we should not dare to *live* in any scene in which we dare not *die*.

But, once realise what the true object *is* in life—that it is *not* pleasure, *not* knowledge, *not* even fame itself, 'that last infirmity of noble minds'—but that it *is* the development of *character*, the rising to a higher, nobler, purer standard, the building-up of the perfect *Man*—and then, so long as we feel that this is going on, and will (we trust) go on for evermore, death has for us no terror; it is not a shadow, but a light; not an end, but a beginning!

One other matter may perhaps seem to call for apology—that I should have treated with such entire want of sympathy the British passion for 'Sport', which no doubt has been in by-gone days, and is still, in some forms of it, an excellent school for hardihood and for coolness in moments of danger. But I am not entirely without sympathy for *genuine* 'Sport': I can heartily admire the courage of the man who, with severe bodily toil, and at the risk of his life, hunts down some 'man-eating' tiger: and I can heartily sympathize with him when he exults in the glorious excitement of the chase and the hand-to-hand struggle with the monster brought to bay. But I can but look with deep wonder and sorrow on the hunter who, at his ease and in safety, can find pleasure in what involves, for some defenceless creature, wild terror and a death of agony: deeper, if the hunter be one who has pledged himself to preach to men the Religion of universal Love: deepest of all, if it be one of those '*tender and delicate*' beings, whose very name serves as a symbol of Love—'*thy love to me was wonderful, passing the love of women*'—whose mission here is surely to help and comfort all that are in pain or sorrow!

'*Farewell, farewell! but this I tell*
To thee, thou Wedding-Guest!
He prayeth well, who loveth well
Both man and bird and beast.

He prayeth best, who loveth best
All things both great and small;
For the dear God who loveth us,
He made and loveth all.'

CONTENTS.

SYLVIE AND BRUNO.

CHAPTER I.

LESS BREAD! MORE TAXES!

——and then all the people cheered again, and one man, who was more excited than the rest, flung his hat high into the air, and shouted (as well as I could make out) "Who roar for the Sub-Warden?" *Everybody* roared, but whether it was for the Sub-Warden, or not, did not clearly appear: some were shouting "Bread!" and some "Taxes!", but no one seemed to know what it was they really wanted.

All this I saw from the open window of the Warden's breakfast-saloon, looking across the shoulder of the Lord Chancellor, who had sprung to his feet the moment the shouting began, almost as if he had been expecting it, and had rushed to the window which commanded the best view of the market-place.

"What *can* it all mean?" he kept repeating to himself, as, with his hands clasped behind him, and his gown floating in the air, he paced rapidly up and down the room. "I never heard such shouting before—and at this time of the morning, too! And with such unanimity! Doesn't it strike *you* as very remarkable?"

I represented, modestly, that to *my* ears it appeared that they were shouting for different things, but the Chancellor would not listen to my suggestion for a moment. "They all shout the same words, I assure you!" he said: then, leaning well out of the window, he whispered to a man who was standing close underneath, "Keep 'em together, ca'n't you? The Warden will be here directly. Give 'em the signal for the march up!" All this was evidently not meant for *my* ears, but I could scarcely help hearing it, considering that my chin was almost on the Chancellor's shoulder.

The 'march up' was a very curious sight:

a straggling procession of men, marching two and two, began from the other side of the market-place, and advanced in an irregular zig-zag fashion towards the Palace, wildly tacking from side to side, like a sailing vessel making way against an unfavourable wind—

so that the head of the procession was often further from us at the end of one tack than it had been at the end of the previous one.

Yet it was evident that all was being done under orders, for I noticed that all eyes were fixed on the man who stood just under the window, and to whom the Chancellor was continually whispering. This man held his hat in one hand and a little green flag in the other: whenever he waved the flag the procession advanced a little nearer, when he dipped it they sidled a little farther off, and whenever he waved his hat they all raised a hoarse cheer. "Hoo-roah!" they cried, carefully keeping time with the hat as it bobbed up and down. "Hoo-roah! Noo! Consti! Tooshun! Less! Bread! More! Taxes!"

"That'll do, that'll do!" the Chancellor whispered. "Let 'em rest a bit till I give you the word. He's not here yet!" But at this moment the great folding-doors of the saloon were flung open, and he turned with a guilty start to receive His High Excellency. However it was only Bruno, and the Chancellor gave a little gasp of relieved anxiety.

"Morning!" said the little fellow, addressing the remark, in a general sort of way, to the Chancellor and the waiters. "Doos oo know where Sylvie is? I's looking for Sylvie!"

"She's with the Warden, I believe, y'reince!" the Chancellor replied with a low bow. There was, no doubt, a certain amount of absurdity in applying this title (which, as of course you see without my telling you, was nothing but 'your Royal Highness' condensed into one syllable) to a small creature whose father was merely the Warden of Outland: still, large excuse must be made for a man who had passed several years at the Court of Fairyland, and had there acquired the almost impossible art of pronouncing five syllables as one.

But the bow was lost upon Bruno, who had run out of the room, even while the great feat of The Unpronounceable Monosyllable was being triumphantly performed.

Just then, a single voice in the distance was understood to shout "A speech from the Chancellor!" "Certainly, my friends!" the Chancellor replied with extraordinary promptitude. "You shall have a speech!" Here one of the waiters, who had been for some minutes busy making a queer-looking mixture of egg and sherry, respectfully presented it on a large silver salver. The Chancellor took it haughtily, drank it off thoughtfully, smiled benevolently on the happy waiter as he set down the empty glass, and began. To the best of my recollection this is what he said.

"Ahem! Ahem! Ahem! Fellow-sufferers, or rather suffering fellows——" ("Don't call 'em names!" muttered the man under the window. "I didn't say *felons!*" the Chancellor explained.) "You may be sure that I always sympa——" ("'Ear, 'ear!" shouted the crowd, so loudly as quite to drown the orator's thin squeaky voice) "—that I always sympa——" he repeated. ("Don't simper quite so much!" said the man under the window. "It makes yer look a hidiot!" And, all this time, "'Ear, 'ear!" went rumbling round the market-place, like a peal of thunder.) "That I always *sympathise!*" yelled the Chancellor, the first moment there was silence. "But your *true* friend is the *Sub-Warden!* Day and night he is brooding on your wrongs—I should say your *rights*——that is to say your *wrongs*——no, I mean your *rights*——" ("Don't talk no more!" growled the man under the window. "You're making a mess of it!") At this moment the Sub-Warden entered the saloon. He was a thin man, with a mean and crafty face, and a greenish-yellow complexion; and he crossed the room very slowly, looking suspiciously about him as if he thought there might be a savage dog hidden somewhere. "Bravo!" he cried, patting the Chancellor on the back. "You did that speech very well indeed. Why, you're a born orator, man!"

"Oh, that's nothing!" the Chancellor replied, modestly, with downcast eyes. "Most orators are *born*, you know."

The Sub-Warden thoughtfully rubbed his chin. "Why, so they are!" he admitted. "I never considered it in that light. Still, you did it very well. A word in your ear!"

The rest of their conversation was all in whispers: so, as I could hear no more, I thought I would go and find Bruno.

I found the little fellow standing in the passage, and being addressed by one of the men in livery, who stood before him, nearly bent double from extreme respectfulness, with his hands hanging in front of him like the fins of a fish. "His High Excellency," this respectful man was saying, "is in his Study, y'reince!" (He didn't pronounce this quite so well as the Chancellor.) Thither Bruno trotted, and I thought it well to follow him.

The Warden, a tall dignified man with a grave but very pleasant face, was seated before a writing-table, which was covered with papers, and holding on his knee one of the sweetest and loveliest little maidens it has ever been my lot to see. She looked four or five years older than Bruno, but she had the same rosy cheeks and sparkling eyes, and the same wealth of curly brown hair. Her eager smiling face was turned upwards towards her father's, and it was a pretty sight to see the mutual love with which the two faces—one in the Spring of Life, the other in its late Autumn—were gazing on each other.

"No, you've never seen him," the old man was saying: "you couldn't, you know, he's been away so long—traveling from land to land, and seeking for health, more years than you've been alive, little Sylvie!"

Here Bruno climbed upon his other knee, and a good deal of kissing, on a rather complicated system, was the result.

"He only came back last night," said the Warden, when the kissing was over: "he's been traveling post-haste, for the last thousand miles or so, in order to be here on Sylvie's birthday. But he's a very early riser, and I dare say he's in the Library already. Come with me and see him. He's always kind to children. You'll be sure to like him."

"Has the Other Professor come too?" Bruno asked in an awe-struck voice.

"Yes, they arrived together. The Other Professor is——well, you won't like him quite so much, perhaps. He's a little more *dreamy*, you know."

"I wiss *Sylvie* was a little more dreamy," said Bruno.

"What *do* you mean, Bruno?" said Sylvie.

Bruno went on addressing his father. "She says she *ca'n't*, oo know. But I thinks it isn't *ca'n't*, it's *wo'n't*."

"Says she *ca'n't* dream!" the puzzled Warden repeated.

"She *do* say it," Bruno persisted. "When I says to her 'Let's stop lessons!', she says 'Oh, I ca'n't *dream* of letting oo stop yet!'"

"He always wants to stop lessons," Sylvie explained, "five minutes after we begin!"

"Five minutes' lessons a day!" said the Warden. "You won't learn much at *that* rate, little man!"

"That's just what Sylvie says," Bruno rejoined. "She says I *wo'n't* learn my lessons. And I tells her, over and over, I *ca'n't* learn 'em. And what doos oo think she says? She says 'It isn't *ca'n't*, it's *wo'n't!*'"

"Let's go and see the Professor," the Warden said, wisely avoiding further discussion. The children got down off his knees, each secured a hand, and the happy trio set off for the Library—followed by me. I had come to the conclusion by this time that none of the party (except, for a few moments, the Lord Chancellor) was in the least able to see me.

"What's the matter with him?" Sylvie asked, walking with a little extra sedateness, by way of example to Bruno at the other side, who never ceased jumping up and down.

"What *was* the matter——but I hope he's all right now——was lumbago, and rheumatism, and that kind of thing. He's been curing *himself*, you know: he's a very learned doctor. Why, he's actually *invented* three new diseases, besides a new way of breaking your collar-bone!"

"Is it a nice way?" said Bruno.

"Well, hum, not *very*," the Warden said, as we entered the Library. "And here *is* the Professor. Good morning, Professor! Hope you're quite rested after your journey!"

A jolly-looking, fat little man, in a flowery dressing-gown, with a large book under each arm, came trotting in at the other end of the room, and was going straight across without taking any notice of the children. "I'm looking for Vol. Three," he said. "Do you happen to have seen it?"

"You don't see my *children*, Professor!" the Warden exclaimed, taking him by the shoulders and turning him round to face them.

The Professor laughed violently: then he gazed at them through his great spectacles, for a minute or two, without speaking.

At last he addressed Bruno. "I hope you have had a good night, my child?"

Bruno looked puzzled. "I's had the same night *oo've* had," he replied. "There's only been *one* night since yesterday!"

It was the Professor's turn to look puzzled now. He took off his spectacles, and rubbed them with his hankerchief. Then he gazed at them again. Then he turned to the Warden. "Are they bound?" he enquired.

"No, we aren't," said Bruno, who thought himself quite able to answer *this* question.

The Professor shook his head sadly. "Not even half-bound?"

"Why *would* we be half-bound?" said Bruno. "We're not prisoners!"

But the Professor had forgotten all about them by this time, and was speaking to the Warden again. "You'll be glad to hear," he was saying, "that the Barometer's beginning to move——"

"Well, which way?" said the Warden——adding to the children, "Not that *I* care, you know. Only *he* thinks it affects the weather. He's a wonderfully clever man, you know. Sometimes he says things that only the Other Professor can understand. Sometimes he says things that *nobody* can understand! Which way is it, Professor? Up or down?"

"Neither!" said the Professor, gently clapping his hands. "It's going sideways——if I may so express myself."

"And what kind of weather does *that* produce?" said the Warden. "Listen, children! Now you'll hear something worth knowing!"

"Horizontal weather," said the Professor, and made straight for the door, very nearly trampling on Bruno, who had only just time to get out of his way.

"*Isn't* he learned?" the Warden said, looking after him with admiring eyes. "Positively he runs over with learning!"

"But he needn't run over *me!*" said Bruno.

The Professor was back in a moment: he had changed his dressing-gown for a frock-coat, and had put on a pair of very strange-looking boots, the tops of which were open umbrellas. "I thought you'd like to see them," he said. "*These* are the boots for horizontal weather!"

"But what's the use of wearing umbrellas round one's knees?"

"In *ordinary* rain," the Professor admitted, "they would *not* be of much use. But if ever it rained *horizontally*, you know, they would be invaluable—simply invaluable!"

"Take the Professor to the breakfast-saloon, children," said the Warden. "And tell them

not to wait for me. I had breakfast early, as I've some business to attend to." The children seized the Professor's hands, as familiarly as if they had known him for years, and hurried him away. I followed respectfully behind.

CHAPTER II.

L'AMIE INCONNUE.

As we entered the breakfast-saloon, the Professor was saying "—and he had breakfast by himself, early: so he begged you wouldn't wait for him, my Lady. This way, my Lady," he added, "this way!" And then, with (as it seemed to me) most superfluous politeness, he flung open the door of my compartment, and ushered in "—a young and lovely lady!" I muttered to myself with some bitterness. "And this is, of course, the opening scene of Vol. I. *She* is the Heroine. And *I* am one of those subordinate characters that only turn up when needed for the development of her destiny, and whose final appearance is outside the church, waiting to greet the Happy Pair!"

"Yes, my Lady, change at Fayfield," were the next words I heard (oh that too obsequious Guard!), "next station but one." And the door closed, and the lady settled down into her corner, and the monotonous throb of the engine (making one feel as if the train were some gigantic monster, whose very circulation we could feel) proclaimed that we were once more speeding on our way. "The lady had a perfectly formed nose," I caught myself saying to myself, "hazel eyes, and lips——" and here it occurred to me that to see, for myself, what "the lady" was really like, would be more satisfactory than much speculation.

I looked round cautiously, and—— was entirely disappointed of my hope. The veil, which shrouded her whole face, was too thick for me to see more than the glitter of bright eyes and the hazy outline of what *might* be a lovely oval face, but might also, unfortunately, be an equally *un*lovely one. I closed my eyes again, saying to myself "——couldn't have a better chance for an experiment in Telepathy! I'll *think out* her face, and afterwards test the portrait with the original."

At first, no result at all crowned my efforts, though I 'divided my swift mind,' now hither, now thither, in a way that I felt sure would have made Æneas green with envy: but the dimly-seen oval remained as provokingly blank as ever—a mere Ellipse, as if in some mathematical diagram, without even the Foci that might be made to do duty as a nose and a mouth. Gradually, however, the conviction came upon me that I could, by a certain concentration of thought, *think the veil away*, and so get a glimpse of the mysterious face——as to which the two questions, "is she pretty?" and "is she plain?", still hung suspended, in my mind, in beautiful equipoise.

Success was partial——and fitful——still there *was* a result: ever and anon, the veil seemed to vanish, in a sudden flash of light: but, before I could fully realise the face, all was dark again. In each such glimpse, the face seemed to grow more childish and more innocent: and, when I had at last *thought* the veil entirely away, it was, unmistakeably, the sweet face of little Sylvie!

"So, either I've been dreaming about Sylvie," I said to myself, "and this is the reality. Or else I've really been with Sylvie, and this is a dream! Is Life itself a dream, I wonder?"

To occupy the time, I got out the letter, which had caused me to take this sudden railway-journey from my London home down to a strange fishing-town on the North coast, and read it over again:—

"*Dear old Friend,*

"*I'm sure it will be as great a pleasure to me, as it can possibly be to you, to meet once more after so many years: and of course I shall be ready to give you all the benefit of such medical skill as I have: only, you know, one mustn't violate professional etiquette! And you are already in the hands of a first-rate London doctor, with whom it would be utter affectation for me to pretend to compete. (I make no doubt he is right in saying the heart is affected: all your symptoms point that way.) One thing, at any rate, I have already done in my doctorial capacity——secured you a bedroom on the ground-floor, so that you will not need to ascend the stairs at all.*

"*I shall expect you by last train on Friday, in accordance with your letter: and, till then, I shall say, in the words of the old song, 'Oh for Friday nicht! Friday's lang a-coming!'*

"*Yours always,*

"*Arthur Forester.*

"*P.S. Do you believe in Fate?*"

This Postscript puzzled me sorely. "He is far too sensible a man," I thought, "to have become a Fatalist. And yet what else can he mean by it?" And, as I folded up the letter and put it away, I inadvertently repeated the words aloud. "Do you believe in Fate?"

The fair 'Incognita' turned her head quickly at the sudden question. "No, I don't!" she said with a smile. "Do you?"

"I——I didn't mean to ask the question!" I stammered, a little taken aback at having begun a conversation in so unconventional a fashion.

The lady's smile became a laugh——not a mocking laugh, but the laugh of a happy child who is perfectly at her ease. "Didn't you?" she said. "Then it was a case of what you Doctors call 'unconscious cerebration'?"

"I am no Doctor," I replied. "Do I look so like one? Or what makes you think it?"

She pointed to the book I had been reading, which was so lying that its title, "Diseases of the Heart," was plainly visible.

"One needn't be a *Doctor*," I said, "to take an interest in medical books. There's another class of readers, who are yet more deeply interested——"

"You mean the *Patients?*" she interrupted, while a look of tender pity gave new sweetness to her face. "But," with an evident wish to avoid a possibly painful topic, "one needn't be *either*, to take an interest in books of *Science*. Which contain the greatest amount of Science, do you think, the books, or the minds?"

"Rather a profound question for a lady!" I said to myself, holding, with the conceit so natural to Man, that Woman's intellect is essentially shallow. And I considered a minute before replying. "If you mean *living* minds, I don't think it's possible to decide. There is so much *written* Science that no living person has ever *read:* and there is so much *thought-out* Science that hasn't yet been *written*. But, if you mean the whole human race, then I think the *minds* have it: everything, recorded in *books*, must have once been in some *mind*, you know."

"Isn't that rather like one of the Rules in Algebra?" my Lady enquired. ("*Algebra* too!" I thought with increasing wonder.) "I mean, if we consider thoughts as *factors*, may we not say that the Least Common Multiple of all the *minds* contains that of all the *books;* but not the other way?"

"Certainly we may!" I replied, delighted with the illustration. "And what a grand thing it would be," I went on dreamily, thinking aloud rather than talking, "if we could only *apply* that Rule to books! You know, in finding the Least Common Multiple, we strike out a quantity wherever it occurs, except in the term where it is raised to its highest power. So we should have to erase every recorded thought, except in the sentence where it is expressed with the greatest intensity."

My Lady laughed merrily. "*Some* books would be reduced to blank paper, I'm afraid!" she said.

"They would. Most libraries would be terribly diminished in *bulk*. But just think what they would gain in *quality!*"

"When will it be done?" she eagerly asked. "If there's any chance of it in *my* time, I think I'll leave off reading, and wait for it!"

"Well, perhaps in another thousand years or so——"

"Then there's no use waiting!" said my Lady. "Let's sit down. Uggug, my pet, come and sit by me!"

"Anywhere but by *me!*" growled the Sub-Warden. "The little wretch always manages to upset his coffee!"

I guessed at once (as perhaps the reader will also have guessed, if, like myself, he is *very* clever at drawing conclusions) that my Lady was the Sub-Warden's wife, and that Uggug (a hideous fat boy, about the same age as Sylvie, with the expression of a prize-pig) was their son. Sylvie and Bruno, with the Lord Chancellor, made up a party of seven.

"And you actually got a plunge-bath every morning?" said the Sub-Warden, seemingly in continuation of a conversation with the Professor. "Even at the little roadside-inns?"

"Oh, certainly, certainly!" the Professor replied with a smile on his jolly face. "Allow me to explain. It is, in fact, a very simple problem in Hydrodynamics. (That means a combination of Water and Strength.) If we take a plunge-bath, and a man of great strength (such as myself) about to plunge into it, we have a perfect example of this science. I am bound to admit," the Professor continued, in a lower tone and with downcast eyes, "that we need a man of *remarkable* strength. He must be able to spring from the floor to about twice his own height, gradually turning over as he rises, so as to come down again head first."

"Why, you need a *flea*, not a *man!*" exclaimed the Sub-Warden.

"Pardon me," said the Professor. "This particular kind of bath is *not* adapted for a flea. Let us suppose," he continued, folding his table-napkin into a graceful festoon, "that this represents what is perhaps *the* necessity of this Age——the Active Tourist's Portable Bath. You may describe it briefly, if you like," looking at the Chancellor, "by the letters A. T. P. B."

The Chancellor, much disconcerted at finding everybody looking at him, could only murmur, in a shy whisper, "Precisely so!"

"One great advantage of this plunge-bath," continued the Professor, "is that it requires only half-a-gallon of water——"

"I don't call it a *plunge*-bath," His Sub-Excellency remarked, "unless your Active Tourist goes *right under!*"

"But he *does* go right under," the old man gently replied. "The A. T. hangs up the P. B. on a nail——*thus*. He then empties the water-jug into it——places the empty jug below the bag——leaps into the air——descends head-first into the bag——the water rises round him to the top of the bag——and there you are!" he triumphantly concluded. "The A. T. is as much under water as if he'd gone a mile or two down into the Atlantic!"

"And he's drowned, let us say, in about four minutes——"

"By no means!" the Professor answered with a proud smile. "After about a minute, he quietly turns a tap at the lower end of the P. B.—all the water runs back into the jug—and there you are again!"

"But how in the world is he to get *out* of the bag again?"

"*That*, I take it," said the Professor, "is the most beautiful part of the whole invention. All the way up the P.B., inside, are loops for the thumbs; so it's something like going up-stairs, only perhaps less comfortable; and, by the time the A. T. has risen out of the bag, all but his head, he's sure to topple over, one way or the other—the Law of Gravity secures *that*. And there he is on the floor again!"

"A little bruised, perhaps?"

"Well, yes, a little bruised; but *having had his plunge-bath*: that's the great thing."

"Wonderful! It's almost beyond belief!" murmured the Sub-Warden. The Professor took it as a compliment, and bowed with a gratified smile.

"*Quite* beyond belief!" my Lady added—meaning, no doubt, to be more complimentary still. The Professor bowed, but he didn't smile *this* time.

"I can assure you," he said earnestly, "that, *provided the bath was made*, I used it every morning. I certainly *ordered* it—*that* I am clear about—my only doubt is, whether the man ever finished making it. It's difficult to remember, after so many years——"

At this moment the door, very slowly and creakingly, began to open, and Sylvie and Bruno jumped up, and ran to meet the well-known footstep.

CHAPTER III.

BIRTHDAY-PRESENTS.

"It's my brother!" the Sub-Warden exclaimed, in a warning whisper. "Speak out, and be quick about it!"

The appeal was evidently addressed to the Lord Chancellor, who instantly replied, in a shrill monotone, like a little boy repeating the alphabet, "As I was remarking, your Sub-Excellency, this portentous movement——"

"You began too soon!" the other interrupted, scarcely able to restrain himself to a whisper, so great was his excitement. "He couldn't have heard you. Begin again!"

"As I was remarking," chanted the obedient Lord Chancellor, "this portentous movement has already assumed the dimensions of a Revolution!"

"And what *are* the dimensions of a Revolution?" The voice was genial and mellow, and the face of the tall dignified old man, who had just entered the room, leading Sylvie by the hand, and with Bruno riding triumphantly on his shoulder, was too noble and gentle to have scared a less guilty man: but the Lord Chancellor turned pale instantly, and could hardly articulate the words "The dimensions—your—your High Excellency? I—I—scarcely comprehend!"

"Well, the length, breadth, and thickness, if you like it better!" And the old man smiled, half-contemptuously.

The Lord Chancellor recovered himself with a great effort, and pointed to the open window. "If your High Excellency will listen for a moment to the shouts of the exasperated populace——" ("of the exasperated populace!" the Sub-Warden repeated in a louder tone, as the Lord Chancellor, being in a state of abject terror, had dropped almost into a whisper) "——you will understand what it is they want."

And at that moment there surged into the room a hoarse confused cry, in which the only clearly audible words were "Less—— bread——More——taxes!" The old man laughed heartily. "What in the world——" he was beginning: but the Chancellor heard him not. "Some mistake!" he muttered, hurrying to the window, from which he shortly returned with an air of relief. "*Now* listen!" he exclaimed, holding up his hand impressively. And now the words came quite distinctly, and with the regularity of the ticking of a clock, "More——bread——Less——taxes!"

"More bread!" the Warden repeated in astonishment. "Why, the new Government Bakery was opened only last week, and I gave orders to sell the bread at cost-price during the present scarcity! What *can* they expect more?"

"The Bakery's closed, y'reince!" the Chancellor said, more loudly and clearly than he had spoken yet. He was emboldened by the consciousness that *here*, at least, he had evidence to produce: and he placed in the Warden's hands a few printed notices, that were lying ready, with some open ledgers, on a side-table.

"Yes, yes, *I* see!" the Warden muttered, glancing carelessly through them. "Order countermanded by my brother, and supposed to be *my* doing! Rather sharp practice! It's all right!" he added in a louder tone. "My name is signed to it: so I take it on myself. But what do they mean by 'Less Taxes'? How *can* they be less? I abolished the last of them a month ago!"

"It's been put on again, y'reince, and by y'reince's own orders!", and other printed notices were submitted for inspection.

The Warden, whilst looking them over, glanced once or twice at the Sub-Warden, who had seated himself before one of the open ledgers, and was quite absorbed in adding it up; but he merely repeated "It's all right. I accept it as my doing."

"And they do say," the Chancellor went on sheepishly—looking much more like a convicted thief than an Officer of State, "that a change of Government, by the abolition of the Sub-Warden——I mean," he hastily added, on seeing the Warden's look of astonishment, "the abolition of the *office* of Sub-Warden, and giving the present holder the right to act as *Vice*-Warden whenever the Warden is absent ——would appease all this seedling discontent. I mean," he added, glancing at a paper he held in his hand, "all this *seething* discontent!"

"For fifteen years," put in a deep but very harsh voice, "my husband has been acting as Sub-Warden. It is too long! It is much too long!" My Lady was a vast creature at all times: but, when she frowned and folded her arms, as now, she looked more gigantic than ever, and made one try to fancy what a haystack would look like, if out of temper.

"He would distinguish himself as a Vice!" my Lady proceeded, being far too stupid to see the double meaning of her words. "There has been no such Vice in Outland for many a long year, as he would be!"

"What course would *you* suggest, Sister?" the Warden mildly enquired.

My Lady stamped, which was undignified: and snorted, which was ungraceful. "This is no *jesting* matter!" she bellowed.

"I will consult my brother," said the Warden. "Brother!"

"——and seven makes a hundred and ninety-four, which is sixteen and twopence," the Sub-Warden replied. "Put down two and carry sixteen."

The Chancellor raised his hands and eyebrows, lost in admiration. "*Such* a man of business!" he murmured.

"Brother, could I have a word with you in my Study?" the Warden said in a louder tone. The Sub-Warden rose with alacrity, and the two left the room together.

My Lady turned to the Professor, who had uncovered the urn, and was taking its temperature with his pocket-thermometer. "Professor!" she began, so loudly and suddenly that even Uggug, who had gone to sleep in his chair, left off snoring and opened one eye. The Professor pocketed his thermometer in a moment, clasped his hands, and put his head on one side with a meek smile.

"You were teaching my son before breakfast, I believe?" my Lady loftily remarked. "I hope he strikes you as having talent?"

"Oh, very much so indeed, my Lady!" the Professor hastily replied, unconsciously rubbing his ear, while some painful recollection seemed to cross his mind. "I was very forcibly struck by His Magnificence, I assure you!"

"He is a charming boy!" my Lady exclaimed. "Even his snores are more musical than those of other boys!"

If that *were* so, the Professor seemed to think, the snores of *other* boys must be something too awful to be endured: but he was a cautious man, and he said nothing.

"And he's so clever!" my Lady continued. "No one will enjoy your Lecture more——by the way, have you fixed the time for it yet? You've never given one, you know: and it was promised years ago, before you——"

"Yes, yes, my Lady, *I* know! Perhaps next Tuesday——or Tuesday week——"

"That will do very well," said my Lady, graciously. "Of course you will let the Other Professor lecture as well?"

"I think *not*, my Lady," the Professor said with some hesitation. "You see, he always stands with his back to the audience. It does very well for *reciting*; but for *lecturing*——"

"You are quite right," said my Lady. "And, now I come to think of it, there would hardly be time for more than *one* Lecture. And it will go off all the better, if we begin with a Banquet, and a Fancy-dress Ball——"

"It will indeed!" the Professor cried, with enthusiasm.

"I shall come as a Grass-hopper," my Lady calmly proceeded. "What shall *you* come as, Professor?"

The Professor smiled feebly. "I shall come as——as early as I can, my Lady!"

"You mustn't come in before the doors are opened," said my Lady.

"I ca'n't," said the Professor. "Excuse me a moment. As this is Lady Sylvie's birthday, I would like to——" and he rushed away.

Bruno began feeling in his pockets, looking more and more melancholy as he did so: then he put his thumb in his mouth, and considered for a minute: then he quietly left the room.

He had hardly done so before the Professor was back again, quite out of breath. "Wishing you many happy returns of the day, my dear child!" he went on, addressing the smiling little girl, who had run to meet him. "Allow me to give you a birthday-present. It's a second-hand pincushion, my dear. And it only cost fourpence-halfpenny!"

"Thank you, it's *very* pretty!" And Sylvie rewarded the old man with a hearty kiss.

"And the *pins* they gave me for nothing!" the Professor added in high glee. "Fifteen of em, and only *one* bent!"

"I'll make the bent one into a *hook!*" said Sylvie. "To catch Bruno with, when he runs away from his lessons!"

"You ca'n't guess what *my* present is!" said Uggug, who had taken the butter-dish from the table, and was standing behind her, with a wicked leer on his face.

"No, I ca'n't guess," Sylvie said without looking up. She was still examining the Professor's pincushion.

"It's *this!*" cried the bad boy, exultingly, as he emptied the dish over her, and then, with a grin of delight at his own cleverness, looked round for applause.

Sylvie coloured crimson, as she shook off the butter from her frock: but she kept her lips tight shut, and walked away to the window, where she stood looking out and trying to recover her temper.

Uggug's triumph was a very short one: the Sub-Warden had returned, just in time to be a witness of his dear child's playfulness, and in another moment a skilfully-applied box on the ear had changed the grin of delight into a howl of pain.

"My darling!" cried his mother, enfolding him in her fat arms. "Did they box his ears for nothing? A precious pet!"

"It's not for *nothing!*" growled the angry father. "Are you aware, Madam, that *I* pay the house-bills, out of a fixed annual sum? The loss of all that wasted butter falls on *me!* Do you hear, Madam!"

"Hold your tongue, Sir!" My Lady spoke very quietly——almost in a whisper. But there was something in her *look* which silenced him. "Don't you see it was only a *joke?* And a very clever one, too! He only meant that he loved nobody *but* her! And, instead of being pleased with the compliment, the spiteful little thing has gone away in a huff!"

The Sub-Warden was a very good hand at changing a subject. He walked across to the window. "My dear," he said, "is that a *pig* that I see down below, rooting about among your flower-beds?"

"A *pig!*" shrieked my Lady, rushing madly to the window, and almost pushing her husband out, in her anxiety to see for herself. "Whose pig is it? How did it get in? Where's that crazy Gardener gone?"

At this moment Bruno re-entered the room, and passing Uggug (who was blubbering his loudest, in the hope of attracting notice) as if he was quite used to that sort of thing, he ran up to Sylvie and threw his arms round her. "I went to my toy-cupboard," he said with a very sorrowful face, "to see if there were *somefin* fit for a present for oo! And there isn't *nuffin!* They's *all* broken, every one! And I haven't got *no* money left, to buy oo a birthday-present! And I ca'n't give oo nuffin but *this!*" ("*This*" was a very earnest hug and a kiss.)

"Oh, thank you, darling!" cried Sylvie. "I like *your* present best of all!" (But if so, why did she give it back so quickly?)

His Sub-Excellency turned and patted the two children on the head with his long lean hands. "Go away, dears!" he said. "There's business to talk over."

Sylvie and Bruno went away hand in hand: but, on reaching the door, Sylvie came back again and went up to Uggug timidly. "I don't mind about the butter," she said, "and I—I'm sorry he hurt you!" And she tried to shake hands with the little ruffian: but Uggug only blubbered louder, and wouldn't make friends. Sylvie left the room with a sigh.

The Sub-Warden glared angrily at his weeping son. "Leave the room, Sirrah!" he said, as loud as he dared. His wife was still leaning out of the window, and kept repeating "I *ca'n't* see that pig! Where *is* it?"

"It's moved to the right——now it's gone a little to the left," said the Sub-Warden: but he had his back to the window, and was making signals to the Lord Chancellor, pointing to Uggug and the door, with many a cunning nod and wink.

The Chancellor caught his meaning at last, and, crossing the room, took that interesting child by the ear—the next moment he and Uggug were out of the room, and the door shut behind them: but not before one piercing yell had rung through the room, and reached the ears of the fond mother.

"What *is* that hideous noise?" she fiercely asked, turning upon her startled husband.

"It's some hyæna——or other," replied the Sub-Warden, looking vaguely up to the ceiling, as if that was where they usually were to be found. "Let us to business, my dear. Here comes the Warden." And he picked up from the floor a wandering scrap of manuscript, on which I just caught the words 'after which Election duly holden the said Sibimet and Tabikat his wife may at their pleasure assume Imperial——' before, with a guilty look, he crumpled it up in his hand.

CHAPTER IV.

A CUNNING CONSPIRACY.

THE Warden entered at this moment: and close behind him came the Lord Chancellor, a little flushed and out of breath, and adjusting his wig, which appeared to have been dragged partly off his head.

"But where is my precious child?" my Lady enquired, as the four took their seats at the small side-table devoted to ledgers and bundles and bills.

"He left the room a few minutes ago—with the Lord Chancellor," the Sub-Warden briefly explained.

"Ah!" said my Lady, graciously smiling on that high official. "Your Lordship has a very *taking* way with children! I doubt if any one could *gain the ear* of my darling Uggug so quickly as *you* can!" For an entirely stupid woman, my Lady's remarks were curiously full of meaning, of which she herself was wholly unconscious.

The Chancellor bowed, but with a very uneasy air. "I think the Warden was about to speak," he remarked, evidently anxious to change the subject.

But my Lady would not be checked. "He is a clever boy," she continued with enthusiasm, "but he needs a man like your Lordship to *draw him out!*"

The Chancellor bit his lip, and was silent. He evidently feared that, stupid as she looked, she understood what she said *this* time, and was having a joke at his expense. He might have spared himself all anxiety: whatever accidental meaning her *words* might have, she *herself* never meant anything at all.

'It is all settled!" the Warden announced, wasting no time over preliminaries. "The

Sub-Wardenship is abolished, and my brother is appointed to act as Vice-Warden whenever I am absent. So, as I am going abroad for a while, he will enter on his new duties at once."

"And there will really be a Vice after all?" my Lady enquired.

"I hope so!" the Warden smilingly replied.

My Lady looked much pleased, and tried to clap her hands: but you might as well have knocked two feather-beds together, for any noise it made. "When my husband is Vice," she said, "it will be the same as if we had a *hundred* Vices!"

"Hear, hear!" cried the Sub-Warden.

"You seem to think it very remarkable," my Lady remarked with some severity, "that your wife should speak the truth!"

"No, not *remarkable* at all!" her husband anxiously explained. "*Nothing* is remarkable that *you* say, sweet one!"

My Lady smiled approval of the sentiment, and went on. "And am I Vice-Wardeness?"

"If you choose to use that title," said the Warden: "but 'Your Excellency' will be the proper style of address. And I trust that both

'*His* Excellency' and '*Her* Excellency' will observe the Agreement I have drawn up. The provision I am *most* anxious about is this." He unrolled a large parchment scroll, and read aloud the words "'*item*, that we will be kind to the poor.' The Chancellor worded it for me," he added, glancing at that great Functionary. "I suppose, now, that word '*item*' has some deep legal meaning?"

"Undoubtedly!" replied the Chancellor, as articulately as he could with a pen between his lips. He was nervously rolling and unrolling several other scrolls, and making room among them for the one the Warden had just handed to him. "These are merely the rough copies," he explained: "and, as soon as I have put in the final corrections——" making a great commotion among the different parchments, "——a semi-colon or two that I have accidentally omitted——" here he darted about, pen in hand, from one part of the scroll to another, spreading sheets of blotting-paper over his corrections, "all will be ready for signing."

"Should it not be read out, first?" my Lady enquired.

"No need, no need!" the Sub-Warden and the Chancellor exclaimed at the same moment, with feverish eagerness.

"No need at all," the Warden gently assented. "Your husband and I have gone through it together. It provides that he shall exercise the full authority of Warden, and shall have the disposal of the annual revenue attached to the office, until my return, or, failing that, until Bruno comes of age: and that he shall then hand over, to myself or to Bruno as the case may be, the Wardenship, the unspent revenue, and the contents of the Treasury, which are to be preserved, intact, under his guardianship."

All this time the Sub-Warden was busy, with the Chancellor's help, shifting the papers from side to side, and pointing out to the Warden the place where he was to sign. He then signed it himself, and my Lady and the Chancellor added their names as witnesses.

"Short partings are best," said the Warden. "All is ready for my journey. My children are waiting below to see me off." He gravely kissed my Lady, shook hands with his brother and the Chancellor, and left the room.

The three waited in silence till the sound of wheels announced that the Warden was out of hearing: then, to my surprise, they broke into peals of uncontrollable laughter.

"What a game, oh, what a game!" cried the Chancellor. And he and the Vice-Warden joined hands, and skipped wildly about the room. My Lady was too dignified to skip, but she laughed like the neighing of a horse, and waved her handkerchief above her head: it was clear to her very limited understanding that *something* very clever had been done, but what it *was* she had yet to learn.

"You said I should hear all about it when the Warden had gone," she remarked, as soon as she could make herself heard.

"And so you shall, Tabby!" her husband graciously replied, as he removed the blotting-paper, and showed the two parchments lying side by side. "This is the one he read but didn't sign: and this is the one he signed but didn't read! You see it was all covered up, except the place for signing the names——"

"Yes, yes!" my Lady interrupted eagerly, and began comparing the two Agreements.

"'*Item*, that he shall exercise the authority of Warden, in the Warden's absence.' Why, that's been changed into 'shall be absolute governor for life, with the title of Emperor, if elected to that office by the people.' What! Are you *Emperor*, darling?"

"Not yet, dear," the Vice-Warden replied. "It won't do to let this paper be seen, just at present. All in good time."

My Lady nodded, and read on. "'*Item*, that we will be kind to the poor.' Why, that's omitted altogether!"

"Course it is!" said her husband. "*We're* not going to bother about the wretches!"

"*Good*," said my Lady, with emphasis, and read on again. "'*Item*, that the contents of the Treasury be preserved intact.' Why, that's altered into 'shall be at the absolute disposal of the Vice-Warden'! "Well, Sibby, that *was* a clever trick! *All* the Jewels, only think! May I go and put them on directly?"

"Well, not *just* yet, Lovey," her husband uneasily replied. "You see the public mind isn't quite *ripe* for it yet. We must feel our way. Of course we'll have the coach-and-four out, at once. And I'll take the title of Emperor, as soon as we can safely hold an Election. But they'll hardly stand our using the *Jewels*, as long as they know the Warden's alive. We must spread a report of his death. A little Conspiracy——"

"A Conspiracy!" cried the delighted lady, clapping her hands. "Of all things, I *do* like a Conspiracy! It's so interesting!"

The Vice-Warden and the Chancellor interchanged a wink or two. "Let her conspire to her heart's content!" the cunning Chancellor whispered. "It'll do no harm!"

"And when will the Conspiracy——"

"Hist!" her husband hastily interrupted her, as the door opened, and Sylvie and Bruno came in, with their arms twined lovingly round each other——Bruno sobbing convulsively, with his face hidden on his sister's shoulder, and Sylvie more grave and quiet, but with tears streaming down her cheeks.

"Mustn't cry like that!" the Vice-Warden said sharply, but without any effect on the weeping children. "Cheer 'em up a bit!" he hinted to my Lady.

"*Cake!*" my Lady muttered to herself with great decision, crossing the room and opening a cupboard, from which she presently returned with two slices of plum-cake. "Eat, and don't cry!" were her short and simple orders: and the poor children sat down side by side, but seemed in no mood for eating.

For the second time the door opened——or rather was *burst* open, this time, as Uggug rushed violently into the room, shouting "that old Beggar's come again!"

"He's not to have any food——" the Vice-Warden was beginning, but the Chancellor interrupted him. "It's all right," he said, in a low voice: "the servants have their orders."

"He's just under here," said Uggug, who had gone to the window, and was looking down into the court-yard.

"Where, my darling?" said his fond mother, flinging her arms round the neck of the little monster. All of us (except Sylvie and Bruno, who took no notice of what was going on) followed her to the window. The old Beggar looked up at us with hungry eyes. "Only a crust of bread, your Highness!" he pleaded.

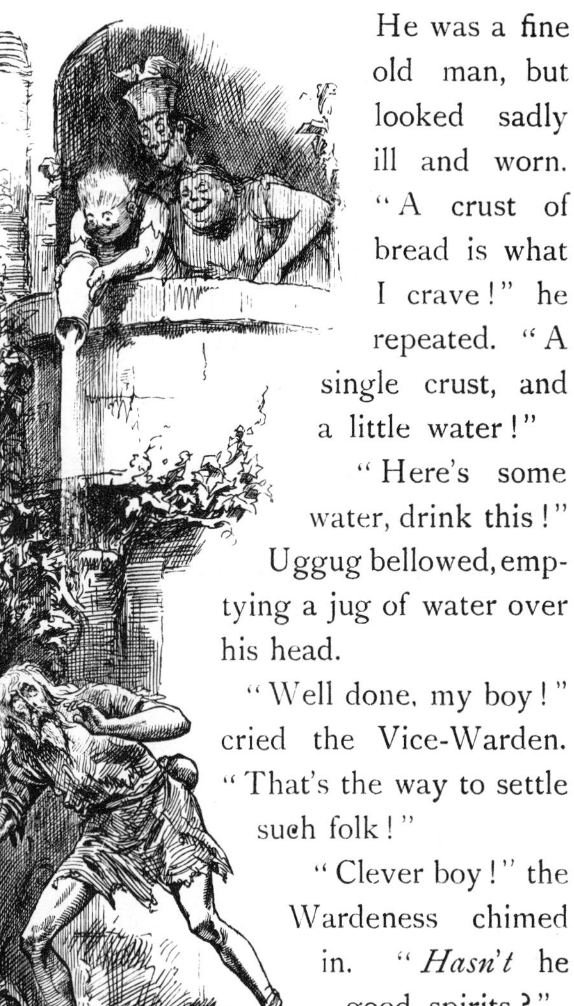

He was a fine old man, but looked sadly ill and worn. "A crust of bread is what I crave!" he repeated. "A single crust, and a little water!"

"Here's some water, drink this!" Uggug bellowed, emptying a jug of water over his head.

"Well done, my boy!" cried the Vice-Warden. "That's the way to settle such folk!"

"Clever boy!" the Wardeness chimed in. "*Hasn't* he good spirits?"

"Take a stick to him!" shouted

the Vice-Warden, as the old Beggar shook the water from his ragged cloak, and again gazed meekly upwards.

"Take a red-hot poker to him!" my Lady again chimed in.

Possibly there was no red-hot poker handy: but some *sticks* were forthcoming in a moment, and threatening faces surrounded the poor old wanderer, who waved them back with quiet dignity. "No need to break my old bones," he said. "I am going. Not even a crust!"

"Poor, *poor* old man!" exclaimed a little voice at my side, half choked with sobs. Bruno was at the window, trying to throw out his slice of plum-cake, but Sylvie held him back.

"He *shall* have my cake!" Bruno cried, passionately struggling out of Sylvie's arms.

"Yes, yes, darling!" Sylvie gently pleaded. "But don't *throw* it out! He's gone away, don't you see? Let's go after him." And she led him out of the room, unnoticed by the rest of the party, who were wholly absorbed in watching the old Beggar.

The Conspirators returned to their seats, and continued their conversation in an undertone, so as not to be heard by Uggug, who was still standing at the window.

"By the way, there was something about Bruno succeeding to the Wardenship," said my Lady. "How does *that* stand in the new Agreement?"

The Chancellor chuckled. "Just the same, word for word," he said, "with *one* exception, my Lady. Instead of 'Bruno,' I've taken the liberty to put in——" he dropped his voice to a whisper, "——to put in 'Uggug,' you know!"

"Uggug, indeed!" I exclaimed, in a burst of indignation I could no longer control. To bring out even that one word seemed a gigantic effort: but, the cry once uttered, all effort ceased at once: a sudden gust swept away the whole scene, and I found myself sitting up, staring at the young lady in the opposite corner of the carriage, who had now thrown back her veil, and was looking at me with an expression of amused surprise.

CHAPTER V.

A BEGGAR'S PALACE.

THAT I had said *something*, in the act of waking, I felt sure: the hoarse stifled cry was still ringing in my ears, even if the startled look of my fellow-traveler had not been evidence enough: but what could I possibly say by way of apology?

"I hope I didn't frighten you?" I stammered out at last. "I have no idea what I said. I was dreaming."

"You said '*Uggug indeed!*'" the young lady replied, with quivering lips that *would* curve themselves into a smile, in spite of all her efforts to look grave. "At least——you didn't *say* it——you *shouted* it!"

"I'm very sorry," was all I could say, feeling very penitent and helpless. "She *has* Sylvie's eyes!" I thought to myself, half-doubting whether, even now, I were fairly awake. "And that sweet look of innocent wonder is all Sylvie's, too. But Sylvie *hasn't* got that calm resolute mouth——nor that far-away look of dreamy sadness, like one that has had some deep sorrow, very long ago——" And the thick-coming fancies almost prevented my hearing the lady's next words.

"If you had had a 'Shilling Dreadful' in your hand," she proceeded, "something about Ghosts——or Dynamite——or Midnight Murder——one could understand it: those things aren't worth the shilling, unless they give one a Nightmare. But really——with only a *medical treatise*, you know——" and she glanced, with a pretty shrug of contempt, at the book over which I had fallen asleep.

Her friendliness, and utter unreserve, took me aback for a moment; yet there was no touch of forwardness, or boldness, about the child——

for child, almost, she seemed to be: I guessed her at scarcely over twenty—all was the innocent frankness of some angelic visitant, new to the ways of earth and the conventionalisms—or, if you will, the barbarisms—of Society. "Even so," I mused, "will *Sylvie* look and speak, in another ten years."

"You don't care for Ghosts, then," I ventured to suggest, "unless they are really terrifying?"

"Quite so," the lady assented. "The regular Railway-Ghosts—I mean the Ghosts of ordinary Railway-literature—are very poor affairs. I feel inclined to say, with Alexander Selkirk, 'Their tameness is shocking to me'! And they never do any Midnight Murders. They couldn't 'welter in gore,' to save their lives!"

"'Weltering in gore' is a very expressive phrase, certainly. Can it be done in *any* fluid, I wonder?"

"I think *not*," the lady readily replied—quite as if she had thought it out, long ago. "It has to be something *thick*. For instance, you might welter in bread-sauce. That, being *white*, would be more suitable for a Ghost, supposing it wished to welter!"

"You have a real good *terrifying* Ghost in that book?" I hinted.

"How *could* you guess?" she exclaimed with the most engaging frankness, and placed the volume in my hands. I opened it eagerly, with a not unpleasant thrill (like what a good ghost-story gives one) at the 'uncanny' coincidence of my having so unexpectedly divined the subject of her studies.

It was a book of Domestic Cookery, open at the article 'Bread Sauce.'

I returned the book, looking, I suppose, a little blank, as the lady laughed merrily at my discomfiture. "It's far more exciting than some of the modern ghosts, I assure you! Now there was a Ghost last month——I don't mean a *real* Ghost in——in Supernature——but in a Magazine. It was a perfectly *flavourless* Ghost. It wouldn't have frightened a mouse! It wasn't a Ghost that one would even offer a chair to!"

"Three score years and ten, baldness, and spectacles, have their advantages after all!" I said to myself. "Instead of a bashful youth and maiden, gasping out monosyllables at awful intervals, here we have an old man and a child, quite at their ease, talking as if they had known each other for years! Then you think," I continued aloud, "that we ought *sometimes* to ask a Ghost to sit down? But have we any authority for it? In Shakespeare, for instance——there are plenty of ghosts *there*——does Shakespeare ever give the stage-direction '*hands chair to Ghost*'?"

The lady looked puzzled and thoughtful for a moment: then she *almost* clapped her hands. "Yes, yes, he *does!*" she cried. "He makes Hamlet say '*Rest, rest, perturbed Spirit!*'"

"And that, I suppose, means an easy-chair?"

"An American rocking-chair, I *think*——"

"Fayfield Junction, my Lady, change for Elveston!" the guard announced, flinging open the door of the carriage: and we soon found ourselves, with all our portable property around us, on the platform.

The accommodation, provided for passengers waiting at this Junction, was distinctly inadequate——a single wooden bench, apparently intended for three sitters only: and even this was already partially occupied by a very old man, in a smock frock, who sat, with rounded shoulders and drooping head, and with hands clasped on the top of his stick so as to make a sort of pillow for that wrinkled face with its look of patient weariness.

"Come, you be off!" the Station-master roughly accosted the poor old man. "You be off, and make way for your betters! This way, my Lady!" he added in a perfectly different tone. "If your Ladyship will take a seat, the train will be up in a few minutes." The cringing servility of his manner was due, no doubt, to the address legible on the pile of luggage, which announced their owner to be "Lady Muriel Orme, passenger to Elveston, *viâ* Fayfield Junction."

As I watched the old man slowly rise to his feet, and hobble a few paces down the platform, the lines came to my lips:—

> "*From sackcloth couch the Monk arose,*
> *With toil his stiffen'd limbs he rear'd;*
> *A hundred years had flung their snows*
> *On his thin locks and floating beard.*"

But the lady scarcely noticed the little incident. After one glance at the 'banished

man,' who stood tremulously leaning on his stick, she turned to me. "This is *not* an

American rocking-chair, by any means! Yet may I say," slightly changing her place, so as to make room for me beside her, "may I say, in Hamlet's words, 'Rest, rest——'" she broke off with a silvery laugh.

"——perturbed Spirit!'" I finished the sentence for her. "Yes, that describes a railway-traveler *exactly!* And here is an instance of it," I added, as the tiny local train drew up alongside the platform, and the porters bustled about, opening carriage-doors——one of them helping the poor old man to hoist himself into a third-class carriage, while another of them obsequiously conducted the lady and myself into a first-class.

She paused, before following him, to watch the progress of the other passenger. "Poor old man!" she said. "How weak and ill he looks! It was a shame to let him be turned away like that. I'm very sorry——" At this moment it dawned on me that these words were not addressed to *me*, but that she was unconsciously thinking aloud. I moved away a few steps, and waited to follow her into the carriage, where I resumed the conversation.

"Shakespeare *must* have traveled by rail, if only in a dream: 'perturbed Spirit' is such a happy phrase."

"'Perturbed' referring, no doubt," she rejoined, "to the sensational booklets peculiar to the Rail. If Steam has done nothing else, it has at least added a whole new Species to English Literature!"

"No doubt of it," I echoed. "The true origin of all our medical books—and all our cookery-books——"

"No, no!" she broke in merrily. "I didn't mean *our* Literature! *We* are quite abnormal. But the booklets——the little thrilling romances, where the Murder comes at page fifteen, and the Wedding at page forty——surely *they* are due to Steam?"

"And when we travel by Electricity——if I may venture to develop your theory——we shall have leaflets instead of booklets, and the Murder and the Wedding will come on the same page."

"A development worthy of Darwin!" the lady exclaimed enthusiastically. "Only *you* reverse his theory. Instead of developing a mouse into an elephant, you would develop an elephant into a mouse!" But here we plunged into a tunnel, and I leaned back and closed my eyes for a moment, trying to recall a few of the incidents of my recent dream.

"I thought I saw——" I murmured sleepily: and then the phrase insisted on conjugating itself, and ran into "you thought you saw—— he thought he saw——" and then it suddenly went off into a song:—

"*He thought he saw an Elephant,*
That practised on a fife:
He looked again, and found it was
A letter from his wife.
'At length I realise,' he said,
'The bitterness of Life!'"

And what a wild being it was who sang these wild words! A Gardener he seemed to be——yet surely a mad one, by the way he brandished his rake——madder, by the way he broke, ever and anon, into a frantic jig—— maddest of all, by the shriek in which he brought out the last words of the stanza!

It was so far a description of himself that he had the *feet* of an Elephant: but the rest of him was skin and bone: and the wisps of loose straw, that bristled all about him, suggested that he had been originally stuffed with it, and that nearly all the stuffing had come out.

Sylvie and Bruno waited patiently till the end of the first verse. Then Sylvie advanced alone (Bruno having suddenly turned shy) and timidly introduced herself with the words "Please, I'm Sylvie!"

"And who's that other thing?" said the Gardener.

"What thing?" said Sylvie, looking round. "Oh, that's Bruno. He's my brother."

"Was he your brother yesterday?" the Gardener anxiously enquired.

"Course I were!" cried Bruno, who had gradually crept nearer, and didn't at all like being talked about without having his share in the conversation.

"Ah, well!" the Gardener said with a kind of groan. "Things change so, here. Whenever I look again, it's sure to be something different! Yet I does my duty! I gets up wriggle-early at five——"

"If I was *oo*," said Bruno, "I wouldn't wriggle so early. It's as bad as being a worm!" he added, in an undertone to Sylvie.

"But you shouldn't be lazy in the morning, Bruno," said Sylvie. "Remember, it's the *early* bird that picks up the worm!"

"It may, if it likes!" Bruno said with a slight yawn. "I don't like eating worms, one bit. I always stop in bed till the early bird has picked them up!"

"I wonder you've the face to tell me such fibs!" cried the Gardener.

To which Bruno wisely replied "Oo don't want a *face* to tell fibs wiz——only a *mouf*."

Sylvie discreetly changed the subject. "And did you plant all these flowers?" she said.

"What a lovely garden you've made! Do you know, I'd like to live here *always!*"

"In the winter-nights——" the Gardener was beginning.

"But I'd nearly forgotten what we came about!" Sylvie interrupted. "Would you please let us through into the road? There's a poor old beggar just gone out——and he's very hungry——and Bruno wants to give him his cake, you know!"

"It's as much as my place is worth!" the Gardener muttered, taking a key from his pocket, and beginning to unlock a door in the garden-wall.

"How much *are* it wurf?" Bruno innocently enquired.

But the Gardener only grinned. "That's a secret!" he said. "Mind you come back quick!" he called after the children, as they passed out into the road. I had just time to follow them, before he shut the door again.

We hurried down the road, and very soon caught sight of the old Beggar, about a quarter of a mile ahead of us, and the children at once set off running to overtake him.

Lightly and swiftly they skimmed over the ground, and I could not in the least understand how it was I kept up with them so easily. But the unsolved problem did not worry me so much as at another time it might have done, there were so many other things to attend to.

The old Beggar must have been very deaf, as he paid no attention whatever to Bruno's eager shouting, but trudged wearily on, never pausing until the child got in front of him and held up the slice of cake. The poor little fellow was quite out of breath, and could only utter the one word "Cake!"——not with the gloomy decision with which Her Excellency had so lately pronounced it, but with a sweet childish timidity, looking up into the old man's face with eyes that loved 'all things both great and small.'

The old man snatched it from him, and devoured it greedily, as some hungry wild beast might have done, but never a word of thanks did he give his little benefactor——only growled "More, more!" and glared at the half-frightened children.

"There *is* no more!" Sylvie said with tears in her eyes. "I'd eaten mine. It was a shame to let you be turned away like that. I'm very sorry——"

I lost the rest of the sentence, for my mind had recurred, with a great shock of surprise, to Lady Muriel Orme, who had so lately uttered these very words of Sylvie's——yes, and in Sylvie's own voice, and with Sylvie's gentle pleading eyes!

"Follow me!" were the next words I heard, as the old man waved his hand, with a dignified grace that ill suited his ragged dress, over a bush, that stood by the road side, which began instantly to sink into the earth. At another time I might have doubted the evidence of my eyes, or at least have felt some astonishment: but, in *this* strange scene, my whole being seemed absorbed in strong curiosity as to what would happen next.

When the bush had sunk quite out of our sight, marble steps were seen, leading downwards into darkness. The old man led the way, and we eagerly followed.

The staircase was so dark, at first, that I could only just see the forms of the children, as, hand-in-hand, they groped their way down after their guide: but it got lighter every moment, with a strange silvery brightness, that seemed to exist in the air, as there were no lamps visible; and, when at last we reached a level floor, the room, in which we found ourselves, was almost as light as day.

It was eight-sided, having in each angle a slender pillar, round which silken draperies were twined. The wall between the pillars was entirely covered, to the height of six or seven feet, with creepers, from which hung quantities of ripe fruit and of brilliant flowers, that almost hid the leaves. In another place, perchance, I might have wondered to see fruit and flowers growing together: here, my chief wonder was that neither fruit nor flowers were such as I had ever seen before. Higher up, each wall contained a circular window of coloured glass; and over all was an arched roof, that seemed to be spangled all over with jewels.

With hardly less wonder, I turned this way and that, trying to make out how in the world we had come in: for there was no door: and all the walls were thickly covered with the lovely creepers.

"We are safe here, my darlings!" said the old man, laying a hand on Sylvie's shoulder, and bending down to kiss her. Sylvie drew back hastily, with an offended air: but in another moment, with a glad cry of "Why, it's *Father!*", she had run into his arms.

"Father! Father!" Bruno repeated: and, while the happy children were being hugged and kissed, I could but rub my eyes and say "Where, then, are the rags gone to?"; for the old man was now dressed in royal robes that glittered with jewels and gold embroidery, and wore a circlet of gold around his head.

CHAPTER VI.

THE MAGIC LOCKET.

"WHERE are we, father?" Sylvie whispered, with her arms twined closely around the old man's neck, and with her rosy cheek lovingly pressed to his.

"In Elfland, darling. It's one of the provinces of Fairyland."

"But I thought Elfland was *ever* so far from Outland: and we've come such a *tiny* little way!"

"You came by the Royal Road, sweet one. Only those of royal blood can travel along it: but *you've* been royal ever since I was made

King of Elfland——that's nearly a month ago. They sent *two* ambassadors, to make sure that their invitation to me, to be their new King, should reach me. One was a Prince; so *he* was able to come by the Royal Road, and to come invisibly to all but me: the other was a Baron; so *he* had to come by the common road, and I dare say he hasn't even *arrived* yet."

"Then how far have we come?" Sylvie enquired.

"Just a thousand miles, sweet one, since the Gardener unlocked that door for you."

"A thousand miles!" Bruno repeated. "And may I eat one?"

"Eat a *mile*, little rogue?"

"No," said Bruno. "I mean may I eat one of that fruits?"

"Yes, child," said his father: "and then you'll find out what *Pleasure* is like——the Pleasure we all seek so madly, and enjoy so mournfully!"

Bruno ran eagerly to the wall, and picked a fruit that was *shaped* something like a banana, but had the *colour* of a strawberry.

He ate it with beaming looks, that became gradually more gloomy, and were very blank indeed by the time he had finished.

"It hasn't got no taste at all!" he complained. "I couldn't feel nuffin in my mouf! It's a—— what's that hard word, Sylvie?"

"It was a *Phlizz*," Sylvie gravely replied. "Are they *all* like that, father?"

"They're all like that to *you*, darling, because you don't belong to Elfland——yet. But to *me* they are real."

Bruno looked puzzled. "I'll try anuvver kind of fruits!" he said, and jumped down off the King's knee. "There's some lovely striped ones, just like a rainbow!" And off he ran.

Meanwhile the Fairy-King and Sylvie were talking together, but in such low tones that I could not catch the words: so I followed Bruno, who was picking and eating other kinds of fruit, in the vain hope of finding *some* that had a taste. I tried to pick some myself——but it was like grasping air, and I soon gave up the attempt and returned to Sylvie.

"Look well at it, my darling," the old man was saying, "and tell me how you like it."

"It's just *lovely*," cried Sylvie, delightedly. "Bruno, come and look!" And she held up, so that he might see the light through it, a heart-shaped Locket, apparently cut out of a single jewel, of a rich blue colour, with a slender gold chain attached to it.

"It are welly pretty," Bruno more soberly remarked: and he began spelling out some words inscribed on it. "All——will——love——Sylvie," he made them out at last. "And so they doos!" he cried, clasping his arms round her neck. "*Everybody* loves Sylvie!"

"But *we* love her best, don't we, Bruno?" said the old King, as he took possession of the Locket. "Now, Sylvie, look at *this*." And he showed her, lying on the palm of his hand, a Locket of a deep crimson colour, the same shape as the blue one and, like it, attached to a slender golden chain.

"Lovelier and lovelier!" exclaimed Sylvie, clasping her hands in ecstasy. "Look, Bruno!"

"And there's words on this one, too," said Bruno. "Sylvie——will——love——all."

"Now you see the difference," said the old man: "different colours and different words.

Choose one of them, darling. I'll give you whichever you like best."

Sylvie whispered the words, several times over, with a thoughtful smile, and then made her decision. "It's *very* nice to be loved," she said: "but it's nicer to love other people! May I have the red one, Father?"

The old man said nothing: but I could see his eyes fill with tears, as he bent his head and pressed his lips to her forehead in a long loving kiss. Then he undid the chain, and showed her how to fasten it round her neck, and to hide it away under the edge of her frock. "It's for you to *keep*, you know," he said in a low voice, "not for other people to *see*. You'll remember how to use it?"

"Yes, I'll remember," said Sylvie.

"And now, darlings, it's time for you to go back, or they'll be missing you, and then that poor Gardener will get into trouble!"

Once more a feeling of wonder rose in my mind as to how in the world we were to *get* back again—since I took it for granted that, wherever the children went, *I* was to go—but no shadow of doubt seemed to cross *their* minds, as they hugged and kissed him, murmuring, over and over again, "Good-bye, darling Father!" And then, suddenly and swiftly, the darkness of midnight seemed to close in upon us, and through the darkness harshly rang a strange wild song:—

"He thought he saw a Buffalo
Upon the chimney-piece:
He looked again, and found it was
His Sister's Husband's Niece.
'Unless you leave this house,' he said,
'I'll send for the Police!'"

"That was *me!*" he added, looking out at us, through the half-opened door, as we stood waiting in the road. "And that's what I'd have done—as sure as potatoes aren't radishes—if she hadn't have tooken herself off! But I always loves my *pay-rints* like anything."

"Who *are* oor *pay-rints?*" said Bruno.

"Them as pay *rint* for me, a course!" the Gardener replied. "You can come in now, if you like."

He flung the door open as he spoke, and we got out, a little dazzled and stupefied (at least *I* felt so) at the sudden transition from the half-darkness of the railway-carriage to the brilliantly-lighted platform of Elveston Station.

A footman, in a handsome livery, came forwards and respectfully touched his hat. "The carriage is here, my Lady," he said, taking from her the wraps and small articles she was carrying: and Lady Muriel, after shaking hands and bidding me "Good-night!" with a pleasant smile, followed him.

It was with a somewhat blank and lonely feeling that I betook myself to the van from which the luggage was being taken out: and, after giving directions to have my boxes sent after me, I made my way on foot to Arthur's lodgings, and soon lost my lonely feeling in the hearty welcome my old friend gave me, and the cozy warmth and cheerful light of the little sitting-room into which he led me.

"Little, as you see, but quite enough for us two. Now, take the easy-chair, old fellow, and let's have another look at you! Well, you *do* look a bit pulled down!" and he put on a solemn professional air. "I prescribe Ozone, *quant. suff.* Social dissipation, *fiant pilulæ quam plurimæ:* to be taken, feasting, three times a day!"

"But, Doctor!" I remonstrated. "Society doesn't 'receive' three times a day!"

"That's all *you* know about it!" the young Doctor gaily replied. "At home, lawn-tennis, 3 P.M. At home, kettledrum, 5 P.M. At home, music (Elveston doesn't give dinners), 8 P.M. Carriages at 10. There you are!"

It sounded very pleasant, I was obliged to admit. "And I know some of the *lady*-society already," I added. "One of them came in the same carriage with me."

"What was she like? Then perhaps I can identify her."

"The *name* was Lady Muriel Orme. As to what she was *like*——well, *I* thought her very beautiful. Do you know her?"

"Yes——I do know her." And the grave Doctor coloured slightly as he added "Yes, I agree with you. She *is* beautiful."

"*I* quite lost my heart to her!" I went on mischievously. "We talked——"

"Have some supper!" Arthur interrupted with an air of relief, as the maid entered with the tray. And he steadily resisted all my attempts to return to the subject of Lady Muriel until the evening had almost worn itself away. Then, as we sat gazing into the fire, and conversation was lapsing into silence, he made a hurried confession.

"I hadn't meant to tell you anything about her," he said (naming no names, as if there were only one 'she' in the world!) "till you had seen more of her, and formed your own judgment of her: but somehow you surprised it out of me. And I've not breathed a word of it to any one else. But I can trust *you* with a secret, old friend! Yes! It's true of *me*, what I suppose *you* said in jest."

"In the merest jest, believe me!" I said earnestly. "Why, man, I'm three times her age! But if she's *your* choice, then I'm sure she's all that is good and——"

"——and sweet," Arthur went on, "and pure, and self-denying, and true-hearted, and——" he broke off hastily, as if he could not trust himself to say more on a subject so sacred and so precious. Silence followed: and I leaned back drowsily in my easy-chair, filled with bright and beautiful imaginings of Arthur and his lady-love, and of all the peace and happiness in store for them.

I pictured them to myself walking together, lingeringly and lovingly, under arching trees, in a sweet garden of their own, and welcomed back by their faithful gardener, on their return from some brief excursion.

It seemed natural enough that the gardener should be filled with exuberant delight at the return of so gracious a master and mistress—and how strangely childlike they looked! I could have taken them for Sylvie and Bruno—less natural that he should show it by such wild dances, such crazy songs!

"*He thought he saw a Rattlesnake*
That questioned him in Greek:
He looked again, and found it was
The Middle of Next Week.
'*The one thing I regret,' he said,*
'*Is that it cannot speak!*'"

—least natural of all that the Vice-Warden and 'my Lady' should be standing close beside me, discussing an open letter, which had just been handed to him by the Professor, who stood, meekly waiting, a few yards off.

"If it were not for those two brats," I heard him mutter, glancing savagely at Sylvie and Bruno, who were courteously listening to the Gardener's song, "there would be no difficulty whatever."

"Let's hear that bit of the letter again," said my Lady. And the Vice-Warden read aloud :—

"—— and we therefore entreat you graciously to accept the Kingship, to which you have been unanimously elected by the Council of Elfland : and that you will allow your son Bruno——of whose goodness, cleverness, and beauty, reports have reached us——to be regarded as Heir-Apparent."

"But what's the difficulty ?" said my Lady.

"Why, don't you see ? The Ambassador, that brought this, is waiting in the house : and he's sure to see Sylvie and Bruno : and then, when he sees Uggug, and remembers all that about 'goodness, cleverness, and beauty,' why, he's sure to——"

"And *where* will you find a better boy than *Uggug?*" my Lady indignantly interrupted. "Or a wittier, or a lovelier?"

To all of which the Vice-Warden simply replied "Don't you be a great blethering goose! Our only chance is to keep those two brats out of sight. If *you* can manage *that*, you may leave the rest to *me*. *I'll* make him believe Uggug to be a model of cleverness and all that."

"We must change his name to Bruno, of course?" said my Lady.

The Vice-Warden rubbed his chin. "Humph! No!" he said musingly. "Wouldn't do. The boy's such an utter idiot, he'd never learn to answer to it."

"*Idiot*, indeed!" cried my Lady. "He's no more an idiot than *I* am!"

"You're right, my dear," the Vice-Warden soothingly replied. "He isn't, indeed!"

My Lady was appeased. "Let's go in and receive the Ambassador," she said, and beckoned to the Professor. "Which room is he waiting in?" she inquired.

"In the Library, Madam."

"And *what* did you say his name was?" said the Vice-Warden.

The Professor referred to a card he held in his hand. "His Adiposity the Baron Doppelgeist."

"Why does he come with such a funny name?" said my Lady.

"He couldn't well change it on the journey," the Professor meekly replied, "because of the luggage."

"*You* go and receive him," my Lady said to the Vice-Warden, "and *I'll* attend to the children."

CHAPTER VII.

THE BARON'S EMBASSY.

I WAS following the Vice-Warden, but, on second thoughts, went after my Lady, being curious to see how she would manage to keep the children out of sight.

I found her holding Sylvie's hand, and with her other hand stroking Bruno's hair in a most tender and motherly fashion: both children were looking bewildered and half-frightened.

" My own darlings," she was saying, " I've been planning a little treat for you! The Professor shall take you a long walk into the woods this beautiful evening: and you shall take a basket of food with you, and have a little picnic down by the river!"

Bruno jumped, and clapped his hands. "That *are* nice!" he cried. "Aren't it, Sylvie?"

Sylvie, who hadn't quite lost her surprised look, put up her mouth for a kiss. "Thank you *very* much," she said earnestly.

My Lady turned her head away to conceal the broad grin of triumph that spread over her vast face, like a ripple on a lake. "Little simpletons!" she muttered to herself, as she marched up to the house. I followed her in.

"Quite so, your Excellency," the Baron was saying as we entered the Library. "All the infantry were under *my* command." He turned, and was duly presented to my Lady.

"A *military* hero?" said my Lady. The fat little man simpered. "Well, yes," he replied, modestly casting down his eyes. "My ancestors were all famous for military genius."

My Lady smiled graciously. "It often runs in families," she remarked: "just as a love for pastry does."

The Baron looked slightly offended, and the Vice-Warden discreetly changed the subject. "Dinner will soon be ready," he said. "May I have the honour of conducting your Adiposity to the guest-chamber?"

"Certainly, certainly!" the Baron eagerly assented. "It would never do to keep *dinner* waiting!" And he almost trotted out of the room after the Vice-Warden.

He was back again so speedily that the Vice-Warden had barely time to explain to my Lady that her remark about "a love for pastry" was "unfortunate. You might have seen, with half an eye," he added, "that that's *his* line. Military genius, indeed! Pooh!"

"Dinner ready yet?" the Baron enquired, as he hurried into the room.

"Will be in a few minutes," the Vice-Warden replied. "Meanwhile, let's take a turn in the garden. You were telling me," he continued, as the trio left the house, "something about a great battle in which you had the command of the infantry——"

"True," said the Baron. "The enemy, as I was saying, far outnumbered us: but I marched my men right into the middle of——what's that?" the Military Hero exclaimed in agitated tones, drawing back behind the Vice-Warden, as a strange creature rushed wildly upon them, brandishing a spade.

"It's only the Gardener!" the Vice-Warden replied in an encouraging tone. "Quite harmless, I assure you. Hark, he's singing! It's his favorite amusement."

And once more those shrill discordant tones rang out:—

> "*He thought he saw a Banker's Clerk*
> *Descending from the bus:*
> *He looked again, and found it was*
> *A Hippopotamus:*
> '*If this should stay to dine,' he said,*
> '*There won't be much for us!*'"

Throwing away the spade, he broke into a frantic jig, snapping his fingers, and repeating, again and again

> "*There won't be much for us!*
> *There won't be much for us!*"

Once more the Baron looked slightly offended, but the Vice-Warden hastily explained that the song had no allusion to *him*, and in fact had no meaning at all. "You didn't mean anything by it, now *did* you?" He appealed to the Gardener, who had finished his song, and stood, balancing himself on one leg, and looking at them, with his mouth open.

"I never means nothing," said the Gardener: and Uggug luckily came up at the moment, and gave the conversation a new turn.

"Allow me to present my son," said the Vice-Warden; adding, in a whisper, "one of the best and cleverest boys that ever lived! I'll contrive for you to see some of his cleverness. He knows everything that other boys *don't* know; and in archery, in fishing, in painting, and in music, his skill is——but you shall judge for yourself. You see that target over there? He shall shoot an arrow at it. Dear boy," he went on aloud, "his Adiposity would like to see you shoot. Bring his Highness' bow and arrows!"

Uggug looked very sulky as he received the bow and arrow, and prepared to shoot. Just as the arrow left the bow, the Vice-Warden trod heavily on the toe of the Baron, who yelled with the pain.

"Ten thousand pardons!" he exclaimed. "I stepped back in my excitement. See! It is a bull's-eye!"

The Baron gazed in astonishment. "He held the bow so awkwardly, it seemed impossible!" he muttered. But there was no room for doubt:

there was the arrow, right in the centre of the bull's-eye!

"The lake is close by," continued the Vice-Warden. "Bring his Highness' fishing-rod!" And Uggug most unwillingly held the rod, and dangled the fly over the water.

"A beetle on your arm!" cried my Lady, pinching the poor Baron's arm worse than if ten lobsters had seized it at once. "*That* kind is poisonous," she explained. "But *what* a pity! You missed seeing the fish pulled out!"

An enormous dead cod-fish was lying on the bank, with the hook in its mouth.

"I had always fancied," the Baron faltered, "that cod were *salt*-water fish?"

"Not in *this* country," said the Vice-Warden. "Shall we go in? Ask my son some question on the way——*any* subject you like!" And the sulky boy was violently shoved forwards, to walk at the Baron's side.

"Could your Highness tell me," the Baron cautiously began, "how much seven times nine would come to?"

"Turn to the left!" cried the Vice-Warden, hastily stepping forwards to show the way——

so hastily, that he ran against his unfortunate guest, who fell heavily on his face.

"*So* sorry!" my Lady exclaimed, as she and her husband helped him to his feet again. "My son was in the act of saying 'sixty-three' as you fell!"

The Baron said nothing: he was covered with dust, and seemed much hurt, both in body and mind. However, when they had got him into the house, and given him a good brushing, matters looked a little better.

Dinner was served in due course, and every fresh dish seemed to increase the good-humour of the Baron: but all efforts, to get him to express his opinion as to Uggug's cleverness, were in vain, until that interesting youth had left the room, and was seen from the open window, prowling about the lawn with a little basket, which he was filling with frogs.

"So fond of Natural History as he is, dear boy!" said the doting mother. "Now *do* tell us, Baron, what you think of him!"

"To be perfectly candid," said the cautious Baron, "I would like a *little* more evidence. I think you mentioned his skill in——"

"Music?" said the Vice-Warden. "Why, he's simply a prodigy! You shall hear him play the piano." And he walked to the window. "Ug——I mean my boy! Come in for a minute, *and bring the music-master with you!* To turn over the music for him," he added as an explanation.

Uggug, having filled his basket with frogs, had no objection to obey, and soon appeared in the room, followed by a fierce-looking little man, who asked the Vice-Warden "Vot music vill you haf?"

"The Sonata that His Highness plays so charmingly," said the Vice-Warden.

"His Highness haf not——" the music-master began, but was sharply stopped by the Vice-Warden.

"Silence, Sir! Go and turn over the music for his Highness. My dear," (to the Wardeness) "will you show him what to do? And meanwhile, Baron, I'll just show you a most interesting map we have——of Outland, and Fairyland, and that sort of thing."

By the time my Lady had returned, from explaining things to the music-master, the map

had been hung up, and the Baron was already much bewildered by the Vice-Warden's habit of pointing to one place while he shouted out the name of another.

My Lady joining in, pointing out other places, and shouting other names, only made matters worse; and at last the Baron, in despair, took to pointing out places for himself, and feebly asked "Is that great yellow splotch *Fairyland?*"

"Yes, that's Fairyland," said the Vice-Warden: "and you might as well give him a hint," he muttered to my Lady, "about going back to-morrow. He eats like a shark! It would hardly do for *me* to mention it."

His wife caught the idea, and at once began giving hints of the most subtle and delicate kind. "Just see what a short way it is back to Fairyland! Why, if you started to-morrow morning, you'd get there in very little more than a week!"

The Baron looked incredulous. "It took me a full month to *come*," he said.

"But it's ever so much shorter, going *back*, you know!"

The Baron looked appealingly to the Vice-Warden, who chimed in readily. "You can go back *five* times, in the time it took you to come here *once*—if you start to-morrow morning!"

All this time the Sonata was pealing through the room. The Baron could not help admitting to himself that it was being magnificently played: but he tried in vain to get a glimpse of the youthful performer. Every time he had nearly succeeded in catching sight of him, either the Vice-Warden or his wife was sure to get in the way, pointing out some new place on the map, and deafening him with some new name.

He gave in at last, wished a hasty good-night, and left the room, while his host and hostess interchanged looks of triumph.

"Deftly done!" cried the Vice-Warden. "Craftily contrived! But what means all that tramping on the stairs?" He half-opened the door, looked out, and added in a tone of dismay, "The Baron's boxes are being carried down!"

"And what means all that rumbling of wheels?" cried my Lady. She peeped through the window curtains. "The Baron's carriage has come round!" she groaned.

At this moment the door opened: a fat, furious face looked in: a voice, hoarse with passion, thundered out the words "My room is full of frogs——I leave you!": and the door closed again.

And still the noble Sonata went pealing through the room: but it was *Arthur's* masterly touch that roused the echoes, and thrilled my very soul with the tender music of the immortal 'Sonata Pathetique': and it was not till the last note had died away that the tired but happy traveler could bring himself to utter the words "good-night!" and to seek his much-needed pillow.

CHAPTER VIII.

A RIDE ON A LION.

THE next day glided away, pleasantly enough, partly in settling myself in my new quarters, and partly in strolling round the neighbourhood, under Arthur's guidance, and trying to form a general idea of Elveston and its inhabitants. When five o'clock arrived, Arthur proposed—without any embarrassment this time—to take me with him up to 'the Hall,' in order that I might make acquaintance with the Earl of Ainslie, who had taken it for the season, and renew acquaintance with his daughter Lady Muriel.

My first impressions of the gentle, dignified, and yet genial old man were entirely favourable: and the *real* satisfaction that showed itself on his daughter's face, as she met me with the words "this is indeed an unlooked-for pleasure!", was very soothing for whatever remains of personal vanity the failures and disappointments of many long years, and much buffeting with a rough world, had left in me.

Yet I noted, and was glad to note, evidence of a far deeper feeling than mere friendly regard, in her meeting with Arthur——though this was, as I gathered, an almost daily occurrence——and the conversation between them, in which the Earl and I were only occasional sharers, had an ease and a spontaneity rarely met with except between *very* old friends: and, as I knew that they had not known each other for a longer period than the summer which was now rounding into autumn, I felt certain that 'Love,' and Love alone, could explain the phenomenon.

"How convenient it would be," Lady Muriel laughingly remarked, *à propos* of my having insisted on saving her the trouble of carrying a cup of tea across the room to the Earl, "if cups of tea had no weight at all! Then perhaps ladies would *sometimes* be permitted to carry them for short distances!"

"One can easily imagine a situation," said Arthur, "where things would *necessarily* have no weight, relatively to each other, though each would have its usual weight, looked at by itself."

"Some desperate paradox!" said the Earl. "Tell us how it could be. We shall never guess it."

"Well, suppose this house, just as it is, placed a few billion miles above a planet, and with nothing else near enough to disturb it: of course it falls *to* the planet?"

The Earl nodded. "Of course—though it might take some centuries to do it."

"And is five-o'clock-tea to be going on all the while?" said Lady Muriel.

"That, and other things," said Arthur. "The inhabitants would live their lives, grow up and die, and still the house would be falling, falling, falling! But now as to the relative weight of things. Nothing can be *heavy*, you know, except by *trying* to fall, and being prevented from doing so. You all grant that?"

We all granted that.

"Well, now, if I take this book, and hold it out at arm's length, of course I feel its *weight*. It is trying to fall, and I prevent it. And, if I let go, it falls to the floor. But, if we were all falling together, it couldn't be *trying* to fall any quicker, you know: for, if I let go, what more could it do than fall? And, as my hand would be falling too—at the same rate—it would never leave it, for that would be to get ahead of it in the race. And it could never overtake the falling floor!"

"I see it clearly," said Lady Muriel. "But it makes one dizzy to think of such things! How *can* you make us do it?"

"There is a more curious idea yet," I ventured to say. "Suppose a cord fastened to the house, from below, and pulled down by some one on the planet. Then of course the *house* goes faster than its natural rate of falling: but the furniture—with our noble selves—would go on falling at their old pace, and would therefore be left behind."

"Practically, we should rise to the ceiling," said the Earl. "The inevitable result of which would be concussion of brain."

"To avoid that," said Arthur, "let us have the furniture fixed to the floor, and ourselves tied down to the furniture. Then the five-o'clock-tea could go on in peace."

"With one little drawback!" Lady Muriel gaily interrupted. "We should take the *cups* down with us: but what about the *tea?*"

"I had forgotten the *tea*," Arthur confessed. "*That*, no doubt, would rise to the ceiling—unless you chose to drink it on the way!"

"Which, I think, is *quite* nonsense enough for one while!" said the Earl. "What news does this gentleman bring us from the great world of London?"

This drew *me* into the conversation, which now took a more conventional tone. After a while, Arthur gave the signal for our departure, and in the cool of the evening we strolled down to the beach, enjoying the silence, broken only by the murmur of the sea and the far-away music of some fishermen's song, almost as much as our late pleasant talk.

We sat down among the rocks, by a little pool, so rich in animal, vegetable, and zoöphytic ——or whatever is the right word——life, that I became entranced in the study of it, and, when Arthur proposed returning to our lodgings, I begged to be left there for a while, to watch and muse alone.

The fishermen's song grew ever nearer and clearer, as their boat stood in for the beach; and I would have gone down to see them land their cargo of fish, had not the microcosm at my feet stirred my curiosity yet more keenly.

One ancient crab, that was for ever shuffling frantically from side to side of the pool, had particularly fascinated me: there was a vacancy in its stare, and an aimless violence in its behaviour, that irresistibly recalled the Gardener who had befriended Sylvie and Bruno: and, as I gazed, I caught the concluding notes of the tune of his crazy song.

The silence that followed was broken by the sweet voice of Sylvie. "Would you please let us out into the road?"

"What! After that old beggar again?" the Gardener yelled, and began singing:—

"*He thought he saw a Kangaroo*
That worked a coffee-mill:
He looked again, and found it was
A Vegetable-Pill.
'*Were I to swallow this,*' *he said,*
'*I should be very ill!*'"

"We don't want him to swallow *anything*," Sylvie explained. "He's not hungry. But we want to see him. So will you please——"

"Certainly!" the Gardener promptly replied. "I *always* please. Never displeases nobody.

There you are!" And he flung the door open, and let us out upon the dusty high-road.

We soon found our way to the bush, which had so mysteriously sunk into the ground: and here Sylvie drew the Magic Locket from its hiding-place, turned it over with a thoughtful air, and at last appealed to Bruno in a rather helpless way. "What *was* it we had to do with it, Bruno? It's all gone out of my head!"

"Kiss it!" was Bruno's invariable recipe in cases of doubt and difficulty. Sylvie kissed it, but no result followed.

"Rub it the wrong way," was Bruno's next suggestion.

"Which *is* the wrong way?" Sylvie most reasonably enquired. The obvious plan was to try *both* ways.

Rubbing from left to right had no visible effect whatever.

From right to left—"Oh, stop, Sylvie!" Bruno cried in sudden alarm. "Whatever *is* going to happen?"

For a number of trees, on the neighbouring hillside, were moving slowly upwards, in solemn procession: while a mild little brook, that had

been rippling at our feet a moment before, began to swell, and foam, and hiss, and bubble, in a truly alarming fashion.

"Rub it some other way!" cried Bruno. "Try up-and-down! Quick!"

It was a happy thought. Up-and-down did it: and the landscape, which had been showing signs of mental aberration in various directions, returned to its normal condition of sobriety—with the exception of a small yellowish-brown mouse, which continued to run wildly up and down the road, lashing its tail like a little lion.

"Let's follow it," said Sylvie: and this also turned out a happy thought. The mouse at once settled down into a business-like jog-trot, with which we could easily keep pace. The only phenomenon, that gave me any uneasiness, was the rapid increase in the *size* of the little creature we were following, which became every moment more and more like a real lion.

Soon the transformation was complete: and a noble lion stood patiently waiting for us to come up with it. No thought of fear seemed to occur to the children, who patted and stroked it as if it had been a Shetland-pony.

"Help me up!" cried Bruno. And in another moment Sylvie had lifted him upon the broad back of the gentle beast, and seated herself behind him, pillion-fashion. Bruno took a good handful of mane in each hand, and made believe to guide this new kind of steed. "Gee-up!" seemed quite sufficient by way of *verbal* direction: the lion at once broke into an easy canter, and we soon found ourselves in the depths of the forest. I say '*we*,' for I am certain that *I* accompanied them——though *how* I managed to keep up with a cantering lion I am wholly unable to explain. But I was certainly one of the party when we came upon an old beggar-man cutting sticks, at whose feet the lion made a profound obeisance, Sylvie and Bruno at the same moment dismounting, and leaping into the arms of their father.

"From bad to worse!" the old man said to himself, dreamily, when the children had finished their rather confused account of the Ambassador's visit, gathered no doubt from general report, as they had not seen him themselves. "From bad to worse! That is their destiny. I see it, but I cannot alter it. The selfishness of a mean and crafty man——the selfishness of an ambitious and silly woman——the selfishness of a spiteful and loveless child——all tend one way, from bad to worse! And you, my darlings, must suffer it awhile, I fear. Yet, when things are at their worst, you can come to me. I can do but little as yet——"

Gathering up a handful of dust and scattering it in the air, he slowly and solemnly pronounced some words that sounded like a charm, the children looking on in awe-struck silence:——

"Let craft, ambition, spite,
Be quenched in Reason's night,
Till weakness turn to might,
Till what is dark be light,
Till what is wrong be right!"

The cloud of dust spread itself out through the air, as if it were alive, forming curious shapes that were for ever changing into others.

"It makes letters! It makes words!" Bruno whispered, as he clung, half-frightened, to Sylvie. "Only I *ca'n't* make them out! Read them, Sylvie!"

"I'll try," Sylvie gravely replied. "Wait a minute—if only I could see that word—"

"I should be very ill!" a discordant voice yelled in our ears.

"'*Were I to swallow this,' he said,*
'*I should be very ill!*'"

CHAPTER IX.

A JESTER AND A BEAR.

YES, we were in the garden once more: and, to escape that horrid discordant voice, we hurried indoors, and found ourselves in the library——Uggug blubbering, the Professor standing by with a bewildered air, and my Lady, with her arms clasped round her son's neck, repeating, over and over again, "and *did* they give him nasty lessons to learn? My own pretty pet!"

"What's all this noise about?" the Vice-Warden angrily enquired, as he strode into the room. "And who put the hat-stand here?"

And he hung his hat up on Bruno, who was standing in the middle of the room, too much astonished by the sudden change of scene to make any attempt at removing it, though it came down to his shoulders, making him look something like a small candle with a large extinguisher over it.

The Professor mildly explained that His Highness had been graciously pleased to say he wouldn't do his lessons.

"Do your lessons this instant, you young cub!" thundered the Vice-Warden. "And take *this!*" and a resounding box on the ear made the unfortunate Professor reel across the room.

"Save me!" faltered the poor old man, as he sank, half-fainting, at my Lady's feet.

"Shave you? Of course I will!" my Lady replied, as she lifted him into a chair, and pinned an anti-macassar round his neck. "Where's the razor?"

The Vice-Warden meanwhile had got hold of Uggug, and was belabouring him with his umbrella. "Who left this loose nail in the floor?" he shouted. "Hammer it in, I say!

Hammer it in!" Blow after blow fell on the writhing Uggug, till he dropped howling to the floor.

Then his father turned to the 'shaving' scene which was being enacted, and roared with laughter. "Excuse me, dear, I ca'n't help it!" he said as soon as he could speak. "You *are* such an utter donkey! Kiss me, Tabby!"

And he flung his arms round the neck of the terrified Professor, who raised a wild shriek, but whether he received the threatened kiss or not I was unable to see, as Bruno, who had by this time released himself from his extinguisher, rushed headlong out of the room, followed by Sylvie ; and I was so fearful of being left alone among all these crazy creatures that I hurried after them.

"We must go to Father!" Sylvie panted, as they ran down the garden. "I'm *sure* things are at their worst! I'll ask the Gardener to let us out again."

"But we ca'n't *walk* all the way!" Bruno whimpered. "How I *wiss* we had a coach-and-four, like Uncle!"

And, shrill and wild, rang through the air the familiar voice :—

"He thought he saw a Coach-and-Four
That stood beside his bed :
He looked again, and found it was
A Bear without a Head.
'Poor thing,' he said, 'poor silly thing!
It's waiting to be fed!'"

"No, I ca'n't let you out again!" he said, before the children could speak. "The Vice-Warden gave it me, he did, for letting you out last time! So be off with you!" And, turning away from them, he began digging frantically in the middle of a gravel-walk, singing, over and over again,

> "'*Poor thing,' he said, 'poor silly thing!*
> *It's waiting to be fed!*'"

but in a more musical tone than the shrill screech in which he had begun.

The music grew fuller and richer at every moment: other manly voices joined in the refrain: and soon I heard the heavy thud that told me the boat had touched the beach, and the harsh grating of the shingle as the men dragged it up. I roused myself, and, after lending them a hand in hauling up their boat, I lingered yet awhile to watch them disembark a goodly assortment of the hard-won 'treasures of the deep.'

When at last I reached our lodgings I was tired and sleepy, and glad enough to settle down again into the easy-chair, while Arthur hospitably went to his cupboard, to get me out some cake and wine, without which, he declared, he could not, as a doctor, permit my going to bed.

And how that cupboard-door *did* creak! It surely could not be *Arthur*, who was opening and shutting it so often, moving so restlessly about, and muttering like the soliloquy of a tragedy-queen!

No, it was a *female* voice. Also the figure—half-hidden by the cupboard-door—was a *female* figure, massive, and in flowing robes.

Could it be the landlady? The door opened, and a strange man entered the room.

"What *is* that donkey doing?" he said to himself, pausing, aghast, on the threshold.

The lady, thus rudely referred to, was his wife. She had got one of the cupboards open, and stood with her back to him, smoothing down a sheet of brown paper on one of the shelves, and whispering to herself "So, so! Deftly done! Craftily contrived!"

Her loving husband stole behind her on tiptoe, and tapped her on the head. "Boh!" he playfully shouted at her ear. "Never tell me again I ca'n't say 'boh' to a goose!"

My Lady wrung her hands. "Discovered!" she groaned. "Yet no—he is one of us! Reveal it not, oh Man! Let it bide its time!"

"Reveal *what* not?" her husband testily replied, dragging out the sheet of brown paper. "What are you hiding here, my Lady? I insist upon knowing!"

My Lady cast down her eyes, and spoke in the littlest of little voices. "Don't make fun of it, Benjamin!" she pleaded. "It's—it's—don't you understand? It's a DAGGER!"

"And what's *that* for?" sneered His Excellency. "We've only got to make people *think* he's dead! We haven't got to *kill* him! And made of tin, too!" he snarled, contemptuously bending the blade round his thumb. Now, Madam, you'll be good enough to explain. First, what do you call me *Benjamin* for?"

"It's part of the Conspiracy, Love! One *must* have an alias, you know——"

"Oh, an *alias*, is it? Well! And next, what did you get this dagger for? Come, no evasions! You ca'n't deceive *me!*"

"I got it for——for——for——" the detected Conspirator stammered, trying her best to put on the assassin-expression that she had been practising at the looking-glass. "For——"

"For *what*, Madam!"

"Well, for eighteenpence, if you *must* know, dearest! That's what I got it for, on my——"

"Now *don't* say your Word and Honour!" groaned the other Conspirator. "Why, they aren't worth half the money, put together!"

"On my *birthday*," my Lady concluded in a meek whisper. "One *must* have a dagger, you know. It's part of the——"

"Oh, don't talk of Conspiracies!" her husband savagely interrupted, as he tossed the dagger into the cupboard. "You know about as much how to manage a Conspiracy as if you were a chicken. Why, the first thing is to get a disguise. Now, just look at this!"

And with pardonable pride he fitted on the cap and bells, and the rest of the Fool's dress, and winked at her, and put his tongue in his cheek. "Is *that* the sort of thing, now?" he demanded.

My Lady's eyes flashed with all a Conspirator's enthusiasm. "The very thing!" she exclaimed, clapping her hands. "You do look, oh, such a *perfect* Fool!"

The Fool smiled a doubtful smile. He was not quite clear whether it was a compliment or not, to express it so plainly. "You mean a Jester? Yes, that's what I intended. And what do you think *your* disguise is to be?" And he proceeded to unfold the parcel, the lady watching him in rapture.

"Oh, how lovely!" she cried, when at last the dress was unfolded. "What a *splendid* disguise! An Esquimaux peasant-woman!"

"An Esquimaux peasant, indeed!" growled the other. "Here, put it on, and look at yourself in the glass. Why, it's a *Bear*, ca'n't you use your eyes?" He checked himself suddenly, as a harsh voice yelled through the room

"*He looked again, and found it was*
A Bear without a Head!"

But it was only the Gardener, singing under the open window. The Vice-Warden stole on tip-toe to the window, and closed it noiselessly, before he ventured to go on. "Yes, Lovey, a *Bear*: but not without a *head*, I hope! You're the Bear, and me the Keeper. And if any one knows us, they'll have sharp eyes, that's all!"

"I shall have to practise the steps a bit," my Lady said, looking out through the Bear's mouth: "one ca'n't help being rather human just at first, you know. And of course you'll say 'Come up, Bruin!', won't you?"

"Yes, of course," replied the Keeper, laying hold of the chain, that hung from the Bear's collar, with one hand, while with the other he cracked a little whip. "Now go round the room in a sort of a dancing attitude. Very good, my dear, very good. Come up, Bruin! Come up, I say!"

He roared out the last words for the benefit of Uggug, who had just come into the room, and was now standing, with his hands spread out, and eyes and mouth wide open, the very picture of stupid amazement. "Oh, my!" was all he could gasp out.

The Keeper pretended to be adjusting the bear's collar, which gave him an opportunity of whispering, unheard by Uggug, "*my* fault, I'm afraid! Quite forgot to fasten the door. Plot's ruined if *he* finds it out! Keep it up a minute or two longer. Be savage!" Then, while seeming to pull it back with all his strength, he let it advance upon the scared boy: my Lady, with admirable presence of mind, kept up what she no doubt intended for a savage growl, though it was more like the purring of a cat: and Uggug backed out of the room with such haste that he tripped over the mat, and was heard to fall heavily outside——an accident to which even his doting mother paid no heed, in the excitement of the moment.

The Vice-Warden shut and bolted the door. "Off with the disguises!" he panted. "There's not a moment to lose. He's sure to fetch the Professor, and we couldn't take *him* in, you know!" And in another minute the disguises were stowed away in the cupboard, the door unbolted, and the two Conspirators seated lovingly side-by-side on the sofa, earnestly discussing a book the Vice-Warden had hastily snatched off the table, which proved to be the City-Directory of the capital of Outland.

The door opened, very slowly and cautiously, and the Professor peeped in, Uggug's stupid face being just visible behind him.

"It is a beautiful arrangement!" the Vice-Warden was saying with enthusiasm. "You see, my precious one, that there are fifteen houses in Green Street, *before* you turn into West Street."

"*Fifteen* houses! Is it *possible?*" my Lady replied. "I thought it was fourteen!" And, so intent were they on this interesting question, that neither of them even looked up till the Professor, leading Uggug by the hand, stood close before them.

My Lady was the first to notice their approach. "Why, here's the Professor!" she exclaimed in her blandest tones. "And my precious child too! Are lessons over?"

"A strange thing has happened!" the Professor began in a trembling tone. "His Exalted Fatness" (this was one of Uggug's many titles) "tells me he has just seen, in this very room, a Dancing-Bear and a Court-Jester!"

The Vice-Warden and his wife shook with well-acted merriment.

"Not in *this* room, darling!" said the fond mother. "We've been sitting here this hour or more, reading——," here she referred to the book lying on her lap, "——reading the——the City-Directory."

"Let me feel your pulse, my boy!" said the anxious father. "Now put out your tongue. Ah, I thought so! He's a little feverish, Professor, and has had a bad dream. Put him to bed at once, and give him a cooling draught."

"I ain't been dreaming!" his Exalted Fatness remonstrated, as the Professor led him away.

"Bad grammar, Sir!" his father remarked with some sternness. "Kindly attend to *that* little matter, Professor, as soon as you have corrected the feverishness. And, by the way, Professor!" (The Professor left his distinguished pupil standing at the door, and meekly returned.) "There is a rumour afloat, that the people wish to elect an——in point of fact, an ——you understand that I mean an——"

"Not *another Professor!*" the poor old man exclaimed in horror.

"No! Certainly not!" the Vice-Warden eagerly explained. "Merely an *Emperor*, you understand."

"An *Emperor!*" cried the astonished Professor, holding his head between his hands, as if he expected it to come to pieces with the shock. "What will the Warden——"

"Why, the *Warden* will most likely *be* the new Emperor!" my Lady explained. "Where could we find a better? Unless, perhaps——" she glanced at her husband.

"Where indeed!" the Professor fervently responded, quite failing to take the hint.

The Vice-Warden resumed the thread of his discourse. "The reason I mentioned it, Professor, was to ask *you* to be so kind as to preside at the Election. You see it would make the thing *respectable*——no suspicion of anything underhand——"

"I fear I ca'n't, your Excellency!" the old man faltered. "What will the Warden——"

"True, true!" the Vice-Warden interrupted. "Your position, as Court-Professor, makes it awkward, I admit. Well, well! Then the Election shall be held without you."

"Better so, than if it were held *within* me!" the Professor murmured with a bewildered air, as if he hardly knew what he was saying. "Bed, I think your Highness said, and a cooling-draught?" And he wandered dreamily back to where Uggug sulkily awaited him.

I followed them out of the room, and down the passage, the Professor murmuring to himself, all the time, as a kind of aid to his feeble memory, "C, C, C; Couch, Cooling-Draught, Correct-Grammar," till, in turning a corner, he met Sylvie and Bruno, so suddenly that the startled Professor let go of his fat pupil, who instantly took to his heels.

CHAPTER X.

THE OTHER PROFESSOR.

"WE were looking for you!" cried Sylvie, in a tone of great relief. "We *do* want you so much, you ca'n't think!"

"What is it, dear children?" the Professor asked, beaming on them with a very different look from what Uggug ever got from him.

"We want you to speak to the Gardener for us," Sylvie said, as she and Bruno took the old man's hands and led him into the hall.

"He's ever so unkind!" Bruno mournfully added. "They's *all* unkind to us, now that Father's gone. The Lion were *much* nicer!"

"But you must explain to me, please," the Professor said with an anxious look, "*which* is the Lion, and *which* is the Gardener. It's *most* important not to get two such animals confused together. And one's very liable to do it in their case—both having mouths, you know——"

"Doos oo *always* confuses two animals together?" Bruno asked.

"Pretty often, I'm afraid," the Professor candidly confessed. "Now, for instance, there's the rabbit-hutch and the hall-clock." The Professor pointed them out. "One gets a little confused with *them*—both having doors, you know. Now, only yesterday—would you believe it?—I put some lettuces into the clock, and tried to wind up the rabbit!"

"Did the rabbit *go*, after oo wounded it up?" said Bruno.

The Professor clasped his hands on the top of his head, and groaned. "Go? I should think it *did* go! Why, it's *gone!* And where ever it's gone to—that's what I *ca'n't* find out! I've done my best—I've read all the article 'Rabbit' in the great dictionary——Come in!"

"Only the tailor, Sir, with your little bill," said a meek voice outside the door.

"Ah, well, I can soon settle *his* business," the Professor said to the children, "if you'll just wait a minute. How much is it, this year, my man?" The tailor had come in while he was speaking.

"Well, it's been a doubling so many years, you see," the tailor replied, a little gruffly, "and I think I'd like the money now. It's two thousand pound, it is!"

"Oh, that's nothing!" the Professor carelessly remarked, feeling in his pocket, as if he always carried at least *that* amount about with him. "But wouldn't you like to wait just another year, and make it *four* thousand? Just think how rich you'd be! Why, you might be a *King*, if you liked!"

"I don't know as I'd care about being a *King*," the man said thoughtfully. "But it *dew* sound a powerful sight o' money! Well, I think I'll wait——"

"Of course you will!" said the Professor. "There's good sense in *you*, I see. Good-day to you, my man!"

"Will you ever have to pay him that four thousand pounds?" Sylvie asked as the door closed on the departing creditor.

"*Never*, my child!" the Professor replied emphatically. "He'll go on doubling it, till he dies. You see it's *always* worth while waiting another year, to get twice as much money! And now what would you like to do, my little friends? Shall I take you to see the Other Professor? This would be an excellent opportunity for a visit," he said to himself, glancing at his watch: "he generally takes a short rest—of fourteen minutes and a half—about this time."

Bruno hastily went round to Sylvie, who was standing at the other side of the Professor, and put his hand into hers. "I *thinks* we'd like to go," he said doubtfully: "only please let's go all together. It's best to be on the safe side, oo know!"

"Why, you talk as if you were *Sylvie!*" exclaimed the Professor.

"I know I did," Bruno replied very humbly. "I quite forgotted I wasn't Sylvie. Only I fought he might be rarver fierce!"

The Professor laughed a jolly laugh. "Oh, he's quite tame!" he said. "He never bites. He's only a little—a little *dreamy*, you know." He took hold of Bruno's other hand, and led the children down a long passage I had never noticed before—not that there was anything remarkable in *that*: I was constantly coming on new rooms and passages in that mysterious Palace, and very seldom succeeded in finding the old ones again.

Near the end of the passage the Professor stopped. "This is his room," he said, pointing to the solid wall.

"We ca'n't get in through *there!*" Bruno exclaimed.

Sylvie said nothing, till she had carefully examined whether the wall opened anywhere. Then she laughed merrily. "You're playing us a trick, you dear old thing!" she said. "There's no *door* here!"

"There isn't any door to the room," said the Professor. "We shall have to climb in at the window."

So we went into the garden, and soon found the window of the Other Professor's

room. It was a ground-floor window, and stood invitingly open: the Professor first lifted the two children in, and then he and I climbed in after them.

The Other Professor was seated at a table, with a large book open before him, on which his forehead was resting: he had clasped his arms round the book, and was snoring heavily. "He usually reads like that," the Professor remarked, "when the book's very interesting: and then sometimes it's very difficult to get him to attend!"

This seemed to be one of the difficult times: the Professor lifted him up, once or twice, and shook him violently: but he always returned to his book the moment he was let go of, and showed by his heavy breathing that the book was as interesting as ever.

"How dreamy he is!" the Professor exclaimed. "He must have got to a *very* interesting part of the book!" And he rained quite a shower of thumps on the Other Professor's back, shouting "Hoy! Hoy!" all the time. "Isn't it *wonderful* that he should be so dreamy?" he said to Bruno.

"If he's always as *sleepy* as that," Bruno remarked, "a *course* he's dreamy!"

"But what are we to *do?*" said the Professor. "You see he's quite wrapped up in the book!"

"Suppose oo *shuts* the book?" Bruno suggested.

"That's it!" cried the delighted Professor. "Of course that'll do it!" And he shut up the book so quickly that he caught the Other Professor's nose between the leaves, and gave it a severe pinch.

The Other Professor instantly rose to his feet, and carried the book away to the end of the room, where he put it back in its place in the book-case. "I've been reading for eighteen hours and three-quarters," he said, "and now I shall rest for fourteen minutes and a half. Is the Lecture all ready?"

"Very nearly," the Professor humbly replied. "I shall ask you to give me a hint or two—there will be a few little difficulties——"

"And a Banquet, I think you said?"

"Oh, yes! The Banquet comes *first*, of course. People never enjoy Abstract Science, you know, when they're ravenous with hunger. And then there's the Fancy-Dress-Ball. Oh, there'll be lots of entertainment!"

"Where will the Ball come in?" said the Other Professor.

"I *think* it had better come at the beginning of the Banquet—it brings people together so nicely, you know."

"Yes, that's the right order. First the Meeting: then the Eating: then the Treating—for I'm sure any Lecture *you* give us will be a treat!" said the Other Professor, who had been standing with his back to us all this time, occupying himself in taking the books out, one by one, and turning them upside-down. An easel, with a black board on it, stood near him: and, every time that he turned a book upside-down, he made a mark on the board with a piece of chalk.

"And as to the 'Pig-Tale'— which *you* have so kindly promised to give us—" the Professor went on, thoughtfully rubbing his chin. "I think that had better come at the *end* of the Banquet: then people can listen to it quietly."

"Shall I *sing* it?" the Other Professor asked, with a smile of delight.

"If you *can*," the Professor replied, cautiously.

"Let me try," said the Other Professor, seating himself at the pianoforte. "For the sake of argument, let us assume that it begins on A flat." And he struck the note in question. "La, la, la! I think that's within an octave of it." He struck the note again, and appealed to Bruno, who was standing at his side. "Did I sing it like *that*, my child?"

"No, oo didn't," Bruno replied with great decision. "It were more like a duck."

"Single notes are apt to have that effect," the Other Professor said with a sigh. "Let me try a whole verse.

There was a Pig, that sat alone,
Beside a ruined Pump.
By day and night he made his moan:
It would have stirred a heart of stone
To see him wring his hoofs and groan,
Because he could not jump.

Would you call that a tune, Professor?" he asked, when he had finished.

The Professor considered a little. "Well," he said at last, "some of the notes are the same as others—and some are different—but I should hardly call it a *tune*."

"Let me try it a bit by myself," said the Other Professor. And he began touching the notes here and there, and humming to himself like an angry bluebottle.

"How do you like his singing?" the Professor asked the children in a low voice.

"It isn't very *beautiful*," Sylvie said, hesitatingly.

"It's very extremely *ugly!*" Bruno said, without any hesitation at all.

"All extremes are bad," the Professor said, very gravely. "For instance, Sobriety is a very good thing, when practised *in moderation*: but even Sobriety, when carried to an *extreme*, has its disadvantages."

"What are its disadvantages?" was the question that rose in my mind—and, as usual, Bruno asked it for me. "What *are* its lizard bandages?"

"Well, this is *one* of them," said the Professor. "When a man's tipsy (that's one extreme, you know), he sees one thing as two. But, when he's *extremely* sober (that's the other extreme), he sees two things as one. It's equally inconvenient, whichever happens."

"What does 'illconvenient' mean?" Bruno whispered to Sylvie.

"The difference between 'convenient' and 'inconvenient' is best explained by an example," said the Other Professor, who had overheard the question. "If you'll just think over any Poem that contains the two words—such as——"

The Professor put his hands over his ears, with a look of dismay. "If you once let him begin a *Poem*," he said to Sylvie, "he'll never leave off again! He never does!"

"Did he ever begin a Poem and not leave off again?" Sylvie enquired.

"Three times," said the Professor.

Bruno raised himself on tiptoe, till his lips were on a level with Sylvie's ear. "What became of them three Poems?" he whispered. "Is he saying them all, now?"

"Hush!" said Sylvie. "The Other Professor is speaking!"

"I'll say it very quick," murmured the Other Professor, with downcast eyes, and melancholy voice, which contrasted oddly with his face, as he had forgotten to leave off smiling. ("At least it wasn't exactly a *smile*," as Sylvie said afterwards: "it looked as if his mouth was made that shape.")

"Go on then," said the Professor. "*What must be must be.*"

"Remember that!" Sylvie whispered to Bruno, "It's a very good rule for whenever you hurt yourself."

"And it's a very good rule for whenever I make a noise," said the saucy little fellow. "So *you* remember it too, Miss!"

"Whatever *do* you mean?" said Sylvie, trying to frown, a thing she never managed particularly well.

"Oftens and oftens," said Bruno, "haven't oo told me 'There mustn't be so much noise, Bruno!' when I've tolded oo 'There *must!*' Why, there isn't no rules at all about 'There mustn't'! But oo never believes *me!*"

"As if any one *could* believe *you*, you wicked wicked boy!" said Sylvie. The *words* were severe enough, but I am of opinion that, when you are really *anxious* to impress a criminal with a sense of his guilt, you ought not to pronounce the sentence with your lips *quite* close to his cheek—since a kiss at the end of it, however accidental, weakens the effect terribly.

CHAPTER XI.

PETER AND PAUL.

"As I was saying," the Other Professor resumed, "if you'll just think over any Poem, that contains the words——such as

'Peter is poor,' said noble Paul,
'And I have always been his friend:
And, though my means to give *are small,*
At least I can afford to lend.
How few, in this cold age of greed,
Do good, except on selfish grounds!
But I can feel for Peter's need,
And I WILL LEND HIM FIFTY POUNDS!'

How great was Peter's joy to find
His friend in such a genial vein!

How cheerfully the bond he signed,
To pay the money back again!
'We ca'n't,' said Paul, 'be too precise:
'Tis best to fix the very day:
So, by a learned friend's advice,
I've made it Noon, the Fourth of May.'

'But this is April!' Peter said.
'The First of April, as I think.
Five little weeks will soon be fled:
One scarcely will have time to wink!
Give me a year to speculate—
To buy and sell—to drive a trade—
Said Paul 'I cannot change the date.
On May the Fourth it must be paid.'

'Well, well!' said Peter, with a sigh.
'Hand me the cash, and I will go.
I'll form a Joint-Stock Company,
And turn an honest pound or so.'
'I'm grieved,' said Paul, 'to seem unkind:
The money shall of course be lent:
But, for a week or two, I find
It will not be convenient.'

So, week by week, poor Peter came
And turned in heaviness away;
For still the answer was the same,
'I cannot manage it to-day.'
And now the April showers were dry—
The five short weeks were nearly spent—
Yet still he got the old reply,
'It is not quite convenient!'

The Fourth arrived, and punctual Paul
Came, with his legal friend, at noon.
'I thought it best,' said he, 'to call:
One cannot settle things too soon.'
Poor Peter shuddered in despair:
His flowing locks he wildly tore:
And very soon his yellow hair
Was lying all about the floor.

The legal friend was standing by,
With sudden pity half unmanned:
The tear-drop trembled in his eye,
The signed agreement in his hand:
But when at length the legal soul
Resumed its customary force,
The Law,' he said, 'we ca'n't control:
Pay, or the Law must take its course!'

Said Paul 'How bitterly I rue
That fatal morning when I called!
Consider, Peter, what you do!
You won't be richer when you're bald!
Think you, by rending curls away,
To make your difficulties less?
Forbear this violence, I pray:
You do but add to my distress!'

'*Not willingly would I inflict,*'
Said Peter, '*on that noble heart*
One needless pang. Yet why so strict?
Is this *to act a friendly part?*
However legal it may be
To pay what never has been lent,

This style of business seems to me
Extremely inconvenient!

'*No Nobleness of soul have I,*
Like some *that in this Age are found!*'
(*Paul blushed in sheer humility,*
And cast his eyes upon the ground.)
'*This debt will simply swallow all,*
And make my life a life of woe!'
'*Nay, nay, my Peter!*' *answered Paul.*
'*You must not rail on Fortune so!*

'*You have enough to eat and drink:*
You are respected in the world:
And at the barber's, as I think,
You often get your whiskers curled.
Though Nobleness you ca'n't attain—
To any very great extent—
The path of Honesty is plain,
However inconvenient!'

''*Tis true,*' *said Peter,* '*I'm alive:*
I keep my station in the world:
Once in the week I just contrive
To get my whiskers oiled and curled.

But my assets are very low:
My little income's overspent:
To trench on capital, you know,
Is always inconvenient!'

'But pay your debts!' cried honest Paul.
'My gentle Peter, pay your debts!
What matter if it swallows all
That you describe as your "assets"?
Already you're an hour behind:
Yet Generosity is best.
It pinches me—but never mind!
I WILL NOT CHARGE YOU INTEREST!'

'How good! How great!' poor Peter cried.
'Yet I must sell my Sunday wig—
The scarf-pin that has been my pride—
My grand piano—and my pig!'
Full soon his property took wings:
And daily, as each treasure went,
He sighed to find the state of things
Grow less and less convenient.

Weeks grew to months, and months to years:
Peter was worn to skin and bone:

And once he even said, with tears,
'Remember, Paul, that promised Loan!'
Said Paul 'I'll lend you, when I can,
All the spare money I have got—
Ah, Peter, you're a happy man!
Yours is an enviable lot!

'I'm getting stout, as you may see:
It is but seldom I am well:
I cannot feel my ancient glee
In listening to the dinner-bell:
But you, you gambol like a boy,
Your figure is so spare and light:
The dinner-bell's a note of joy
To such a healthy appetite!'

Said Peter 'I am well aware
Mine is a state of happiness:
And yet how gladly could I spare
Some of the comforts I possess!
What you *call healthy appetite*
I *feel as Hunger's savage tooth:*
And, when no dinner is in sight,
The dinner-bell's a sound of ruth!

'No scare-crow would accept this coat:
Such boots as these you seldom see.
Ah, Paul, a single five-pound-note
Would make another man of me!'
Said Paul 'It fills me with surprise
To hear you talk in such a tone:
I fear you scarcely realise
The blessings that are all your own!

'You're safe from being overfed:
You're sweetly picturesque in rags:
You never know the aching head
That comes along with money-bags:
And you have time to cultivate
That best of qualities, Content—
For which you'll find your present state
Remarkably convenient!'

Said Peter 'Though I cannot sound
The depths of such a man as you,
Yet in your character I've found
An inconsistency or two.
You seem to have long years to spare
When there's a promise to fulfil:
And yet how punctual you were
In calling with that little bill!'

'One can't be too deliberate,'
Said Paul, 'in parting with one's pelf,
With bills, as you correctly state,
I'm punctuality itself.
A man may surely claim his dues:
But, when there's money to be lent,
A man must be allowed to choose
Such times as are convenient!'

It chanced one day, as Peter sat
Gnawing a crust—his usual meal—
Paul bustled in to have a chat,
And grasped his hand with friendly zeal.
'I knew,' said he, 'your frugal ways:
So, that I might not wound your pride
By bringing strangers in to gaze,
I've left my legal friend outside!

'You well remember, I am sure,
When first your wealth began to go,
And people sneered at one so poor,
I *never used my Peter so!*
And when you'd lost your little all,
And found yourself a thing despised,
I need not ask you to recall
How tenderly I sympathised!

'Then the advice I've poured on you,
So full of wisdom and of wit:
All given gratis, though 'tis true
I might have fairly charged for it!
But I refrain from mentioning
Full many a deed I might relate—
For boasting is a kind of thing
That I particularly hate.

'How vast the total sum appears
Of all the kindnesses I've done,
From Childhood's half-forgotten years
Down to that Loan of April One!
That Fifty Pounds! You little guessed
How deep it drained my slender store:

But there's a heart within this breast,
And I WILL LEND YOU FIFTY MORE!'

'Not so,' was Peter's mild reply,
His cheeks all wet with grateful tears;
'No man recalls, so well as I,
Your services in bygone years:
And this new offer, I admit,
Is very very kindly meant—
Still, to avail myself of it
Would not be quite convenient!'

You'll see in a moment what the difference is between 'convenient' and 'inconvenient.' You quite understand it now, don't you?" he added, looking kindly at Bruno, who was sitting, at Sylvie's side, on the floor.

"Yes," said Bruno, very quietly. Such a short speech was very unusual, for him: but just then he seemed, I fancied, a little exhausted. In fact, he climbed up into Sylvie's lap as he spoke, and rested his head against her shoulder. "What a many verses it was!" he whispered.

CHAPTER XII.

A MUSICAL GARDENER.

The Other Professor regarded him with some anxiety. "The smaller animal ought to go to bed *at once*," he said with an air of authority.

"Why *at once?*" said the Professor.

"Because he can't go at twice," said the Other Professor.

The Professor gently clapped his hands. "Isn't he *wonderful!*" he said to Sylvie. "Nobody else could have thought of the reason, so quick. Why, *of course* he ca'n't go at twice! It would hurt him to be divided."

This remark woke up Bruno, suddenly and completely. "I don't want to be *divided*," he said decisively.

"It does very well on a *diagram*," said the Other Professor. "I could show it you in a minute, only the chalk's a little blunt."

"Take care!" Sylvie anxiously exclaimed, as he began, rather clumsily, to point it. "You'll cut your finger off, if you hold the knife so!"

"If oo cuts it off, will oo give it to *me*, please?" Bruno thoughtfully added.

"It's like this," said the Other Professor, hastily drawing a long line upon the black board, and marking the letters '*A*,' '*B*,' at the two ends, and '*C*' in the middle: "let me explain it to you. If *AB* were to be divided into two parts at *C*——"

"It would be drownded," Bruno pronounced confidently.

The Other Professor gasped. "*What* would be drownded?"

"Why the bumble-bee, of course!" said Bruno. "And the two bits would sink down in the sea!"

Here the Professor interfered, as the Other Professor was evidently too much puzzled to go on with his diagram.

"When I said it would *hurt* him, I was merely referring to the action of the nerves——"

The Other Professor brightened up in a moment. "The action of the nerves," he began eagerly, "is curiously slow in some people. I had a friend, once, that, if you burnt him with a red-hot poker, it would take years and years before he felt it!"

"And if you only *pinched* him?" queried Sylvie.

"Then it would take ever so much longer, of course. In fact, I doubt if the man *himself* would ever feel it, at all. His grandchildren might."

"I wouldn't like to be the grandchild of a pinched grandfather, would *you*, Mister Sir?" Bruno whispered. "It might come just when you wanted to be happy!"

That would be awkward, I admitted, taking it quite as a matter of course that he had so suddenly caught sight of me. "But don't you *always* want to be happy, Bruno?"

"Not *always*," Bruno said thoughtfully. "Sometimes, when I's *too* happy, I wants to be a little miserable. Then I just tell Sylvie about it, oo know, and Sylvie sets me some lessons. Then it's all right."

"I'm sorry you don't like lessons," I said. "You should copy Sylvie. *She's* always as busy as the day is long!"

"Well, so am *I!*" said Bruno.

"No, no!" Sylvie corrected him. "*You're* as busy as the day is *short!*"

"Well, what's the difference?" Bruno asked. "Mister Sir, isn't the day as short as it's long? I mean, isn't it the *same* length?"

Never having considered the question in this light, I suggested that they had better ask the Professor; and they ran off in a moment to appeal to their old friend. The Professor left off polishing his spectacles to consider. "My dears," he said after a minute, "the day is the same length as anything that is the same length as *it*." And he resumed his never-ending task of polishing.

The children returned, slowly and thoughtfully, to report his answer. "*Isn't* he wise?"

Sylvie asked in an awestruck whisper. "If *I* was as wise as *that*, I should have a head-ache all day long. I *know* I should!"

"You appear to be talking to somebody—that isn't here," the Professor said, turning round to the children. "Who is it?"

Bruno looked puzzled. "I never talks to nobody when he isn't here!" he replied. "It isn't good manners. Oo should always wait till he comes, before oo talks to him!"

The Professor looked anxiously in my direction, and seemed to look through and through me without seeing me. "Then who are you talking to?" he said. "There isn't anybody here, you know, except the Other Professor—and *he* isn't here!" he added wildly, turning round and round like a teetotum. "Children! Help to look for him! Quick! He's got lost again!"

The children were on their feet in a moment.

"Where shall we look?" said Sylvie.

"Anywhere!" shouted the excited Professor. "Only be quick about it!" And he began trotting round and round the room, lifting up the chairs, and shaking them.

Bruno took a very small book out of the bookcase, opened it, and shook it in imitation of the Professor. "He isn't *here*," he said.

"He *ca'n't* be there, Bruno!" Sylvie said indignantly.

"Course he ca'n't!" said Bruno. "I should have shooked him out, if he'd been in there!"

"Has he ever been lost before?" Sylvie enquired, turning up a corner of the hearth-rug, and peeping under it.

"Once before," said the Professor: "he once lost himself in a wood——"

"And couldn't he find his-self again?" said Bruno. "Why didn't he shout? He'd be sure to hear his-self, 'cause he couldn't be far off, oo know."

"Let's try shouting," said the Professor.

"What shall we shout?" said Sylvie.

"On second thoughts, *don't* shout," the Professor replied. "The Vice-Warden might hear you. He's getting awfully strict!"

This reminded the poor children of all the troubles, about which they had come to their old friend. Bruno sat down on the floor and began crying. "He *is* so cruel!" he sobbed. "And he lets Uggug take away *all* my toys! And such horrid meals!"

"What did you have for dinner to-day?" said the Professor.

"A little piece of a dead crow," was Bruno's mournful reply.

"He means rook-pie," Sylvie explained.

"It *were* a dead crow," Bruno persisted. "And there were a apple-pudding——and Uggug ate it all——and I got nuffin but a crust! And I asked for a orange——and——didn't get it!" And the poor little fellow buried his face in Sylvie's lap, who kept gently stroking his hair, as she went on. "It's all true, Professor dear! They *do* treat my darling Bruno very badly! And they're not kind to *me* either," she added in a lower tone, as if *that* were a thing of much less importance.

The Professor got out a large red silk handkerchief, and wiped his eyes. "I wish I could help you, dear children!" he said. "But what *can* I do?"

"We know the way to Fairyland——where Father's gone——quite well," said Sylvie: "if only the Gardener would let us out."

"Won't he open the door for you?" said the Professor.

"Not for *us*," said Sylvie: "but I'm sure he would for *you*. Do come and ask him, Professor dear!"

"I'll come this minute!" said the Professor.

Bruno sat up and dried his eyes. "*Isn't* he kind, Mister Sir?"

"He is *indeed*," said I. But the Professor took no notice of my remark. He had put on a beautiful cap with a long tassel, and was selecting one of the Other Professor's walking-sticks, from a stand in the corner of the room. "A thick stick in one's hand makes people respectful," he was saying to himself. "Come along, dear children!" And we all went out into the garden together.

"I shall address him, first of all," the Professor explained as we went along, "with a few playful remarks on the weather. I shall then question him about the Other Professor. This will have a double advantage. First, it will open the conversation (you can't even drink a bottle of wine without opening it first): and secondly, if he's seen the Other Professor, we shall find him that way : and, if he hasn't, we sha'n't."

On our way, we passed the target, at which Uggug had been made to shoot during the Ambassador's visit.

"See!" said the Professor, pointing out a hole in the middle of the bull's-eye. "His Imperial Fatness had only *one* shot at it; and he went in just *here!*"

Bruno carefully examined the hole. "Couldn't go in *there*," he whispered to me. "He are too *fat!*"

We had no sort of difficulty in *finding* the Gardener. Though he was hidden from us by some trees, that harsh voice of his served to direct us; and, as we drew nearer, the words of his song became more and more plainly audible :——

"He thought he saw an Albatross
That fluttered round the lamp:
He looked again, and found it was
A Penny-Postage-Stamp.
'You'd best be getting home,' he said:
'The nights are very damp!'"

"Would it be afraid of catching cold?" said Bruno.

"If it got *very* damp," Sylvie suggested, "it might stick to something, you know."

"And *that* somefin would have to go by the post, whatever it was!" Bruno eagerly exclaimed. "Suppose it was a cow! Wouldn't it be *dreadful* for the other things!"

"And all these things happened to *him*," said the Professor. "That's what makes the song so interesting."

"He must have had a very curious life," said Sylvie.

"You may say that!" the Professor heartily rejoined.

"Of course she may!" cried Bruno.

By this time we had come up to the Gardener, who was standing on one leg, as usual, and busily employed in watering a bed of flowers with an empty watering-can.

"It hasn't got no water in it!" Bruno explained to him, pulling his sleeve to attract his attention.

"It's lighter to hold," said the Gardener. "A lot of water in it makes one's arms ache." And he went on with his work, singing softly to himself

"The nights are very damp!"

"In digging things out of the ground—which you probably do now and then," the Professor began in a loud voice; "in making things into heaps—which no doubt you often do; and in kicking things about with one heel—which you seem never to leave off doing; have you ever happened to notice another Professor, something like me, but different?"

"Never!" shouted the Gardener, so loudly and violently that we all drew back in alarm. "There ain't such a thing!"

"We will try a less exciting topic," the Professor mildly remarked to the children. "You were asking——"

"We asked him to let us through the garden-door," said Sylvie: "but he wouldn't: but perhaps he would for *you!*"

The Professor put the request, very humbly and courteously.

"I wouldn't mind letting *you* out," said the Gardener. "But I mustn't open the door for *children.* D'you think I'd disobey the *Rules?* Not for one-and-sixpence!"

The Professor cautiously produced a couple of shillings.

"That'll do it!" the Gardener shouted, as he hurled the watering-can across the flower-bed, and produced a handful of keys——one large one, and a number of small ones.

"But look here, Professor dear!" whispered Sylvie. "He needn't open the door for *us,* at all. We can go out with *you.*"

"True, dear child!" the Professor thankfully replied, as he replaced the coins in his pocket. "That saves two shillings!" And he took the children's hands, that they might all go out together when the door was opened. This, however, did not seem a very likely event, though the Gardener patiently tried all the small keys, over and over again.

At last the Professor ventured on a gentle suggestion. "Why not try the *large* one? I have often observed that a door unlocks *much* more nicely with its *own* key."

The very first trial of the large key proved a success: the Gardener opened the door, and held out his hand for the money.

The Professor shook his head. "You are acting by *Rule*," he explained, "in opening the door for *me*. And now it's open, we are going out by *Rule*—the Rule of *Three*."

The Gardener looked puzzled, and let us go out; but, as he locked the door behind us, we heard him singing thoughtfully to himself

"He thought he saw a Garden-Door
That opened with a key:
He looked again, and found it was
A Double Rule of Three:
'And all its mystery,' he said,
'Is clear as day to me!'"

"I shall now return," said the Professor, when we had walked a few yards: "you see, it's impossible to read *here*, for all my books are in the house."

But the children still kept fast hold of his hands. "*Do* come with us!" Sylvie entreated with tears in her eyes.

"Well, well!" said the good-natured old man. "Perhaps I'll come after you, some day soon. But I *must* go back *now*. You see I left off at a comma, and it's so awkward not knowing how the sentence finishes! Besides, you've got to go through Dogland first, and I'm always a little nervous about dogs. But it'll be quite easy to come, as soon as I've completed my new invention—for carrying one's-*self*, you know. It wants just a *little* more working out."

"Won't that be very tiring, to carry *yourself?*" Sylvie enquired.

"Well, no, my child. You see, whatever fatigue one incurs by *carrying*, one saves by *being carried!* Good-bye, dears! Good-bye, Sir!" he added to my intense surprise, giving my hand an affectionate squeeze.

"Good-bye, Professor!" I replied: but my voice sounded strange and far away, and the children took not the slightest notice of our farewell. Evidently they neither saw me nor heard me, as, with their arms lovingly twined round each other, they marched boldly on.

CHAPTER XIII.

A VISIT TO DOGLAND.

"THERE'S a house, away there to the left," said Sylvie, after we had walked what seemed to me about fifty miles. "Let's go and ask for a night's lodging."

"It looks a very comfable house," Bruno said, as we turned into the road leading up to it. "I doos hope the Dogs will be kind to us, I *is* so tired and hungry!"

A Mastiff, dressed in a scarlet collar, and carrying a musket, was pacing up and down, like a sentinel, in front of the entrance. He started, on catching sight of the children, and came forwards to meet them, keeping his musket pointed straight at Bruno, who stood quite still, though he turned pale and kept tight hold of Sylvie's hand, while the Sentinel walked solemnly round and round them, and looked at them from all points of view.

"Oobooh, hooh boohooyah!" He growled at last. "Woobah yahwah oobooh! Bow wahbah woobooyah? Bow wow?" he asked Bruno, severely.

Of course *Bruno* understood all this, easily enough. All Fairies understand Doggee—that is, Dog-language. But, as *you* may find it a little difficult, just at first, I had better put it into English for you. "Humans, I verily believe! A couple of stray Humans! What Dog do you belong to? What do you want?"

"We don't belong to a *Dog!*" Bruno began, in Doggee. ("Peoples *never* belongs to Dogs!" he whispered to Sylvie.)

But Sylvie hastily checked him, for fear of hurting the Mastiff's feelings. "Please, we want a little food, and a night's lodging—if there's room in the house," she added timidly. Sylvie spoke Doggee very prettily: but I think it's almost better, for *you*, to give the conversation in English.

"The *house*, indeed!" growled the Sentinel. "Have you never seen a *Palace* in your life? Come along with me! His Majesty must settle what's to be done with you."

They followed him through the entrance-hall, down a long passage, and into a magnificent Saloon, around which were grouped dogs of all sorts and sizes. Two splendid Blood-hounds were solemnly sitting up, one on each side of the crown-bearer. Two or three Bull-dogs—whom I guessed to be the Body-Guard of the King—were waiting in grim silence: in fact the only voices at all plainly audible were those of two little dogs, who had mounted a settee, and were holding a lively discussion that looked very like a quarrel.

"Lords and Ladies in Waiting, and various Court Officials," our guide gruffly remarked, as he led us in. Of *me* the Courtiers took no notice whatever: but Sylvie and Bruno were the subject of many inquisitive looks, and many whispered remarks, of which I only distinctly caught *one*—made by a sly-looking Dachshund to his friend—"Bah wooh wahyah hoobah Oobooh, *hah* bah?" ("She's not such a bad-looking Human, *is* she?")

Leaving the new arrivals in the centre of the Saloon, the Sentinel advanced to a door, at the further end of it, which bore an inscription, painted on it in Doggee, "Royal Kennel—Scratch and Yell."

Before doing this, the Sentinel turned to the children, and said "Give me your names."

"We'd rather not!" Bruno exclaimed, pulling Sylvie away from the door. "We want them ourselves. Come back, Sylvie! Come quick!"

"Nonsense!" said Sylvie very decidedly: and gave their names in Doggee.

Then the Sentinel scratched violently at the door, and gave a yell that made Bruno shiver from head to foot.

"Hooyah wah!" said a deep voice inside. (That's Doggee for "Come in!")

"It's the King himself!" the Mastiff whispered in an awestruck tone. "Take off your wigs, and lay them humbly at his paws." (What *we* should call "at his *feet*.")

Sylvie was just going to explain, very politely, that really they *couldn't* perform *that* ceremony, because their wigs wouldn't come off, when the door of the Royal Kennel opened, and an enormous Newfoundland Dog put his head out. "Bow wow?" was his first question.

"When His Majesty speaks to you," the Sentinel hastily whispered to Bruno, "you should prick up your ears!"

Bruno looked doubtfully at Sylvie. "I'd rather not, please," he said. "It would hurt."

SWAIN Sc

"It doesn't hurt a bit!" the Sentinel said with some indignation. "Look! It's like this!" And he pricked up his ears like two railway signals.

Sylvie gently explained matters. "I'm afraid we ca'n't manage it," she said in a low voice. "I'm very sorry: but our ears haven't got the right——" she wanted to say "machinery" in Doggee: but she had forgotten the word, and could only think of "steam-engine."

The Sentinel repeated Sylvie's explanation to the King.

"Can't prick up their ears without a steam-engine!" His Majesty exclaimed. "They *must* be curious creatures! I must have a look at them!" And he came out of his Kennel, and walked solemnly up to the children.

What was the amazement——not to say the horror——of the whole assembly, when Sylvie actually *patted His Majesty on the head*, while Bruno seized his long ears and pretended to tie them together under his chin!

The Sentinel groaned aloud: a beautiful Greyhound——who appeared to be one of the Ladies in Waiting——fainted away: and all the other Courtiers hastily drew back, and left plenty of room for the huge Newfoundland to spring upon the audacious strangers, and tear them limb from limb.

Only——he didn't. On the contrary his Majesty actually *smiled*——so far as a Dog *can* smile——and (the other Dogs couldn't believe their eyes, but it was true, all the same) his Majesty *wagged his tail!*

"Yah! Hooh hahwooh!" (that is "Well! I never!") was the universal cry.

His Majesty looked round him severely, and gave a slight growl, which produced instant silence. "Conduct *my friends* to the banqueting-hall!" he said, laying such an emphasis on "*my friends*" that several of the dogs rolled over helplessly on their backs and began to lick Bruno's feet.

A procession was formed, but I only ventured to follow as far as the *door* of the banqueting-hall, so furious was the uproar of barking dogs within. So I sat down by the King, who seemed to have gone to sleep, and waited till the children returned to say good-night, when His Majesty got up and shook himself.

"Time for bed!" he said with a sleepy yawn. "The attendants will show you your room," he added, aside, to Sylvie and Bruno. "Bring lights!" And, with a dignified air, he held out his paw for them to kiss.

But the children were evidently not well practised in Court-manners. Sylvie simply stroked the great paw: Bruno hugged it: the Master of the Ceremonies looked shocked.

All this time Dog-waiters, in splendid livery, were running up with lighted candles: but, as fast as they put them upon the table, other waiters ran away with them, so that there never seemed to be one for *me*, though the Master kept nudging me with his elbow, and repeating "I ca'n't let you sleep *here!* You're not in *bed*, you know!"

I made a great effort, and just succeeded in getting out the words "I know I'm not. I'm in an arm-chair."

"Well, forty winks will do you no harm," the Master said, and left me. I could scarcely hear his words: and no wonder: he was leaning over the side of a ship, that was miles away from the pier on which I stood. The ship passed over the horizon, and I sank back into the arm-chair.

The next thing I remember is that it was morning: breakfast was just over: Sylvie was lifting Bruno down from a high chair, and saying to a Spaniel, who was regarding them with a most benevolent smile, "Yes, thank you, we've had a *very* nice breakfast. Haven't we, Bruno?"

"There was too many bones in the——" Bruno began, but Sylvie frowned at him, and laid her finger on her lips, for, at this moment, the travelers were waited on by a very dignified officer, the Head-Growler, whose duty it was, first to conduct them to the King to bid him farewell, and then to escort them to the boundary of Dogland. The great Newfoundland received them most affably, but, instead of saying "good-bye," he startled the Head-Growler into giving three savage growls, by announcing that he would escort them himself.

"It is a most unusual proceeding, your Majesty!" the Head-Growler exclaimed, almost choking with vexation at being set aside, for he had put on his best Court-suit, made entirely of cat-skins, for the occasion.

"I shall escort them myself," his Majesty repeated, gently but firmly, laying aside the Royal robes, and changing his crown for a small coronet, "and you may stay at home."

"I *are* glad!" Bruno whispered to Sylvie, when they had got well out of hearing. "He were so *welly* cross!" And he not only patted their Royal escort, but even hugged him round the neck in the exuberance of his delight.

His Majesty calmly wagged the Royal tail. "It's quite a relief," he said, "getting away from that Palace now and then! Royal Dogs have a dull life of it, I can tell you! Would you mind" (this to Sylvie, in a low voice, and looking a little shy and embarrassed) "would you mind the trouble of just throwing that stick for me to fetch?"

Sylvie was too much astonished to do anything for a moment: it sounded such a monstrous impossibility that a *King* should wish to run after a stick. But *Bruno* was equal to the occasion, and with a glad shout of "Hi then! Fetch it, good Doggie!" he hurled it over a clump of bushes. The next moment the Monarch of Dogland had bounded over the bushes, and picked up the stick, and came galloping back to the children with it in his mouth. Bruno took it from him with great decision. "Beg for it!" he insisted; and His Majesty begged. "Paw!" commanded Sylvie; and His Majesty gave his paw. In short, the solemn ceremony of escorting the travelers to the boundaries of Dogland became one long uproarious game of play!

"But business is business!" the Dog-King said at last. "And I must go back to mine. I couldn't come any further," he added, consulting a dog-watch, which hung on a chain round his neck, "not even if there were a *Cat* in sight!"

They took an affectionate farewell of His Majesty, and trudged on.

"That *were* a dear dog!" Bruno exclaimed. "Has we to go far, Sylvie? I's tired!"

"Not much further, darling!" Sylvie gently replied. "Do you see that shining, just beyond those trees? I'm almost *sure* it's the gate of Fairyland! I know it's all golden——Father told me so——and so bright, so bright!" she went on dreamily.

"It dazzles!" said Bruno, shading his eyes with one little hand, while the other clung tightly to Sylvie's hand, as if he were half-alarmed at her strange manner.

For the child moved on as if walking in her sleep, her large eyes gazing into the far distance, and her breath coming and going in quick pantings of eager delight. I knew, by some mysterious mental light, that a great change was taking place in my sweet little friend (for such I loved to think her) and that she was passing from the condition of a mere Outland Sprite into the true Fairy-nature.

Upon Bruno the change came later: but it was completed in both before they reached the golden gate, through which I knew it would be impossible for *me* to follow. I could but stand outside, and take a last look at the two sweet children, ere they disappeared within, and the golden gate closed with a bang.

And with *such* a bang! "It never *will* shut like any other cupboard-door," Arthur explained. "There's something wrong with the hinge. However, here's the cake and wine. And you've had your forty winks. So you really *must* get off to bed, old man! You're fit for nothing else. Witness my hand, Arthur Forester, M.D."

By this time I was wide-awake again. "Not *quite* yet!" I pleaded. "Really I'm not sleepy now. And it isn't midnight yet."

"Well, I did want to say another word to you," Arthur replied in a relenting tone, as he supplied me with the supper he had prescribed. "Only I thought you were too sleepy for it to-night."

We took our midnight meal almost in silence; for an unusual nervousness seemed to have seized on my old friend.

"What kind of a night is it?" he asked, rising and undrawing the window-curtains, apparently to change the subject for a minute. I followed him to the window, and we stood together, looking out, in silence.

"When I first spoke to you about——" Arthur began, after a long and embarrassing silence, "that is, when we first talked about her—for I think it was *you* that introduced the subject—my own position in life forbade me to do more than worship her from a distance:

and I was turning over plans for leaving this place finally, and settling somewhere out of all chance of meeting her again. That seemed to be my only chance of usefulness in life."

"Would that have been wise?" I said. "To leave yourself no hope at all?"

"There *was* no hope to leave," Arthur firmly replied, though his eyes glittered with tears as he gazed upwards into the midnight sky, from which one solitary star, the glorious 'Vega,' blazed out in fitful splendour through the driving clouds. "She was like that star to me——bright, beautiful, and pure, but out of reach, out of reach!"

He drew the curtains again, and we returned to our places by the fireside.

"What I wanted to tell you was this," he resumed. "I heard this evening from my solicitor. I can't go into the details of the business, but the upshot is that my worldly wealth is much more than I thought, and I am (or shall soon be) in a position to offer marriage, without imprudence, to any lady, even if she brought nothing. I doubt if there would be anything on *her* side: the Earl is poor, I believe. But I should have enough for both, even if health failed."

"I wish you all happiness in your married life!" I cried. "Shall you speak to the Earl to-morrow?"

"Not yet awhile," said Arthur. "He is very friendly, but I dare not think he means more than that, as yet. And as for——as for Lady Muriel, try as I may, I *cannot* read her feelings towards me. If there *is* love, she is hiding it! No, I must wait, I must wait!"

I did not like to press any further advice on my friend, whose judgment, I felt, was so much more sober and thoughtful than my own; and we parted without more words on the subject that had now absorbed his thoughts, nay, his very life.

The next morning a letter from *my* solicitor arrived, summoning me to town on important business.

CHAPTER XIV.

FAIRY-SYLVIE.

For a full month the business, for which I had returned to London, detained me there: and even then it was only the urgent advice of my physician that induced me to leave it unfinished and pay another visit to Elveston.

Arthur had written once or twice during the month; but in none of his letters was there any mention of Lady Muriel. Still, I did not augur ill from his silence: to me it looked like the natural action of a lover, who, even while his heart was singing "She is mine!", would fear to paint his happiness in the cold phrases of a written letter, but would wait to tell it by word of mouth. "Yes," I thought, "I am to hear his song of triumph from his own lips!"

The night I arrived we had much to say on other matters: and, tired with the journey, I went to bed early, leaving the happy secret still untold. Next day, however, as we chatted on over the remains of luncheon, I ventured to put the momentous question. "Well, old friend, you have told me nothing of Lady Muriel—nor when the happy day is to be?"

"The happy day," Arthur said, looking unexpectedly grave, "is yet in the dim future. We need to know—or, rather, *she* needs to know *me* better. I know *her* sweet nature, thoroughly, by this time. But I dare not speak till I am sure that my love is returned."

"Don't wait too long!" I said gaily. "Faint heart never won fair lady!"

"It *is* 'faint heart,' perhaps. But really I *dare* not speak just yet."

"But meanwhile,' I pleaded, "you are running a risk that perhaps you have not thought of. Some other man——"

"No," said Arthur firmly. "She is heart-whole: I am sure of that. Yet, if she loves another better than me, so be it! I will not spoil her happiness. The secret shall die with me. But she is my first—and my *only* love!"

"That is all very beautiful *sentiment*," I said, "but it is not *practical*. It is not like *you*.

He either fears his fate too much,
Or his desert is small,
Who dares not put it to the touch,
To win or lose it all."

"I *dare* not ask the question whether there is another!" he said passionately. "It would break my heart to know it!"

"Yet is it wise to leave it unasked? You must not waste your life upon an 'if'!"

"I tell you I *dare* not!"

"May *I* find it out for you?" I asked, with the freedom of an old friend.

"No, no!" he replied with a pained look. "I entreat you to say nothing. Let it wait."

"As you please," I said: and judged it best to say no more just then. "But this evening," I thought, "I will call on the Earl. I may be able to *see* how the land lies, without so much as saying a word!"

It was a very hot afternoon——too hot to go for a walk or do anything——or else it wouldn't have happened, I believe.

In the first place, I want to know——dear Child who reads this!——why Fairies should always be teaching *us* to do our duty, and lecturing *us* when we go wrong, and we should never teach *them* anything? You can't mean to say that Fairies are never greedy, or selfish, or cross, or deceitful, because that would be nonsense, you know. Well then, don't you think they might be all the better for a little lecturing and punishing now and then?

I really don't see why it shouldn't be tried, and I'm almost sure that, if you could only catch a Fairy, and put it in the corner, and give it nothing but bread and water for a day or two, you'd find it quite an improved character——it would take down its conceit a little, at all events.

The next question is, what is the best time for seeing Fairies? I believe I can tell you all about that.

The first rule is, that it must be a *very* hot day——that we may consider as settled: and you must be just a *little* sleepy——but not too sleepy to keep your eyes open, mind. Well, and you ought to feel a little——what one may call "fairyish"——the Scotch call it "eerie," and perhaps that's a prettier word; if you don't know what it means, I'm afraid I can hardly explain it; you must wait till you meet a Fairy, and then you'll know.

And the last rule is, that the crickets should not be chirping. I can't stop to explain that: you must take it on trust for the present.

So, if all these things happen together, you have a good chance of seeing a Fairy——or at least a much better chance than if they didn't.

The first thing I noticed, as I went lazily along through an open place in the wood, was a large Beetle lying struggling on its back, and I went down upon one knee to help the poor thing to its feet again. In some things, you know, you ca'n't be quite sure what an insect would like: for instance, I never could quite settle, supposing I were a moth, whether I would rather be kept out of the candle, or be allowed to fly straight in and get burnt——or again, supposing I were a spider, I'm not sure if I should be *quite* pleased to have my web torn down, and the fly let loose——but I feel quite certain that, if I were a beetle and had rolled over on my back, I should always be glad to be helped up again.

So, as I was saying, I had gone down upon one knee, and was just reaching out a little stick to turn the Beetle over, when I saw a sight that made me draw back hastily and hold my breath, for fear of making any noise and frightening the little creature away.

Not that she looked as if she would be easily frightened: she seemed so good and gentle that I'm sure she would never expect that any one could wish to hurt her. She was only a few inches high, and was dressed in green, so that you really would hardly have noticed her among the long grass; and she was so delicate and graceful that she quite seemed to belong to the place, almost as if she were one of the flowers. I may tell you, besides, that she had no wings (I don't believe in Fairies with wings), and that she had quantities of long brown hair and large earnest brown eyes, and then I shall have done all I can to give you an idea of her.

Sylvie (I found out her name afterwards) had knelt down, just as I was doing, to help the Beetle; but it needed more than a little stick for *her* to get it on its legs again; it was as much as she could do, with both arms, to roll the heavy thing over; and all the while she was talking to it, half scolding and half comforting, as a nurse might do with a child that had fallen down.

"There, there! You needn't cry so much about it. You're not killed yet—though if you were, you couldn't cry, you know, and so it's a general rule against crying, my dear! And how did you come to tumble over? But I can see well enough how it was—I needn't ask you that—walking over sand-pits with your chin in the air, as usual. Of course if you go among sand-pits like that, you must expect to tumble. You should look."

The Beetle murmured something that sounded like "I *did* look," and Sylvie went on again.

"But I know you didn't! You never do! You always walk with your chin up—you're so dreadfully conceited. Well, let's see how many legs are broken this time. Why, none of them, I declare! And what's the good of having six legs, my dear, if you can only kick them all about in the air when you tumble? Legs are meant to walk with, you know. Now don't begin putting out your wings yet; I've more to say. Go to the frog that lives behind that buttercup—give him my compliments—Sylvie's compliments—can you say 'compliments'?"

The Beetle tried and, I suppose, succeeded.

"Yes, that's right. And tell him he's to give you some of that salve I left with him yesterday. And you'd better get him to rub it in for you. He's got rather cold hands, but you mustn't mind that."

I think the Beetle must have shuddered at this idea, for Sylvie went on in a graver tone. "Now you needn't pretend to be so particular as all that, as if you were too grand to be rubbed by a frog. The fact is, you ought to be very much obliged to him. Suppose you could get nobody but a toad to do it, how would you like *that?*"

There was a little pause, and then Sylvie added "Now you may go. Be a good beetle, and don't keep your chin in the air." And then began one of those performances of humming, and whizzing, and restless banging about, such as a beetle indulges in when it has decided on flying, but hasn't quite made up its mind which way to go. At last, in one of its awkward zigzags, it managed to fly right into my face, and, by the time I had recovered from the shock, the little Fairy was gone.

I looked about in all directions for the little creature, but there was no trace of her——and my 'eerie' feeling was quite gone off, and the crickets were chirping again merrily——so I knew she was really gone.

And now I've got time to tell you the rule about the crickets. They always leave off chirping when a Fairy goes by——because a Fairy's a kind of queen over them, I suppose——at all events it's a much grander thing than a cricket ——so whenever you're walking out, and the crickets suddenly leave off chirping, you may be sure that they see a Fairy.

I walked on sadly enough, you may be sure. However, I comforted myself with thinking "It's been a very wonderful afternoon, so far. I'll just go quietly on and look about me, and I shouldn't wonder if I were to come across another Fairy somewhere."

Peering about in this way, I happened to notice a plant with rounded leaves, and with queer little holes cut in the middle of several of them. "Ah, the leafcutter bee!" I carelessly remarked——you know I am very learned in Natural History (for instance, I can always tell kittens from chickens at one glance)—and I was passing on, when a sudden thought made me stoop down and examine the leaves.

Then a little thrill of delight ran through me—for I noticed that the holes were all arranged so as to form letters; there were three leaves side by side, with "B," "R," and "U" marked on them, and after some search I found two more, which contained an "N" and an "O."

And then, all in a moment, a flash of inner light seemed to illumine a part of my life that had all but faded into oblivion—the strange visions I had experienced during my journey to Elveston: and with a thrill of delight I thought "Those visions are destined to be linked with my waking life!"

By this time the 'eerie' feeling had come back again, and I suddenly observed that no crickets were chirping; so I felt quite sure that "Bruno" was somewhere very near.

And so indeed he was—so near that I had very nearly walked over him without seeing him; which would have been dreadful, always supposing that Fairies *can* be walked over—my own belief is that they are something of the nature of Will-o'-the-Wisps: and there's no walking over *them*.

Think of any pretty little boy you know, with rosy cheeks, large dark eyes, and tangled brown hair, and then fancy him made small enough to go comfortably into a coffee-cup, and you'll have a very fair idea of him.

"What's your name, little one?" I began, in as soft a voice as I could manage. And, by the way, why is it we always begin by asking little children their names? Is it because we fancy a name will help to make them a little bigger? You never thought of asking a real large man his name, now, did you? But, however that may be, I felt it quite necessary to know *his* name; so, as he didn't answer my question, I asked it again a little louder. "What's your name, my little man?"

"What's oors?" he said, without looking up.

I told him my name quite gently, for he was much too small to be angry with.

"Duke of Anything?" he asked, just looking at me for a moment, and then going on with his work.

"Not Duke at all," I said, a little ashamed of having to confess it.

"Oo're big enough to be two Dukes," said the little creature. "I suppose oo're Sir Something, then?"

"No," I said, feeling more and more ashamed. "I haven't got any title."

The Fairy seemed to think that in that case I really wasn't worth the trouble of talking to, for he quietly went on digging, and tearing the flowers to pieces.

After a few minutes I tried again. "*Please* tell me what your name is."

"Bruno," the little fellow answered, very readily. "Why didn't oo say 'please' before?"

"That's something like what we used to be taught in the nursery," I thought to myself, looking back through the long years (about a hundred of them, since you ask the question), to the time when I was a little child. And here an idea came into my head, and I asked him "Aren't you one of the Fairies that teach children to be good?"

"Well, we have to do that sometimes," said Bruno, "and a dreadful bother it is." As he said this, he savagely tore a heartsease in two, and trampled on the pieces.

"What *are* you doing there, Bruno?" I said.

"Spoiling Sylvie's garden," was all the answer Bruno would give at first. But, as he went on tearing up the flowers, he muttered to himself "The nasty cross thing—wouldn't let me go and play this morning,—said I must finish my lessons first—lessons, indeed! I'll vex her finely, though!"

"Oh, Bruno, you shouldn't do that!" I cried. "Don't you know that's revenge? And revenge is a wicked, cruel, dangerous thing!"

"River-edge?" said Bruno. "What a funny word! I suppose oo call it cruel and dangerous 'cause, if oo wented too far and tumbleded in, oo'd get drownded."

"No, not river-edge," I explained: "revenge" (saying the word very slowly). But I couldn't help thinking that Bruno's explanation did very well for either word.

"Oh!" said Bruno, opening his eyes very wide, but without trying to repeat the word.

"Come! Try and pronounce it, Bruno!" I said, cheerfully. "Re-venge, re-venge."

But Bruno only tossed his little head, and said he couldn't; that his mouth wasn't the right shape for words of that kind. And the more I laughed, the more sulky the little fellow got about it.

"Well, never mind, my little man!" I said. "Shall I help you with that job?"

"Yes, please," Bruno said, quite pacified. "Only I wiss I could think of somefin to vex her more than this. Oo don't know how hard it is to make her angry!"

"Now listen to me, Bruno, and I'll teach you quite a splendid kind of revenge!"

"Somefin that'll vex her finely?" he asked with gleaming eyes.

"Something that will vex her finely. First, we'll get up all the weeds in her garden. See, there are a good many at this end—quite hiding the flowers."

"But *that* won't vex her!" said Bruno.

"After that," I said, without noticing the remark, "we'll water this highest bed—up here. You see it's getting quite dry and dusty."

Bruno looked at me inquisitively, but he said nothing this time.

"Then after that," I went on, "the walks want sweeping a bit; and I think you might cut down that tall nettle——it's so close to the garden that it's quite in the way——"

"What *is* oo talking about?" Bruno impatiently interrupted me. "All that won't vex her a bit!"

"Won't it?" I said, innocently. "Then, after that, suppose we put in some of these coloured pebbles—just to mark the divisions between the different kinds of flowers, you know. That'll have a very pretty effect."

Bruno turned round and had another good stare at me. At last there came an odd little twinkle into his eyes, and he said, with quite a new meaning in his voice, "That'll do nicely. Let's put 'em in rows——all the red together, and all the blue together."

"That'll do capitally," I said; "and then——what kind of flowers does Sylvie like best?"

Bruno had to put his thumb in his mouth and consider a little before he could answer. "Violets," he said, at last.

"There's a beautiful bed of violets down by the brook——"

"Oh, let's fetch 'em!" cried Bruno, giving a little skip into the air. "Here! Catch hold of my hand, and I'll help oo along. The grass is rather thick down that way."

I couldn't help laughing at his having so entirely forgotten what a big creature he was talking to. "No, not yet, Bruno," I said: "we must consider what's the right thing to do first. You see we've got quite a business before us."

"Yes, let's consider," said Bruno, putting his thumb into his mouth again, and sitting down upon a dead mouse.

"What do you keep that mouse for?" I said. "You should either bury it, or else throw it into the brook."

"Why, it's to measure with!" cried Bruno. "How ever would oo do a garden without one? We make each bed three mouses and a half long, and two mouses wide."

I stopped him, as he was dragging it off by the tail to show me how it was used, for I was half afraid the 'eerie' feeling might go off before we had finished the garden, and in that case I should see no more of him or Sylvie. "I think the best way will be for *you* to weed the beds, while *I* sort out these pebbles, ready to mark the walks with."

"That's it!" cried Bruno. "And I'll tell oo about the caterpillars while we work."

"Ah, let's hear about the caterpillars," I said, as I drew the pebbles together into a heap and began dividing them into colours.

And Bruno went on in a low, rapid tone, more as if he were talking to himself. "Yesterday I saw two little caterpillars, when I was sitting by the brook, just where oo go into the wood. They were quite green, and they had yellow eyes, and they didn't see *me*. And one of them had got a moth's wing to carry—a great brown moth's wing, oo know, all dry, with feathers. So he couldn't want it to eat, I should think—perhaps he meant to make a cloak for the winter?"

"Perhaps," I said, for Bruno had twisted up the last word into a sort of question, and was looking at me for an answer.

One word was quite enough for the little fellow, and he went on merrily. "Well, and so he didn't want the other caterpillar to see the moth's wing, oo know—so what must he do but try to carry it with all his left legs, and he tried to walk on the other set. Of course he toppled over after that."

"After what?" I said, catching at the last word, for, to tell the truth, I hadn't been attending much.

"He toppled over," Bruno repeated, very gravely, "and if *oo* ever saw a caterpillar topple over, oo'd know it's a welly serious thing, and not sit grinning like that—and I sha'n't tell oo no more!"

"Indeed and indeed, Bruno, I didn't mean to grin. See, I'm quite grave again now."

But Bruno only folded his arms, and said "Don't tell *me*. I see a little twinkle in one of oor eyes—just like the moon."

"Why do you think I'm like the moon, Bruno?" I asked.

"Oor face is large and round like the moon," Bruno answered, looking at me thoughtfully. "It doosn't shine quite so bright—but it's more cleaner."

I couldn't help smiling at this. "You know I sometimes wash *my* face, Bruno. The moon never does that."

"Oh, doosn't she though!" cried Bruno; and he leant forwards and added in a solemn whisper, "The moon's face gets dirtier and dirtier every night, till it's black all across. And then, when it's dirty all over—*so*—" (he passed his hand across his own rosy cheeks as he spoke) "then she washes it."

"Then it's all clean again, isn't it?"

"Not all in a moment," said Bruno. "What a deal of teaching oo wants! She washes it little by little—only she begins at the other edge, oo know."

By this time he was sitting quietly on the dead mouse with his arms folded, and the weeding wasn't getting on a bit: so I had to say "Work first, pleasure afterwards: no more talking till that bed's finished."

CHAPTER XV.

BRUNO'S REVENGE.

After that we had a few minutes of silence, while I sorted out the pebbles, and amused myself with watching Bruno's plan of gardening. It was quite a new plan to me: he always measured each bed before he weeded it, as if he was afraid the weeding would make it shrink; and once, when it came out longer than he wished, he set to work to thump the mouse with his little fist, crying out "There now! It's all gone wrong again! Why don't oo keep oor tail straight when I tell oo!"

"I'll tell you what I'll do," Bruno said in a half-whisper, as we worked. "Oo like Fairies, don't oo?"

"Yes," I said: "of course I do, or I shouldn't have come here. I should have gone to some place where there are no Fairies."

Bruno laughed contemptuously. "Why, oo might as well say oo'd go to some place where there wasn't any air—supposing oo didn't like air!"

This was a rather difficult idea to grasp. I tried a change of subject. "You're nearly the first Fairy I ever saw. Have *you* ever seen any people besides me?"

"Plenty!" said Bruno. "We see 'em when we walk in the road."

"But they ca'n't see *you*. How is it they never tread on you?"

"Ca'n't *tread* on us," said Bruno, looking amused at my ignorance. "Why, suppose oo're walking, here—so—" (making little marks on the ground) "and suppose there's a Fairy—that's me—walking *here*. Very well then, oo put one foot here, and one foot here, so oo doosn't tread on the Fairy."

This was all very well as an explanation, but it didn't convince me. "Why shouldn't I put one foot *on* the Fairy?" I asked.

"I don't know *why*," the little fellow said in a thoughtful tone. "But I know oo *wouldn't*. Nobody never walked on the top of a Fairy. Now I'll tell oo what I'll do, as oo're so fond of Fairies. I'll get oo an invitation to the Fairy-King's dinner-party. I know one of the head-waiters."

I couldn't help laughing at this idea. "Do the waiters invite the guests?" I asked.

"Oh, not *to sit down!*" Bruno said. "But to wait at table. Oo'd like that, wouldn't oo? To hand about plates, and so on."

"Well, but that's not so nice as sitting at the table, is it?"

"Of course it isn't," Bruno said, in a tone as if he rather pitied my ignorance; "but if oo're not even Sir Anything, oo ca'n't expect to be allowed to sit at the table, oo know."

I said, as meekly as I could, that I didn't expect it, but it was the only way of going to a dinner-party that I really enjoyed. And Bruno tossed his head, and said, in a rather offended tone, that I might do as I pleased—there were many he knew that would give their ears to go.

"Have you ever been yourself, Bruno?"

"They invited me once, last week," Bruno said, very gravely. "It was to wash up the soup-plates—no, the cheese-plates I mean—that was grand enough. And I waited at table. And I didn't hardly make only *one* mistake."

"What was it?" I said. "You needn't mind telling *me*."

"Only bringing scissors to cut the beef with," Bruno said carelessly. "But the grandest thing of all was, *I* fetched the King a glass of cider!"

"That *was* grand!" I said, biting my lip to keep myself from laughing.

"Wasn't it?" said Bruno, very earnestly. "Oo know it isn't every one that's had such an honour as *that!*"

This set me thinking of the various queer things we call "an honour" in this world, but which, after all, haven't a bit more honour in them than what Bruno enjoyed, when he took the King a glass of cider.

I don't know how long I might not have dreamed on in this way, if Bruno hadn't suddenly roused me. "Oh, come here quick!" he cried, in a state of the wildest excitement. "Catch hold of his other horn! I ca'n't hold him more than a minute!"

He was struggling desperately with a great snail, clinging to one of its horns, and nearly breaking his poor little back in his efforts to drag it over a blade of grass.

I saw we should have no more gardening if I let this sort of thing go on, so I quietly took the snail away, and put it on a bank where he couldn't reach it. "We'll hunt it afterwards, Bruno," I said, "if you really want to catch it. But what's the use of it when you've got it?"

"What's the use of a fox when oo've got it?" said Bruno. "I know oo big things hunt foxes."

I tried to think of some good reason why "big things" should hunt foxes, and he should not hunt snails, but none came into my head: so I said at last, "Well, I suppose one's as good as the other. I'll go snail-hunting myself some day."

"I should think oo wouldn't be so silly," said Bruno, "as to go snail-hunting by oor-self. Why, oo'd never get the snail along, if oo hadn't somebody to hold on to his other horn!"

"Of course I sha'n't go *alone*," I said, quite gravely. "By the way, is that the best kind to hunt, or do you recommend the ones without shells?"

"Oh, no, we never hunt the ones without shells," Bruno said, with a little shudder at the thought of it. "They're always so cross about it; and then, if oo tumbles over them, they're ever so sticky!"

By this time we had nearly finished the garden. I had fetched some violets, and Bruno was just helping me to put in the last, when he suddenly stopped and said "I'm tired."

"Rest then," I said: "I can go on without you, quite well."

Bruno needed no second invitation: he at once began arranging the dead mouse as a kind of sofa. "And I'll sing oo a little song," he said, as he rolled it about.

"Do," said I: "I like songs very much."

"Which song will oo choose?" Bruno said, as he dragged the mouse into a place where he could get a good view of me. "'Ting, ting, ting' is the nicest."

There was no resisting such a strong hint as this: however, I pretended to think about it for a moment, and then said "Well, I like 'Ting, ting, ting,' best of all."

"That shows oo're a good judge of music," Bruno said, with a pleased look. "How many hare-bells would oo like?" And he put his thumb into his mouth to help me to consider.

As there was only one cluster of hare-bells within easy reach, I said very gravely that I thought one would do *this* time, and I picked it and gave it to him. Bruno ran his hand once or twice up and down the flowers, like a musician trying an instrument, producing a most delicious delicate tinkling as he did so. I had never heard flower-music before——I don't think one can, unless one's in the 'eerie' state——and I don't know quite how to give you an idea of what it was like, except by saying that it sounded like a peal of bells a thousand miles off. When he had satisfied himself that the flowers were in tune, he seated himself on the dead mouse (he never seemed really comfortable anywhere else), and, looking up at me with a merry twinkle in his eyes, he began. By the way, the tune was rather a curious one, and you might like to try it for yourself, so here are the notes.

"*Rise, oh, rise! The daylight dies:*
The owls are hooting, ting, ting, ting!
Wake, oh, wake! Beside the lake
The elves are fluting, ting, ting, ting!
Welcoming our Fairy King,
We sing, sing, sing."

He sang the first four lines briskly and merrily, making the hare-bells chime in time with the music; but the last two he sang quite slowly and gently, and merely waved the flowers backwards and forwards. Then he left off to explain. "The Fairy-King is Oberon, and he lives across the lake——and sometimes he comes in a little boat——and we go and meet him——and then we sing this song, you know."

"And then you go and dine with him?" I said, mischievously.

"Oo shouldn't talk," Bruno hastily said: "it interrupts the song so."

I said I wouldn't do it again.

"I never talk myself when I'm singing," he went on very gravely: "so *oo* shouldn't either." Then he tuned the hare-bells once more, and sang:—

"*Hear, oh, hear! From far and near*
The music stealing, ting, ting, ting!
Fairy bells adown the dells
Are merrily pealing, ting, ting, ting!
Welcoming our Fairy King,
We ring, ring, ring.

"*See, oh, see! On every tree*
What lamps are shining, ting, ting, ting!
They are eyes of fiery flies
To light our dining, ting, ting, ting!
Welcoming our Fairy King
They swing, swing, swing.

"*Haste, oh haste, to take and taste*
The dainties waiting, ting, ting, ting!
Honey-dew is stored——"

"Hush, Bruno!" I interrupted in a warning whisper. "She's coming!"

Bruno checked his song, and, as she slowly made her way through the long grass, he suddenly rushed out headlong at her like a little bull, shouting "Look the other way! Look the other way!"

"Which way?" Sylvie asked, in rather a frightened tone, as she looked round in all directions to see where the danger could be.

"*That* way!" said Bruno, carefully turning her round with her face to the wood. "Now, walk backwards——walk gently——don't be frightened: oo sha'n't trip!"

But Sylvie *did* trip notwithstanding: in fact he led her, in his hurry, across so many little sticks and stones, that it was really a wonder the poor child could keep on her feet at all. But he was far too much excited to think of what he was doing.

I silently pointed out to Bruno the best place to lead her to, so as to get a view of the whole garden at once: it was a little rising ground, about the height of a potato; and, when they had mounted it, I drew back into the shade, that Sylvie mightn't see me.

I heard Bruno cry out triumphantly "*Now* oo may look!" and then followed a clapping of hands, but it was all done by Bruno himself. Sylvie was silent——she only stood and gazed with her hands clasped together, and I was half afraid she didn't like it after all.

Bruno too was watching her anxiously, and when she jumped down off the mound, and began wandering up and down the little walks, he cautiously followed her about, evidently anxious that she should form her own opinion of it all, without any hint from him. And when at last she drew a long breath, and gave her verdict—in a hurried whisper, and without the slightest regard to grammar—"It's the loveliest thing as I never saw in all my life before!" the little fellow looked as well pleased as if it had been given by all the judges and juries in England put together.

"And did you really do it all by yourself, Bruno?" said Sylvie. "And all for me?"

"I was helped a bit," Bruno began, with a merry little laugh at her surprise. "We've been at it all the afternoon—I thought oo'd like—" and here the poor little fellow's lip began to quiver, and all in a moment he burst out crying, and running up to Sylvie he flung his arms passionately round her neck, and hid his face on her shoulder.

There was a little quiver in Sylvie's voice too, as she whispered "Why, what's the matter, darling?" and tried to lift up his head and kiss him.

But Bruno only clung to her, sobbing, and wouldn't be comforted till he had confessed. "I tried——to spoil oor garden——first——but I'll never——never——" and then came another burst of tears, which drowned the rest of the sentence. At last he got out the words "I liked——putting in the flowers——for *oo*, Sylvie——and I never was so happy before." And the rosy little face came up at last to be kissed, all wet with tears as it was.

Sylvie was crying too by this time, and she said nothing but "Bruno, dear!" and "*I* never was so happy before," though why these two children who had never been so happy before should both be crying was a mystery to *me*.

I felt very happy too, but of course I didn't cry: "big things" never do, you know——we leave all that to the Fairies. Only I think it must have been raining a little just then, for I found a drop or two on my cheeks.

After that they went through the whole garden again, flower by flower, as if it were a long sentence they were spelling out, with kisses for commas, and a great hug by way of a full-stop when they got to the end.

"Doos oo know, that was my river-edge, Sylvie?" Bruno solemnly began.

Sylvie laughed merrily. "What *do* you mean?" she said. And she pushed back her heavy brown hair with both hands, and looked at him with dancing eyes in which the big tear-drops were still glittering.

Bruno drew in a long breath, and made up his mouth for a great effort. "I mean re—venge," he said: "now oo under'tand." And he looked so happy and proud at having said the word right at last, that I quite envied him. I rather think Sylvie didn't "under'tand" at all; but she gave him a little kiss on each cheek, which seemed to do just as well.

So they wandered off lovingly together, in among the buttercups, each with an arm twined round the other, whispering and laughing as they went, and never so much as once looked back at poor me. Yes, once, just before I quite lost sight of them, Bruno half turned his head, and nodded me a saucy little good-bye over one shoulder. And that was all the thanks I got for *my* trouble. The very last thing I saw of them was this——Sylvie was stooping down with her arms round Bruno's neck, and saying coaxingly in his ear, "Do you know, Bruno, I've quite forgotten that hard word. Do say it once more. Come! Only this once, dear!"

But Bruno wouldn't try it again.

CHAPTER XVI.

A CHANGED CROCODILE.

THE Marvellous—the Mysterious—had quite passed out of my life for the moment: and the Common-place reigned supreme. I turned in the direction of the Earl's house, as it was now 'the witching hour' of five, and I knew I should find them ready for a cup of tea and a quiet chat.

Lady Muriel and her father gave me a delightfully warm welcome. They were not of the folk we meet in fashionable drawing-rooms—who conceal all such feelings as they may chance to possess beneath the impenetrable mask of a conventional placidity. 'The Man with the Iron Mask' was, no doubt, a rarity and a marvel in his own age: in modern London no one would turn his head to give him a second look! No, these were *real* people. When they *looked* pleased, it meant that they *were* pleased: and when Lady Muriel said, with a bright smile, "I'm *very* glad to see you again!", I knew that it was *true*.

Still I did not venture to disobey the injunctions——crazy as I felt them to be——of the love-sick young Doctor, by so much as alluding to his existence: and it was only after they had given me full details of a projected picnic, to which they invited me, that Lady Muriel exclaimed, almost as an after-thought, "and *do*, if you can, bring Doctor Forester with you! I'm sure a day in the country would do him good. I'm afraid he studies too much——"

It was 'on the tip of my tongue' to quote the words "His only books are woman's looks!" but I checked myself just in time——with something of the feeling of one who has crossed a street, and has been all but run over by a passing 'Hansom.'

"——and I think he has too lonely a life," she went on, with a gentle earnestness that left no room whatever to suspect a double meaning. "*Do* get him to come! And don't forget the day, Tuesday week. We can drive you over. It would be a pity to go by rail——there is so much pretty scenery on the road. And our open carriage just holds four."

"Oh, *I'll* persuade him to come!" I said with confidence——thinking "it would take all *my* powers of persuasion to keep him away!"

The picnic was to take place in ten days: and though Arthur readily accepted the invitation I brought him, nothing that I could say would induce him to call——either with me or without me——on the Earl and his daughter in the meanwhile. No: he feared to "wear out his welcome," he said: they had "seen enough of him for one while": and, when at last the day for the expedition arrived, he was so childishly nervous and uneasy that I thought it best so to arrange our plans that we should go separately to the house——my intention being to arrive some time after him, so as to give him time to get over a meeting.

With this object I purposely made a considerable circuit on my way to the Hall (as we called the Earl's house): "and if I could only manage to lose my way a bit," I thought to myself, "that would suit me capitally!"

In this I succeeded better, and sooner, than I had ventured to hope for. The path through the wood had been made familiar to me, by many a solitary stroll, in my former visit to Elveston; and how I could have so suddenly and so entirely lost it—even though I *was* so engrossed in thinking of Arthur and his lady-love that I heeded little else—was a mystery to me. "And this open place," I said to myself, "seems to have some memory about it I cannot distinctly recall—surely it is the very spot where I saw those Fairy-Children! But I hope there are no snakes about!" I mused aloud, taking my seat on a fallen tree. "I certainly do *not* like snakes—and I don't suppose *Bruno* likes them, either!"

"No, he *doesn't* like them!" said a demure little voice at my side. "He's not *afraid* of them, you know. But he doesn't *like* them. He says they're too waggly!"

Words fail me to describe the beauty of the little group——couched on a patch of moss, on the trunk of the fallen tree, that met my eager gaze: Sylvie reclining with her elbow buried in the moss, and her rosy cheek resting in the palm of her hand, and Bruno stretched at her feet with his head in her lap.

"Too waggly?" was all I could say in so sudden an emergency.

"I'm not praticular," Bruno said, carelessly: "but I *do* like straight animals best——"

"But you like a dog when it wags its tail," Sylvie interrupted. "You *know* you do, Bruno!"

"But there's more of a dog, isn't there, Mister Sir?" Bruno appealed to me. "*You* wouldn't like to have a dog if it hadn't got nuffin but a head and a tail?"

I admitted that a dog of that kind would be uninteresting.

"There *isn't* such a dog as that," Sylvie thoughtfully remarked.

"But there *would* be," cried Bruno, "if the Professor shortened it up for us!"

"Shortened it up?" I said. "That's something new. How does he do it?"

"He's got a curious machine——" Sylvie was beginning to explain.

"A *welly* curious machine," Bruno broke in, not at all willing to have the story thus taken out of his mouth, "and if oo puts in——somefinoruvver——at *one* end, oo know——and he turns the handle——and it comes out at the uvver end, oh, ever so short!"

"As short as short!" Sylvie echoed.

"And one day——when we was in Outland, oo know——before we came to Fairyland——me and Sylvie took him a big Crocodile. And he shortened it up for us. And it *did* look so funny! And it kept looking round, and saying 'wherever *is* the rest of me got to?' And then its eyes looked unhappy——"

"Not *both* its eyes," Sylvie interrupted.

"Course not!" said the little fellow. "Only the eye that *couldn't* see wherever the rest of it had got to. But the eye that *could* see wherever——"

"How short *was* the crocodile?" I asked, as the story was getting a little complicated.

"Half as short again as when we caught it——*so* long," said Bruno, spreading out his arms to their full stretch.

I tried to calculate what this would come to, but it was too hard for me. Please make it out for me, dear Child who reads this!

"But you didn't leave the poor thing so short as that, did you?"

"Well, no. Sylvie and me took it back again and we got it stretched to——to——how much was it, Sylvie?"

"Two times and a half, and a little bit more," said Sylvie.

"It wouldn't like that better than the other way, I'm afraid?"

"Oh, but it did though!" Bruno put in eagerly. "It *were* proud of its new tail! Oo never saw a Crocodile so proud! Why, it could go round and walk on the top of its tail, and along its back, all the way to its head!"

"Not *quite* all the way," said Sylvie. "It couldn't, you know."

"Ah, but it *did*, once!" Bruno cried triumphantly. "Oo weren't looking——but *I* watched it. And it walked on tipplety toe, so as it wouldn't wake itself, 'cause it thought it were asleep. And it got both its paws on its tail. And it walked and it walked all the way along its back. And it walked and it walked on its forehead. And it walked a tiny little way down its nose! There now!"

This was a good deal worse than the last puzzle. Please, dear Child, help again!

"I don't believe no Crocodile never walked along its own forehead!" Sylvie cried, too much excited by the controversy to limit the number of her negatives.

"Oo don't know the *reason* why it did it!" Bruno scornfully retorted. "It had a welly good reason. I *heerd* it say 'Why *shouldn't* I walk on my own forehead?' So a course it *did*, oo know!"

"If *that's* a good reason, Bruno," I said, "why shouldn't *you* get up that tree?"

"*Shall*, in a minute," said Bruno: "soon as we've done talking. Only two peoples *ca'n't* talk comfably togevver, when one's getting up a tree, and the other isn't!"

It appeared to me that a conversation would scarcely be 'comfable' while trees were being climbed, even if *both* the 'peoples' were doing it: but it was evidently dangerous to oppose any theory of Bruno's; so I thought it best to let the question drop, and to ask for an account of the machine that made things *longer*.

This time Bruno was at a loss, and left it to Sylvie. "It's like a mangle," she said: "if things are put in, they get squoze——"

"Squeezeled!" Bruno interrupted.

"Yes." Sylvie accepted the correction, but did not attempt to pronounce the word, which was evidently new to her. "They get——like that——and they come out, oh, ever so long!"

"Once," Bruno began again, "Sylvie and me writed——"

"Wrote!" Sylvie whispered.

"Well, we *wroted* a Nursery-Song, and the Professor mangled it longer for us. It were '*There was a little Man, And he had a little gun, And the bullets——*'"

"I know the rest," I interrupted. "But would you say it *long*——I mean the way that it came *out* of the mangle?"

"We'll get the Professor to *sing* it for you," said Sylvie. "It would spoil it to *say* it."

"I would like to meet the Professor," I said. "And I would like to take you all with me, to see some friends of mine, that live near here. Would you like to come?"

"I don't think the *Professor* would like to come," said Sylvie. "He's *very* shy. But *we'd* like it very much. Only we'd better not come *this* size, you know."

The difficulty had occurred to me already: and I had felt that perhaps there *would* be a slight awkwardness in introducing two such tiny friends into Society. "What size will you be?" I enquired.

"We'd better come as——common *children*," Sylvie thoughtfully replied. "That's the easiest size to manage."

"Could you come to-day?" I said, thinking "then we could have you at the picnic!"

Sylvie considered a little. "Not *to-day*," she replied. "We haven't got the things ready. We'll come on——Tuesday next, if you like. And now, *really*, Bruno, you must come and do your lessons."

"I *wiss* oo wouldn't say '*really* Bruno!'" the little fellow pleaded, with pouting lips that made him look prettier than ever. "It *always* shows there's something horrid coming! And I won't kiss you, if you're so unkind."

"Ah, but you *have* kissed me!" Sylvie exclaimed in merry triumph.

"Well then, I'll *un*kiss you!" And he threw his arms round her neck for this novel, but apparently not *very* painful, operation.

"It's *very* like *kissing!*" Sylvie remarked, as soon as her lips were again free for speech.

"Oo don't know *nuffin* about it! It were just the *conkery!*" Bruno replied with much severity, as he marched away.

Sylvie turned her laughing face to me. "Shall we come on Tuesday?" she said.

"Very well," I said: "let it be Tuesday next. But where *is* the Professor? Did he come with you to Fairyland?"

"No," said Sylvie. "But he promised he'd come and see us, *some* day. He's getting his Lecture ready. So he has to stay at home."

"At home?" I said dreamily, not feeling quite sure what she had said.

"Yes, Sir. His Lordship and Lady Muriel *are* at home. Please to walk this way."

CHAPTER XVII.

THE THREE BADGERS.

STILL more dreamily I found myself following this imperious voice into a room where the Earl, his daughter, and Arthur, were seated. "So you're come *at last!*" said Lady Muriel, in a tone of playful reproach.

"I was delayed," I stammered. Though *what* it was that had delayed me I should have been puzzled to explain! Luckily no questions were asked.

The carriage was ordered round, the hamper, containing our contribution to the Picnic, was duly stowed away, and we set forth.

There was no need for *me* to maintain the conversation. Lady Muriel and Arthur were evidently on those most delightful of terms, where one has no need to check thought after thought, as it rises to the lips, with the fear '*this* will not be appreciated——*this* will give offence——*this* will sound too serious——this will sound flippant': like very old friends, in fullest sympathy, their talk rippled on.

"Why shouldn't we desert the Picnic and go in some other direction?" she suddenly suggested. "A party of four is surely self-sufficing? And as for *food*, our hamper——"

"Why *shouldn't* we? What a genuine *lady's* argument!" laughed Authur. "A lady never knows on which side the *onus probandi* ——the burden of proving——lies!"

"Do *men* always know?" she asked with a pretty assumption of meek docility.

"With *one* exception——the only one I can think of——Dr. Watts, who has asked the senseless question

Why should I deprive my neighbour
Of his goods against his will?'

Fancy *that* as an argument for Honesty! His position seems to be 'I'm only honest because I see no reason to steal.' And the *thief's* answer is of course complete and crushing. 'I deprive my neighbour of his goods because I want them myself. And I do it against his will because there's no chance of getting him to consent to it!'"

"I can give you one other exception," I said: "an argument I heard only to-day—and *not* by a lady. 'Why shouldn't I walk on my own forehead?'"

"What a curious subject for speculation!" said Lady Muriel, turning to me, with eyes brimming over with laughter. "May we know who propounded the question? And *did* he walk on his own forehead?"

"I ca'n't remember *who* it was that said it!" I faltered. "Nor *where* I heard it!"

"Whoever it was, I hope we shall meet him at the Picnic!" said Lady Muriel. "It's a *far* more interesting question than '*Isn't* this a picturesque ruin?' '*Aren't* those autumn-tints lovely?' I shall have to answer those two questions *ten* times, at least, this afternoon!"

"That's one of the miseries of Society!" said Arthur. "Why ca'n't people let one enjoy the beauties of Nature without having to *say* so every minute? Why should Life be one long Catechism?"

"It's just as bad at a picture-gallery," the Earl remarked. "I went to the R.A. last May, with a conceited young artist: and he *did* torment me! I wouldn't have minded his criticizing the pictures *himself*: but *I* had to agree with him——or else to argue the point, which would have been worse!"

"It was *depreciatory* criticism, of course?" said Arthur.

"I don't see the 'of course' at all."

"Why, did you ever know a conceited man dare to *praise* a picture? The one thing he dreads (next to not being noticed) is *to be proved fallible!* If you once *praise* a picture, your character for *infallibility* hangs by a thread. Suppose it's a figure-picture, and you venture to say 'draws well.' Somebody measures it, and finds one of the proportions an eighth of an inch wrong. *You* are disposed of as a critic! 'Did you say he draws *well?*'

your friends enquire sarcastically, while you hang your head and blush. No. The only *safe* course, if any one says 'draws well,' is to shrug your shoulders. '*Draws* well?' you repeat thoughtfully. 'Draws *well?* Humph!' That's the way to become a great critic!"

Thus airily chatting, after a pleasant drive through a few miles of beautiful scenery, we reached the *rendezvous*——a ruined castle——where the rest of the picnic-party were already assembled. We spent an hour or two in sauntering about the ruins: gathering at last, by common consent, into a few random groups, seated on the side of a mound, which commanded a good view of the old castle and its surroundings.

The momentary silence, that ensued, was promptly taken possession of——or, more correctly, taken into custody——by a Voice; a voice so smooth, so monotonous, so sonorous, that one felt, with a shudder, that any other conversation was precluded, and that, unless some desperate remedy were adopted, we were fated to listen to a Lecture, of which no man could foresee the end!

The speaker was a broadly-built man, whose large, flat, pale face was bounded on the North by a fringe of hair, on the East and West by a fringe of whisker, and on the South by a fringe of beard—the whole constituting a uniform halo of stubbly whitey-brown bristles. His features were so entirely destitute of expression that I could not help saying to myself—helplessly, as if in the clutches of a night-mare—"they are only penciled in: no final touches as yet!" And he had a way of ending every sentence with a sudden smile, which spread like a ripple over that vast blank surface, and was gone in a moment, leaving behind it such absolute solemnity that I felt impelled to murmur "it was not *he:* it was somebody else that smiled!"

"Do you observe?" (such was the phrase with which the wretch began each sentence) "Do you observe the way in which that broken arch, at the very top of the ruin, stands out against the clear sky? It is placed *exactly* right: and there is *exactly* enough of it. A little more, or a little less, and all would be utterly spoiled!"

"Oh gifted architect!" murmured Arthur, inaudibly to all but Lady Muriel and myself. "Foreseeing the exact effect his work would have, when in ruins, centuries after his death!"

"And do you observe, where those trees slope down the hill," (indicating them with a sweep of the hand, and with all the patronising air of the man who has himself arranged the landscape), "how the mists rising from the river fill up *exactly* those intervals where we *need* indistinctness, for artistic effect? Here, in the foreground, a few clear touches are not amiss: but a *back*-ground without mist, you know! It is simply barbarous! Yes, we *need* indistinctness!"

The orator looked so pointedly at *me* as he uttered these words, that I felt bound to reply, by murmuring something to the effect that I hardly felt the need *myself*——and that I enjoyed looking at a thing, better, when I could *see* it.

"Quite so!" the great man sharply took me up. "From *your* point of view, that is correctly put. But for any one who has a soul for *Art*, such a view is preposterous. *Nature* is one thing. *Art* is another. *Nature* shows us the world as it *is*. But *Art*——as a Latin author tells us——*Art*, you know——the words have escaped my memory——"

"*Ars est celare Naturam*," Arthur interposed with a delightful promptitude.

"Quite so!" the orator replied with an air of relief. "I thank you! *Ars est celare*

Naturam——but that isn't it." And, for a few peaceful moments, the orator brooded, frowningly, over the quotation. The welcome opportunity was seized, and *another* voice struck into the silence.

"What a *lovely* old ruin it is!" cried a young lady in spectacles, the very embodiment of the March of Mind, looking at Lady Muriel, as the proper recipient of all really *original* remarks. "And *don't* you admire those autumn-tints on the trees? *I* do, *intensely!*"

Lady Muriel shot a meaning glance at me; but replied with admirable gravity. "Oh yes indeed, indeed! *So* true!"

"And isn't it strange," said the young lady, passing with startling suddenness from Sentiment to Science, "that the mere impact of certain coloured rays upon the Retina should give us such exquisite pleasure?"

"You have studied Physiology, then?" a certain young Doctor courteously enquired.

"Oh, *yes!* Isn't it a *sweet* Science?"

Arthur slightly smiled. "It seems a paradox, does it not," he went on, "that the image formed on the Retina should be inverted?"

"It *is* puzzling," she candidly admitted. "Why is it we do not *see* things upside-down?"

"You have never heard the Theory, then, that the *Brain* also is inverted?"

"No *indeed!* What a *beautiful* fact! But how is it *proved?*"

"*Thus,*" replied Arthur, with all the gravity of ten Professors rolled into one. "What we call the *vertex* of the Brain is really its *base:* and what we call its *base* is really its *vertex:* it is simply a question of *nomenclature.*"

This last polysyllable settled the matter. "How truly delightful!" the fair Scientist exclaimed with enthusiasm. "I shall ask our Physiological Lecturer why he never gave us that *exquisite* Theory!"

"I'd give something to be present when the question is asked!" Arthur whispered to me, as, at a signal from Lady Muriel, we moved on to where the hampers had been collected, and devoted ourselves to the more *substantial* business of the day.

We 'waited' on ourselves, as the modern barbarism (combining two good things in such a way as to secure the discomforts of both and the advantages of neither) of having a picnic with servants to wait upon you, had not yet reached this out-of-the-way region——and of course the gentlemen did not even take their places until the ladies had been duly provided with all imaginable creature-comforts. Then I supplied myself with a plate of something solid and a glass of something fluid, and found a place next to Lady Muriel.

It had been left vacant——apparently for Arthur, as a distinguished stranger: but he had turned shy, and had placed himself next to the young lady in spectacles, whose high rasping voice had already cast loose upon Society such ominous phrases as "Man is a bundle of Qualities!", "the Objective is only attainable through the Subjective!". Arthur was bearing it bravely: but several faces wore a look of alarm, and I thought it high time to start some less metaphysical topic.

"In my nursery days," I began, "when the weather didn't suit for an out-of-doors picnic, we were allowed to have a peculiar kind, that we enjoyed hugely. The table cloth was laid *under* the table, instead of upon it: we sat round it on the floor: and I believe we really enjoyed that extremely uncomfortable kind of dinner more than we ever did the orthodox arrangement!"

"I've no doubt of it," Lady Muriel replied. "There's nothing a well-regulated child hates so much as regularity. I believe a really healthy boy would thoroughly enjoy Greek Grammar—if only he might stand on his head to learn it! And your carpet-dinner certainly spared you *one* feature of a picnic, which is to me its chief drawback."

"The chance of a shower?" I suggested.

"No, the chance—or rather the certainty—of *live* things occurring in combination with one's food! *Spiders* are *my* bugbear. Now my father has *no* sympathy with that sentiment—*have* you, dear?" For the Earl had caught the word and turned to listen.

"To each his sufferings, all are men," he replied in the sweet sad tones that seemed natural to him: "each has his pet aversion."

"But you'll never guess *his!*" Lady Muriel said, with that delicate silvery laugh that was music to my ears.

I declined to attempt the impossible.

"He doesn't like *snakes!*" she said, in a stage whisper. "Now, isn't *that* an unreasonable aversion? Fancy not liking such a dear, coaxingly, *clingingly* affectionate creature as a snake!"

"Not like *snakes!*" I exclaimed. "Is such a thing possible?"

"No, he *doesn't* like them," she repeated with a pretty mock-gravity. "He's not *afraid* of them, you know. But he doesn't *like* them. He says they're too waggly!"

I was more startled than I liked to show. There was something so *uncanny* in this echo of the very words I had so lately heard from that little forest-sprite, that it was only by a great effort I succeeded in saying, carelessly, "Let us banish so unpleasant a topic. Won't you sing us something, Lady Muriel? I know you *do* sing without music."

"The only songs I know——without music——are *desperately* sentimental, I'm afraid! Are your tears all ready?"

"Quite ready! Quite ready!" came from all sides, and Lady Muriel——not being one of those lady-singers who think it *de rigueur* to decline to sing till they have been petitioned three or four times, and have pleaded failure of memory, loss of voice, and other conclusive reasons for silence——began at once :—

" There be three Badgers on a mossy stone,
Beside a dark and covered way:
Each dreams himself a monarch on his throne,
And so they stay and stay——
Though their old Father languishes alone,
They stay, and stay, and stay.

"*There be three Herrings loitering around,*
Longing to share that mossy seat:
Each Herring tries to sing what she has found
That makes Life seem so sweet.
Thus, with a grating and uncertain sound,
They bleat, and bleat, and bleat.

"*The Mother-Herring, on the salt sea-wave,*
Sought vainly for her absent ones:
The Father-Badger, writhing in a cave,
Shrieked out 'Return, my sons!
You shall have buns,' he shrieked, 'if you'll behave!
Yea, buns, and buns, and buns!'

"'*I fear,' said she, 'your sons have gone astray?*
My daughters left me while I slept.'
'Yes 'm,' the Badger said: 'it's as you say.'
'They should be better kept.'
Thus the poor parents talked the time away,
And wept, and wept, and wept."

Here Bruno broke off suddenly. "The Herrings' Song wants anuvver tune, Sylvie," he said. "And I ca'n't sing it—not wizout oo plays it for me!"

Instantly Sylvie seated herself upon a tiny mushroom, that happened to grow in front of a daisy, as if it were the most ordinary musical instrument in the world, and played on the petals as if they were the notes of an organ. And such delicious *tiny* music it was! Such teeny-tiny music!

Bruno held his head on one side, and listened very gravely for a few moments until he had caught the melody. Then the sweet childish voice rang out once more:—

"Oh, dear beyond our dearest dreams,
Fairer than all that fairest seems!
To feast the rosy hours away,
To revel in a roundelay!
How blest would be
A life so free—
Ipwergis-Pudding to consume,
And drink the subtle Azzigoom!

"And if, in other days and hours,
Mid other fluffs and other flowers,
The choice were given me how to dine—
'Name what thou wilt: it shall be thine!'
Oh, then I see
The life for me—
Ipwergis-Pudding to consume,
And drink the subtle Azzigoom!"

"Oo may leave off playing *now*, Sylvie. I can do the uvver tune much better wizout a compliment."

"He means 'without *accompaniment*,'" Sylvie whispered, smiling at my puzzled look: and she pretended to shut up the stops of the organ.

"*The Badgers did not care to talk to Fish:*
They did not dote on Herrings' songs:
They never had experienced the dish
To which that name belongs:
'*And oh, to pinch their tails,*' (*this was their wish,*)
'*With tongs, yea, tongs, and tongs!*'"

I ought to mention that he marked the parenthesis, in the air, with his finger. It seemed to me a very good plan. You know there's no *sound* to represent it——any more than there is for a question.

Suppose you have said to your friend "You are better to-day," and that you want him to understand that you are asking him a *question*, what can be simpler than just to make a "?" in the air with your finger? He would understand you in a moment!

"'*And are not these the Fish,*' *the Eldest sighed,*
'*Whose Mother dwells beneath the foam?*'
'*They* are *the Fish!*' *the Second one replied.*
'*And they have left their home!*'
'*Oh wicked Fish,*' *the Youngest Badger cried,*
'*To roam, yea, roam, and roam!*'

"*Gently the Badgers trotted to the shore—*
The sandy shore that fringed the bay:
Each in his mouth a living Herring bore—
Those aged ones waxed gay:
Clear rang their voices through the ocean's roar,
'*Hooray, hooray, hooray!*'"

"So they all got safe home again," Bruno said, after waiting a minute to see if *I* had anything to say: he evidently felt that *some* remark ought to be made. And I couldn't help wishing there were some such rule in Society, at the conclusion of a song—that the singer *herself* should say the right thing, and not leave it to the audience. Suppose a young lady has just been warbling ('with a grating and uncertain sound') Shelley's exquisite lyric '*I arise from dreams of thee*': how much nicer it would be, instead of *your* having to say "Oh, *thank* you, *thank* you!" for the young lady herself to remark, as she draws on her gloves, while the impassioned words '*Oh, press it to thine own, or it will break at last!*' are still ringing in your ears, "—but she wouldn't do it, you know. So it *did* break at last."

"And I *knew* it would!" she added quietly, as I started at the sudden crash of broken glass. "You've been holding it sideways for the last minute, and letting all the champagne run out! Were you asleep, I wonder? I'm *so* sorry my singing has such a narcotic effect!"

CHAPTER XVIII.

QUEER STREET, NUMBER FORTY.

Lady Muriel was the speaker. And, for the moment, that was the only fact I could clearly realise. But how she came to be there——and how *I* came to be there——and how the glass of champagne came to be there——all these were questions which I felt it better to think out in silence, and not commit myself to any statement till I understood things a little more clearly.

'First accumulate a mass of Facts: and *then* construct a Theory.' *That*, I believe, is the true Scientific Method. I sat up, rubbed my eyes, and began to accumulate Facts.

A smooth grassy slope, bounded, at the upper end, by venerable ruins half buried in ivy, at the lower, by a stream seen through arching trees—a dozen gaily-dressed people, seated in little groups here and there—some open hampers—the *débris* of a picnic—such were the *Facts* accumulated by the Scientific Researcher. And now, what deep, far-reaching *Theory* was he to construct from them? The Researcher found himself at fault. Yet stay! One Fact had escaped his notice. While all the rest were grouped in twos and in threes, *Arthur* was alone: while all tongues were talking, *his* was silent: while all faces were gay, *his* was gloomy and despondent. Here was a *Fact* indeed! The Researcher felt that a *Theory* must be constructed without delay.

Lady Muriel had just risen and left the party. Could *that* be the cause of his despondency? The Theory hardly rose to the dignity of a Working Hypothesis. Clearly more Facts were needed.

The Researcher looked round him once more: and now the Facts accumulated in such bewildering profusion, that the Theory was lost among them. For Lady Muriel had gone to meet a strange gentleman, just visible in the distance: and now she was returning with him, both of them talking eagerly and joyfully, like old friends who have been long parted: and now she was moving from group to group, introducing the new hero of the hour: and he, young, tall, and handsome, moved gracefully at her side, with the erect bearing and firm tread of a soldier. Verily, the Theory looked gloomy for Arthur! His eye caught mine, and he crossed to me.

"He is very handsome," I said.

"Abominably handsome!" muttered Arthur: then smiled at his own bitter words. "Lucky no one heard me but you!"

"Doctor Forester," said Lady Muriel, who had just joined us, "let me introduce to you my cousin Eric Lindon—*Captain* Lindon, I should say."

Arthur shook off his ill-temper instantly and completely, as he rose and gave the young soldier his hand. "I have heard of you," he said. "I'm very glad to make the acquaintance of Lady Muriel's cousin."

"Yes, that's all I'm distinguished for, *as yet!*" said Eric (so we soon got to call him) with a winning smile. "And I doubt," glancing at Lady Muriel, "if it even amounts to a good-conduct-badge! But it's something to begin with."

"You must come to my father, Eric," said Lady Muriel. "I think he's wandering among the ruins." And the pair moved on.

The gloomy look returned to Arthur's face: and I could see it was only to distract his thoughts that he took his place at the side of the metaphysical young lady, and resumed their interrupted discussion.

"Talking of Herbert Spencer," he began, "do you really find no *logical* difficulty in regarding Nature as a process of involution, passing from definite coherent homogeneity to indefinite incoherent heterogeneity?"

Amused as I was at the ingenious jumble he had made of Spencer's words, I kept as grave a face as I could.

"No *physical* difficulty," she confidently replied: "but I haven't studied *Logic* much. Would you *state* the difficulty?"

"Well," said Arthur, "do you accept it as self-evident? Is it as obvious, for instance, as that 'things that are greater than the same are greater than one another'?"

"To *my* mind," she modestly replied, "it seems *quite* as obvious. I grasp *both* truths by intuition. But *other* minds may need some logical——I forget the technical terms."

"For a *complete* logical argument," Arthur began with admirable solemnity, "we need two prim Misses——"

"Of course!" she interrupted. "I remember that word now. And they produce——?"

"A Delusion," said Arthur.

"Ye——es?" she said dubiously. "I don't seem to remember that so well. But what is the *whole* argument called?"

"A Sillygism."

"Ah, yes! I remember now. But I don't need a Sillygism, you know, to prove that mathematical axiom you mentioned."

"Nor to prove that 'all angles are equal', I suppose?"

"Why, of course not! One takes such a simple truth as that for granted!"

Here I ventured to interpose, and to offer her a plate of strawberries and cream. I felt really uneasy at the thought that she *might* detect the trick: and I contrived, unperceived by her, to shake my head reprovingly at the pseudo-philosopher. Equally unperceived by her, Arthur slightly raised his shoulders, and spread his hands abroad, as who should say "What else can I say to her?" and moved away, leaving her to discuss her strawberries by 'involution,' or any other way she preferred.

By this time the carriages, that were to convey the revelers to their respective homes, had begun to assemble outside the Castle-grounds: and it became evident—now that Lady Muriel's cousin had joined our party—that the problem, how to convey five people to Elveston, with a carriage that would only hold four, must somehow be solved.

The Honorable Eric Lindon, who was at this moment walking up and down with Lady Muriel, might have solved it at once, no doubt, by announcing his intention of returning on foot. Of *this* solution there did not seem to be the very smallest probability.

The next best solution, it seemed to me, was that *I* should walk home: and this I at once proposed.

"You're sure you don't mind?" said the Earl. "I'm afraid the carriage won't take us all, and I don't like to suggest to Eric to desert his cousin so soon."

"So far from minding it," I said, "I should prefer it. It will give me time to sketch this beautiful old ruin."

"I'll keep you company," Arthur suddenly said. And, in answer to what I suppose was a look of surprise on my face, he said in a low voice, "I *really* would rather. I shall be quite *de trop* in the carriage!"

"I think I'll walk too," said the Earl. "You'll have to be content with *Eric* as your escort," he added, to Lady Muriel, who had joined us while he was speaking.

"You must be as entertaining as Cerberus—'three gentlemen rolled into one'——" Lady Muriel said to her companion. "It will be a grand military exploit!"

"A sort of Forlorn Hope?" the Captain modestly suggested.

"You *do* pay pretty compliments!" laughed his fair cousin. "Good day to you, gentlemen three——or rather deserters three!" And the two young folk entered the carriage and were driven away.

"How long will your sketch take?" said Arthur.

"Well," I said, "I should like an hour for it. Don't you think you had better go without me? I'll return by train. I know there's one in about an hour's time."

"Perhaps that *would* be best," said the Earl. "The Station is quite close."

So I was left to my own devices, and soon found a comfortable seat, at the foot of a tree, from which I had a good view of the ruins.

"It is a very drowsy day," I said to myself, idly turning over the leaves of the sketch-book to find a blank page. "Why, I thought you were a mile off by this time!" For, to my surprise, the two walkers were back again.

"I came back to remind you," Arthur said, "that the trains go every ten minutes——"

"Nonsense!" I said. "It isn't the Metropolitan Railway!"

"It *is* the Metropolitan Railway," the Earl insisted. "This is a part of Kensington."

"Why do you talk with your eyes shut?" said Arthur. "Wake up!"

"I think it's the heat makes me so drowsy," I said, hoping, but not feeling quite sure, that I was talking sense. "Am I awake now?"

"I think *not*," the Earl judicially pronounced. "What do *you* think, Doctor? He's only got one eye open!"

"And he's snoring like anything!" cried Bruno. "Do wake up, you dear old thing!" And he and Sylvie set to work, rolling the heavy head from side to side, as if its connection with the shoulders was a matter of no sort of importance.

And at last the Professor opened his eyes, and sat up, blinking at us with eyes of utter bewilderment. "Would you have the kindness to mention," he said, addressing me with his usual old-fashioned courtesy, "whereabouts we are just now——and *who* we are, beginning with me?"

I thought it best to begin with the children. "This is Sylvie, Sir; and *this* is Bruno."

"Ah, yes! I know *them* well enough!" the old man murmured. "It's *myself* I'm most anxious about. And perhaps you'll be good enough to mention, at the same time, how I got here?"

"A harder problem occurs to *me*," I ventured to say: "and that is, how you're to get back again."

"True, true!" the Professor replied. "That's *the* Problem, no doubt. Viewed *as* a Problem, outside of oneself, it is a *most* interesting one. Viewed as a portion of one's own biography, it is, I must admit, very distressing!" He groaned, but instantly added, with a chuckle, "As to *myself*, I think you mentioned that I am——"

"Oo're the *Professor!*" Bruno shouted in his ear. "Didn't oo know *that?* Oo've come from *Outland!* And it's *ever* so far away from here!"

The Professor leapt to his feet with the agility of a boy. "Then there's no time to lose!" he exclaimed anxiously. "I'll just ask this guileless peasant, with his brace of buckets that contain (apparently) water, if he'll be so kind as to direct us. Guileless peasant!" he proceeded in a louder voice. "Would you tell us the way to Outland?"

The guileless peasant turned with a sheepish grin. "Hey?" was all he said.

"The——way——to——Outland!" the Professor repeated.

The guileless peasant set down his buckets and considered. "Ah dunnot——"

"I ought to mention," the Professor hastily put in, "that whatever you say will be used in evidence against you."

The guileless peasant instantly resumed his buckets. "Then ah says nowt!" he answered briskly, and walked away at a great pace.

The children gazed sadly at the rapidly vanishing figure. "He goes very quick!" the Professor said with a sigh. "But I *know* that was the right thing to say. I've studied your English Laws. However, let's ask this next man that's coming. He is *not* guileless, and he is *not* a peasant——but I don't know that either point is of vital importance."

It was, in fact, the Honourable Eric Lindon, who had apparently fulfilled his task of escorting Lady Muriel home, and was now strolling leisurely up and down the road outside the house, enjoying a solitary cigar.

"Might I trouble you, Sir, to tell us the nearest way to Outland!" Oddity as he was, in outward appearance, the Professor was, in that essential nature which no outward disguise could conceal, a thorough gentleman.

And, as such, Eric Lindon accepted him instantly. He took the cigar from his mouth, and delicately shook off the ash, while he considered. "The name sounds strange to me," he said. "I doubt if I can help you."

"It is not *very* far from *Fairyland*," the Professor suggested.

Eric Lindon's eye-brows were slightly raised at these words, and an amused smile, which he courteously tried to repress, flitted across his handsome face. "A trifle *cracked!*" he muttered to himself. "But what a jolly old patriarch it is!" Then he turned to the children. "And ca'n't *you* help him, little folk?" he said, with a gentleness of tone that seemed to win their hearts at once. "Surely *you* know all about it?

'How many miles to Babylon?
Three-score miles and ten.
Can I get there by candlelight?
Yes, and back again!'"

To my surprise, Bruno ran forwards to him, as if he were some old friend of theirs, seized the disengaged hand and hung on to it with both of his own: and there stood this tall dignified officer in the middle of the road, gravely swinging a little boy to and fro, while Sylvie stood ready to push him, exactly as if a real swing had suddenly been provided for their pastime.

"We don't want to get to *Babylon*, oo know!" Bruno explained as he swung.

"And it isn't *candlelight:* it's *daylight!*" Sylvie added, giving the swing a push of extra vigour, which nearly took the whole machine off its balance.

By this time it was clear to me that Eric Lindon was quite unconscious of my presence. Even the Professor and the children seemed to have lost sight of me: and I stood in the midst of the group, as unconcernedly as a ghost, seeing but unseen.

"How perfectly isochronous!" the Professor exclaimed with enthusiasm. He had his watch in his hand, and was carefully counting Bruno's oscillations. "He measures time quite as accurately as a pendulum!"

"Yet even pendulums," the good-natured young soldier observed, as he carefully released his hand from Bruno's grasp, "are not a joy *for ever!* Come, that's enough for one bout, little man! Next time we meet, you shall have another. Meanwhile you'd better take this old gentleman to Queer Street, Number——"

"*We'll* find it!" cried Bruno eagerly, as they dragged the Professor away.

"We are much indebted to you!" the Professor said, looking over his shoulder.

"Don't mention it!" replied the officer, raising his hat as a parting salute.

"*What* number did you say!" the Professor called from the distance.

The officer made a trumpet of his two hands. "Forty!" he shouted in stentorian tones. "And not *piano*, by any means!" he added to himself. "It's a mad world, my masters, a mad world!" He lit another cigar, and strolled on towards his hotel.

"What a lovely evening!" I said, joining him as he passed me.

"Lovely indeed," he said. "Where did *you* come from? Dropped from the clouds?"

"I'm strolling your way," I said; and no further explanation seemed necessary.

"Have a cigar?"

"Thanks: I'm not a smoker."

"Is there a Lunatic Asylum near here?"

"Not that I know of."

"Thought there might be. Met a lunatic just now. Queer old fish as ever I saw!"

And so, in friendly chat, we took our homeward ways, and wished each other 'good-night' at the door of his hotel.

Left to myself, I felt the 'eerie' feeling rush over me again, and saw, standing at the door of Number Forty, the three figures I knew so well.

"Then it's the wrong house?" Bruno was saying.

"No, no! It's the right *house*," the Professor cheerfully replied: "but it's the wrong *street*. *That's* where we've made our mistake! Our best plan, now, will be to——"

It was over. The street was empty, Commonplace life was around me, and the 'eerie' feeling had fled.

CHAPTER XIX.

HOW TO MAKE A PHLIZZ.

THE week passed without any further communication with the 'Hall,' as Arthur was evidently fearful that we might 'wear out our welcome'; but when, on Sunday morning, we were setting out for church, I gladly agreed to his proposal to go round and enquire after the Earl, who was said to be unwell.

Eric, who was strolling in the garden, gave us a good report of the invalid, who was still in bed, with Lady Muriel in attendance.

"Are you coming with us to church?" I enquired.

"Thanks, no," he courteously replied. "It's not—exactly—in my line, you know. It's an excellent institution—for the *poor*. When I'm with my own folk, I go, just to set them an example. But I'm not known *here*: so I think I'll excuse myself sitting out a sermon. Country-preachers are always so dull!"

Arthur was silent till we were out of hearing. Then he said to himself, almost inaudibly, "*Where two or three are gathered together in my name, there am I in the midst of them.*"

"Yes," I assented: "no doubt that *is* the principle on which church-going rests."

"And when he *does* go," he continued (our thoughts ran so much together, that our conversation was often slightly elliptical), "I suppose he repeats the words '*I believe in the Communion of Saints*'?"

But by this time we had reached the little church, into which a goodly stream of worshipers, consisting mainly of fishermen and their families, was flowing.

The service would have been pronounced by any modern æsthetic religionist—or religious æsthete, which is it?—to be crude and cold:

to me, coming fresh from the ever-advancing developments of a London church under a *soi-disant* 'Catholic' Rector, it was unspeakably refreshing.

There was no theatrical procession of demure little choristers, trying their best not to simper under the admiring gaze of the congregation: the people's share in the service was taken by the people themselves, unaided, except that a few good voices, judiciously posted here and there among them, kept the singing from going too far astray.

There was no murdering of the noble music, contained in the Bible and the Liturgy, by its recital in a dead monotone, with no more expression than a mechanical talking-doll.

No, the prayers were *prayed*, the lessons were *read*, and——best of all——the sermon was *talked;* and I found myself repeating, as we left the church, the words of Jacob,. when he '*awaked out of his sleep.*' "'*Surely the Lord is in this place! This is none other but the house of God, and this is the gate of heaven.*'"

"Yes," said Arthur, apparently in answer. to my thoughts, "those 'high' services are fast becoming pure Formalism. More and more the people are beginning to regard them as 'performances,' in which they only 'assist' in the French sense. And it is *specially* bad for the little boys. They'd be much less self-conscious as pantomime-fairies. With all that dressing-up, and stagy-entrances and exits, and being always *en evidence*, no wonder if they're eaten up with vanity, the blatant little coxcombs!"

When we passed the Hall on our return, we found the Earl and Lady Muriel sitting out in the garden. Eric had gone for a stroll.

We joined them, and the conversation soon turned on the sermon we had just heard, the subject of which was 'selfishness.'

"What a change has come over our pulpits," Arthur remarked, "since the time when Paley gave that utterly selfish definition of virtue, '*the doing good to mankind, in obedience to the will of God, and for the sake of everlasting happiness*'!"

Lady Muriel looked at him enquiringly, but she seemed to have learned by intuition, what years of experience had taught *me*, that the way to elicit Arthur's deepest thoughts was neither to assent nor dissent, but simply to *listen*.

"At that time," he went on, "a great tidal wave of selfishness was sweeping over human thought. Right and Wrong had somehow been transformed into Gain and Loss, and Religion had become a sort of commercial transaction. We may be thankful that our preachers are beginning to take a nobler view of life."

"But is it not taught again and again in the *Bible?*" I ventured to ask.

"Not in the Bible as a *whole*," said Arthur. "In the Old Testament, no doubt, rewards and punishments are constantly appealed to as motives for action. That teaching is best for *children*, and the Israelites seem to have been, mentally, *utter* children. We guide our children thus, at first: but we appeal, as soon as possible, to their innate sense of Right and Wrong: and, when *that* stage is safely past, we appeal to the highest motive of all, the desire for likeness to, and union with, the Supreme Good. I think you will find that to be the teaching of the Bible, *as a whole*, beginning with '*that thy days may be long in the land*,' and ending with '*be ye perfect, even as your Father which is in heaven is perfect*.'"

We were silent for awhile, and then Arthur went off on another tack. "Look at the literature of Hymns, now. How cankered it is, through and through, with selfishness! There are few human compositions more utterly degraded than some modern Hymns!"

I quoted the stanza

> "*Whatever, Lord, we lend to Thee,*
> *Repaid a thousandfold shall be,*
> *Then gladly will we give to Thee,*
> *Giver of all!*"

"Yes," he said grimly: "that is the typical stanza. And the very last charity-sermon I heard was infected with it. After giving many good reasons for charity, the preacher wound up with 'and, for all you give, you will be repaid a thousandfold!' Oh the utter meanness of such a motive, to be put before men who *do* know what self-sacrifice is, who *can* appreciate generosity and heroism! Talk of Original *Sin!*" he went on with increasing bitterness. "Can you have a stronger proof of the Original Goodness there must be in this nation, than the fact that Religion has been preached to us, as a commercial speculation, for a century, and that we still believe in a God?"

"It couldn't have gone on so long," Lady Muriel musingly remarked, "if the Opposition hadn't been practically silenced—put under what the French call *la clôture*. Surely in any lecture-hall, or in private society, such teaching would soon have been hooted down?"

"I trust so," said Arthur: "and, though I don't want to see 'brawling in church' legalised, I must say that our preachers enjoy an *enormous* privilege—which they ill deserve, and which they misuse terribly. We put our man into a pulpit, and we virtually tell him 'Now, you may stand there and talk to us for half-an-hour. We won't interrupt you by so much as a *word!* You shall have it all your own way!' And what does he give us in return? Shallow twaddle, that, if it were addressed to you over a dinner-table, you would think 'Does the man take me for a *fool?*'"

The return of Eric from his walk checked the tide of Arthur's eloquence, and, after a few minutes' talk on more conventional topics, we took our leave. Lady Muriel walked with us to the gate. "You have given me much to think about," she said earnestly, as she gave Arthur her hand. "I'm so glad you came in!" And her words brought a real glow of pleasure into that pale worn face of his.

On the Tuesday, as Arthur did not seem equal to more walking, I took a long stroll by myself, having stipulated that he was not to give the *whole* day to his books, but was to meet me at the Hall at about tea-time. On my way back, I passed the Station just as the afternoon-train came in sight, and sauntered down the stairs to see it come in. But there was little to gratify my idle curiosity: and, when the train was empty, and the platform clear, I found it was about time to be moving on, if I meant to reach the Hall by five.

As I approached the end of the platform, from which a steep irregular wooden staircase conducted to the upper world, I noticed two passengers, who had evidently arrived by the train, but who, oddly enough, had entirely escaped my notice, though the arrivals had been so few. They were a young woman and a little girl: the former, so far as one could judge by appearances, was a nursemaid, or possibly a nursery-governess, in attendance on the child, whose refined face, even more than her dress, distinguished her as of a higher class than her companion.

The child's face was refined, but it was also a worn and sad one, and told a tale (or so I seemed to read it) of much illness and suffering, sweetly and patiently borne. She had a little crutch to help herself along with: and she was now standing, looking wistfully up the long staircase, and apparently waiting till she could muster courage to begin the toilsome ascent.

There are some things one *says* in life——as well as things one *does*——which come automatically, by *reflex action*, as the physiologists say (meaning, no doubt, action *without* reflection, just as *lucus* is said to be derived '*a non lucendo*'). Closing one's eyelids, when something seems to be flying into the eye, is one of those actions, and saying "May I carry the little girl up the stairs?" was another. It wasn't that any thought of offering help occurred to me, and that *then* I spoke: the

first intimation I had, of being likely to make that offer, was the sound of my own voice, and the discovery that the offer had been made. The servant paused, doubtfully glancing from her charge to me, and then back again to the child. "Would you like it, dear?" she asked her. But no such doubt appeared to cross the child's mind: she lifted her arms eagerly to be taken up. "Please!" was all she said, while a faint smile flickered on the weary little face. I took her up with scrupulous care, and her little arm was at once clasped trustfully round my neck.

She was a *very* light weight——so light, in fact, that the ridiculous idea crossed my mind that it was rather easier going up, with her in my arms, than it would have been without her: and, when we reached the road above, with its cart-ruts and loose stones——all formidable obstacles for a lame child——I found that I had said "I'd better carry her over this rough place," before I had formed any *mental* connection between its roughness and my gentle little burden. "Indeed it's troubling you too much, Sir!" the maid exclaimed. "She can walk very well on the flat." But the arm, that was twined about my neck, clung just an atom more closely at the suggestion, and decided me to say "She's no weight, really. I'll carry her a little further. I'm going your way."

The nurse raised no further objection: and the next speaker was a ragged little boy, with bare feet, and a broom over his shoulder, who ran across the road, and pretended to sweep the perfectly dry road in front of us. "Give us a 'ap'ny!" the little urchin pleaded, with a broad grin on his dirty face.

"*Don't* give him a 'ap'ny!" said the little lady in my arms. The *words* sounded harsh: but the *tone* was gentleness itself. "He's an *idle* little boy!" And she laughed a laugh of such silvery sweetness as I had never yet heard from any lips but Sylvie's. To my astonishment, the boy actually *joined* in the laugh, as if there were some subtle sympathy between them, as he ran away down the road and vanished through a gap in the hedge.

But he was back in a few moments, having discarded his broom and provided himself, from some mysterious source, with an exquisite bouquet of flowers. "Buy a posy, buy a posy! Only a 'ap'ny!" he chanted, with the melancholy drawl of a professional beggar.

"*Don't* buy it!" was Her Majesty's edict as she looked down, with a lofty scorn that seemed curiously mixed with tender interest, on the ragged creature at her feet.

But this time I turned rebel, and ignored the royal commands. Such lovely flowers, and of forms so entirely new to me, were not to be abandoned at the bidding of any little maid, however imperious. I bought the bouquet: and the little boy, after popping the halfpenny into his mouth, turned head-over-heels, as if to ascertain whether the human mouth is really adapted to serve as a money-box.

With wonder, that increased every moment, I turned over the flowers, and examined them one by one: there was not a single one among them that I could remember having ever seen before. At last I turned to the nursemaid. "Do these flowers grow wild about here? I never saw——" but the speech died away on my lips. The nursemaid had vanished!

"You can put me down, *now*, if you like," Sylvie quietly remarked.

I obeyed in silence, and could only ask myself "Is this a *dream?*", on finding Sylvie and Bruno walking one on either side of me, and clinging to my hands with the ready confidence of childhood.

"You're larger than when I saw you last!" I began. "Really I think we ought to be introduced again! There's so much of you that I never met before, you know."

"Very well!" Sylvie merrily replied. "This is *Bruno*. It doesn't take long. He's only got one name!"

"There's *another* name to me!" Bruno protested, with a reproachful look at the Mistress of the Ceremonies. "And it's—'*Esquire*'!"

"Oh, of course. I forgot," said Sylvie. "Bruno—*Esquire!*"

"And did you come here to meet *me*, my children?" I enquired.

"You know I *said* we'd come on Tuesday," Sylvie explained. "Are we the proper size for common children?"

"Quite the right size for *children*," I replied, (adding mentally "though not *common* children, by any means!") "But what became of the nursemaid?"

"It are *gone!*" Bruno solemnly replied.

"Then it wasn't solid, like Sylvie and you?"

"No. Oo couldn't *touch* it, oo know. If oo walked *at* it, oo'd go right froo!"

"I quite expected you'd find it out, once," said Sylvie. "Bruno ran it against a telegraph post, by accident. And it went in two halves. But you were looking the other way."

I felt that I had indeed missed an opportunity: to witness such an event as a nursemaid going 'in two halves' does not occur twice in a life-time!

"When did oo guess it were Sylvie?" Bruno enquired.

"I didn't guess it, till it *was* Sylvie," I said. "But how did you manage the nursemaid?"

"*Bruno* managed it," said Sylvie. "It's called a Phlizz."

"And how do you make a Phlizz, Bruno?"

"The Professor teached me how," said Bruno. "First oo takes a lot of air——"

"Oh, *Bruno!*" Sylvie interposed. "The Professor said you weren't to tell!"

"But who did her *voice?*" I asked.

"Indeed it's troubling you too much, Sir! She can walk very well on the flat."

Bruno laughed merrily as I turned hastily from side to side, looking in all directions for the speaker. "That were *me!*" he gleefully proclaimed, in his own voice.

"She can indeed walk very well on the flat," I said. "And I think *I* was the Flat."

By this time we were near the Hall. "This is where my friends live," I said. "Will you come in and have some tea with them?"

Bruno gave a little jump of joy: and Sylvie said "Yes, please. You'd like some tea, Bruno, wouldn't you? He hasn't tasted *tea,*" she explained to me, "since we left Outland."

"And *that* weren't *good* tea!" said Bruno. "It were so *welly* weak!"

CHAPTER XX.

LIGHT COME, LIGHT GO.

LADY MURIEL'S smile of welcome could not *quite* conceal the look of surprise with which she regarded my new companions.

I presented them in due form. "This is *Sylvie*, Lady Muriel. And this is *Bruno*."

"Any surname?" she enquired, her eyes twinkling with fun.

"No," I said gravely. "No surname."

She laughed, evidently thinking I said it in fun; and stooped to kiss the children—a salute to which *Bruno* submitted with reluctance: *Sylvie* returned it with interest.

While she and Arthur (who had arrived before me) supplied the children with tea and cake, I tried to engage the Earl in conversation: but he was restless and *distrait*, and we made little progress. At last, by a sudden question, he betrayed the cause of his disquiet.

"*Would* you let me look at those flowers you have in your hand?"

"Willingly!" I said, handing him the bouquet. Botany was, I knew, a favourite study of his: and these flowers were to me so entirely new and mysterious, that I was really curious to see what a botanist would say of them.

They did *not* diminish his disquiet. On the contrary, he became every moment more excited as he turned them over. "*These* are all from Central India!" he said, laying aside part of the bouquet. "They are rare, even there: and I have never seen them in any other part of the world. *These* two are Mexican——*This* one——" (He rose hastily, and carried it to the window, to examine it in a better light, the flush of excitement mounting to his very forehead) "——is, I am nearly sure——but I have a book of Indian Botany here——" He took a volume from the book-shelves, and turned the leaves with trembling fingers. "Yes! Compare it with this picture! It is the exact duplicate! This is the flower of the Upas-tree, which usually grows only in the depths of forests; and the flower fades so quickly after being plucked, that it is scarcely possible to keep its form or colour even so far as the outskirts of the forest! Yet this is in full bloom! *Where* did you get these flowers?" he added with breathless eagerness.

I glanced at Sylvie, who, gravely and silently, laid her finger on her lips, then beckoned to Bruno to follow her, and ran out into the garden; and I found myself in the position of a defendant whose two most important witnesses have been suddenly taken away. "Let me give you the flowers!" I stammered out at last, quite 'at my wit's end' as to how to get out of the difficulty. "You know much more about them than I do!"

"I accept them most gratefully! But you have not yet told me——" the Earl was beginning, when we were interrupted, to my great relief, by the arrival of Eric Lindon.

To *Arthur*, however, the new-comer was, I saw clearly, anything but welcome. His face clouded over : he drew a little back from the circle, and took no further part in the conversation, which was wholly maintained, for some minutes, by Lady Muriel and her lively cousin, who were discussing some new music that had just arrived from London.

"Do just try this one!" he pleaded. "The music looks easy to sing at sight, and the song's quite appropriate to the occasion."

"Then I suppose it's

> '*Five o'clock tea!*
> *Ever to thee*
> *Faithful I'll be,*
> *Five o'clock tea!*'"

laughed Lady Muriel, as she sat down to the piano, and lightly struck a few random chords.

"Not quite: and yet it *is* a kind of 'ever to thee faithful I'll be!' It's a pair of hapless lovers : *he* crosses the briny deep : and *she* is left lamenting."

"That is *indeed* appropriate!" she replied mockingly, as he placed the song before her.

"And am *I* to do the lamenting? And who for, if you please?"

She played the air once or twice through, first in quick, and finally in slow, time; and then gave us the whole song with as much graceful ease as if she had been familiar with it all her life:—

"He stept so lightly to the land,
All in his manly pridė:
He kissed her cheek, he pressed her hand,
Yet still she glanced aside.
'Too gay he seems,' she darkly dreams,
'Too gallant and too gay
To think of me——poor simple me——
When he is far away!'

'I bring my Love this goodly pearl
Across the seas,' he said:
'A gem to deck the dearest girl
That ever sailor wed!'
She clasps it tight: her eyes are bright:
Her throbbing heart would say
'He thought of me——he thought of me——
When he was far away!'

The ship has sailed into the West :
Her ocean-bird is flown :
A dull dead pain is in her breast,
And she is weak and lone :
Yet there's a smile upon her face,
A smile that seems to say
'He'll think of me—he'll think of me—
When he is far away !

'Though waters wide between us glide,
Our lives are warm and near :
No distance parts two faithful hearts—
Two hearts that love so dear :
And I will trust my sailor-lad,
For ever and a day,
To think of me—to think of me—
When he is far away !'"

The look of displeasure, which had begun to come over Arthur's face when the young Captain spoke of Love so lightly, faded away as the song proceeded, and he listened with evident delight. But his face darkened again when Eric demurely remarked "Don't you think 'my *soldier*-lad' would have fitted the tune just as well!"

"Why, so it would!" Lady Muriel gaily retorted. "Soldiers, sailors, tinkers, tailors, what a lot of words would fit in! I think 'my *tinker*-lad' sounds best. Don't *you?*"

To spare my friend further pain, I rose to go, just as the Earl was beginning to repeat his particularly embarrassing question about the flowers.

"You have not yet——"

"Yes, I've *had* some tea, thank you!" I hastily interrupted him. "And now we really *must* be going. Good evening, Lady Muriel!" And we made our adieux, and escaped, while the Earl was still absorbed in examining the mysterious bouquet.

Lady Muriel accompanied us to the door. "You *couldn't* have given my father a more acceptable present!" she said, warmly. "He is so passionately fond of Botany. I'm afraid *I* know nothing of the *theory* of it, but I keep his *Hortus Siccus* in order. I must get some sheets of blotting-paper, and dry these new treasures for him before they fade."

"*That* won't be no good at all!" said Bruno, who was waiting for us in the garden.

"Why won't it?" said I. "You know I *had* to give the flowers, to stop questions."

"Yes, it ca'n't be helped," said Sylvie: "but they *will* be sorry when they find them gone!"

"But how will they go?"

"Well, I don't know *how*. But they *will* go. The nosegay was only a *Phlizz*, you know. Bruno made it up."

These last words were in a whisper, as she evidently did not wish Arthur to hear. But of this there seemed to be little risk: he hardly seemed to notice the children, but paced on, silent and abstracted; and when, at the entrance to the wood, they bid us a hasty farewell and ran off, he seemed to wake out of a day-dream.

The bouquet vanished, as Sylvie had predicted; and when, a day or two afterwards, Arthur and I once more visited the Hall, we found the Earl and his daughter, with the old housekeeper, out in the garden, examining the fastenings of the drawing-room window.

"We are holding an Inquest," Lady Muriel said, advancing to meet us: "and we admit you, as Accessories before the Fact, to tell us all you know about those flowers."

"The Accessories before the Fact decline to answer *any* questions," I gravely replied. "And they reserve their defence."

"Well then, turn Queen's Evidence, please! The flowers have disappeared in the night," she went on, turning to Arthur, "and we are *quite* sure no one in the house has meddled with them. Somebody must have entered by the window——"

"But the fastenings have not been tampered with," said the Earl.

"It must have been while you were dining, my Lady," said the housekeeper.

"That was it," said the Earl. "The thief must have seen you bring the flowers," turning to me, "and have noticed that you did *not* take them away. And he must have known their great value—they are simply *priceless!*" he exclaimed, in sudden excitement.

"And you never told us how you got them!" said Lady Muriel.

"Some day," I stammered, "I may be free to tell you. Just now, would you excuse me?"

The Earl looked disappointed, but kindly said "Very well, we will ask no questions."

"But we consider you a *very* bad Queen's Evidence," Lady Muriel added playfully, as we entered the arbour. "We pronounce you to be an accomplice: and we sentence you to solitary confinement, and to be fed on bread and——butter. Do you take sugar?"

"It is disquieting, certainly," she resumed, when all 'creature-comforts' had been duly supplied, "to find that the house has been entered by a thief——in this out-of-the-way place. If only the flowers had been *eatables*, one might have suspected a thief of quite another shape——"

"You mean that universal explanation for all mysterious disappearances, 'the *cat* did it'?" said Arthur.

"Yes," she replied. "What a convenient thing it would be if all thieves had the same shape! It's so confusing to have some of them quadrupeds and others bipeds!"

"It has occurred to me," said Arthur, "as a curious problem in Teleology——the Science of Final Causes," he added, in answer to an enquiring look from Lady Muriel.

"And a Final Cause is——?"

"Well, suppose we say——the last of a series of connected events——each of the series being the cause of the next——for whose sake the first event takes place."

"But the last event is practically an *effect* of the first, isn't it? And yet you call it a *cause* of it!"

Arthur pondered a moment. "The words are rather confusing, I grant you," he said. "Will this do? The last event is an effect of the first: but the *necessity* for that event is a cause of the *necessity* for the first."

"That seems clear enough," said Lady Muriel. "Now let us have the problem."

"It's merely this. What object can we imagine in the arrangement by which each different size (roughly speaking) of living creatures has its special shape? For instance, the human race has one kind of shape——bipeds. Another set, ranging from the lion to the mouse, are quadrupeds. Go down a step or two further, and you come to insects with six legs ——hexapods——a beautiful name, is it not? But beauty, in our sense of the word, seems to diminish as we go down: the creature becomes more——I won't say 'ugly' of any of God's creatures——more uncouth. And, when we take the microscope, and go a few steps lower still, we come upon animalculæ, terribly uncouth, and with a terrible number of legs!"

"The other alternative," said the Earl, "would be a *diminuendo* series of repetitions of the same type. Never mind the monotony of it: let's see how it would work in other ways. Begin with the race of men, and the creatures they require: let us say horses, cattle, sheep, and dogs——we don't exactly require frogs and spiders, do we, Muriel?"

Lady Muriel shuddered perceptibly: it was evidently a painful subject. "We can dispense with *them*," she said gravely.

"Well, then we'll have a second race of men, half-a-yard high——"

"——who would have *one* source of exquisite enjoyment, not possessed by ordinary men!" Arthur interrupted.

"*What* source?" said the Earl.

"Why, the grandeur of scenery! Surely the grandeur of a mountain, to *me*, depends on its *size*, relative to me? Double the height of the mountain, and of course it's twice as grand. Halve *my* height, and you produce the same effect."

"Happy, happy, happy Small!" Lady Muriel murmured rapturously. "None but the Short, none but the Short, none but the Short enjoy the Tall!"

"But let me go on," said the Earl. "We'll have a third race of men, five inches high; a fourth race, an inch high——"

"They couldn't eat common beef and mutton, I'm sure!" Lady Muriel interrupted.

"True, my child, I was forgetting. Each set must have its own cattle and sheep."

"And its own vegetation," I added. "What could a cow, an inch high, do with grass that waved far above its head?"

"That is true. We must have a pasture within a pasture, so to speak. The common grass would serve our inch-high cows as a green forest of palms, while round the root of each tall stem would stretch a tiny carpet of microscopic grass. Yes, I think our scheme will work fairly well. And it would be very interesting, coming into contact with the races below us. What sweet little things the inch-high bull-dogs would be! I doubt if even *Muriel* would run away from one of them!"

"Don't you think we ought to have a *crescendo* series, as well?" said Lady Muriel. "Only fancy being a hundred yards high! One could use an elephant as a paper-weight, and a crocodile as a pair of scissors!"

"And would you have races of different sizes communicate with one another?" I enquired. "Would they make war on one another, for instance, or enter into treaties?"

"*War* we must exclude, I think. When you could crush a whole nation with one blow of your fist, you couldn't conduct war on equal terms. But anything, involving a collision of *minds* only, would be possible in our ideal world—for of course we must allow *mental* powers to all, irrespective of size. Perhaps the fairest rule would be that, the *smaller* the race, the *greater* should be its intellectual development!"

"Do you mean to say," said Lady Muriel, "that these manikins of an inch high are to *argue* with me?"

"Surely, surely!" said the Earl. "An argument doesn't depend for its logical force on the *size* of the creature that utters it!"

She tossed her head indignantly. "I would *not* argue with any man less than six inches high!" she cried. "I'd make him *work!*"

"What at?" said Arthur, listening to all this nonsense with an amused smile.

"*Embroidery!*" she readily replied. "What *lovely* embroidery they would do!"

"Yet, if they did it wrong," I said, "you couldn't *argue* the question. I don't know *why:* but I agree that it couldn't be done."

"The reason is," said Lady Muriel, "one couldn't sacrifice one's *dignity* so far."

"Of course one couldn't!" echoed Arthur. "Any more than one could argue with a potato. It would be altogether—excuse the ancient pun—*infra dig.!*"

"I doubt it," said I. "Even a pun doesn't *quite* convince me."

"Well, if that is *not* the reason," said Lady Muriel, "what reason would you give?"

I tried hard to understand the meaning of this question: but the persistent humming of the bees confused me, and there was a drowsiness in the air that made every thought stop and go to sleep before it had got well thought out: so all I could say was "That must depend on the *weight* of the potato."

I felt the remark was not so sensible as I should have liked it to be. But Lady Muriel seemed to take it quite as a matter of course. "In that case——" she began, but suddenly started, and turned away to listen. "Don't you hear him?" she said. "He's crying. We must go to him, somehow."

And I said to myself "That's very strange! I quite thought it was *Lady Muriel* talking to me. Why, it's *Sylvie* all the while!" And I made another great effort to say something that should have some meaning in it. "Is it about the potato?"

CHAPTER XXI.

THROUGH THE IVORY DOOR.

"I DON'T know," said Sylvie. "Hush! I must think. I could go to him, by myself, well enough. But I want *you* to come too."

"Let me go with you," I pleaded. "I can walk as fast as *you* can, I'm sure."

Sylvie laughed merrily. "What nonsense!" she cried. "Why, you ca'n't walk a bit! You're lying quite flat on your back! You don't understand these things."

"I can walk as well as *you* can," I repeated. And I tried my best to walk a few steps: but the ground slipped away backwards, quite as fast as I could walk, so that I made no progress at all. Sylvie laughed again.

"There, I told you so! You've no idea how funny you look, moving your feet about in the air, as if you were walking! Wait a bit. I'll ask the Professor what we'd better do." And she knocked at his study-door.

The door opened, and the Professor looked out. "What's that crying I heard just now?" he asked. "Is it a human animal?"

"It's a boy," Sylvie said.

"I'm afraid you've been teasing him?"

"No, *indeed* I haven't!" Sylvie said, very earnestly. "I *never* tease him!"

"Well, I must ask the Other Professor about it." He went back into the study, and we heard him whispering "small human animal——says she hasn't been teasing him——the kind that's called Boy——"

"Ask her *which* Boy," said a new voice. The Professor came out again.

"*Which* Boy is it that you haven't been teasing?"

Sylvie looked at me with twinkling eyes. "You dear old thing!" she exclaimed, standing on tiptoe to kiss him, while he gravely stooped to receive the salute. "How you *do* puzzle me! Why, there are *several* boys I haven't been teasing!"

The Professor returned to his friend: and this time the voice said "Tell her to bring them here——*all* of them!"

"I ca'n't, and I won't!" Sylvie exclaimed, the moment he reappeared. "It's *Bruno* that's crying: and he's my brother: and, please, we *both* want to go: he ca'n't walk, you know: he's——he's *dreaming*, you know" (this in a whisper, for fear of hurting my feelings). "*Do* let's go through the Ivory Door!"

"I'll ask him," said the Professor, disappearing again. He returned directly. "He says you may. Follow me, and walk on tip-toe."

The difficulty with me would have been, just then, *not* to walk on tip-toe. It seemed very hard to reach down far enough to just touch the floor, as Sylvie led me through the study.

The Professor went before us to unlock the Ivory Door. I had just time to glance at the Other Professor, who was sitting reading, with his back to us, before the Professor showed us out through the door, and locked it behind us. Bruno was standing with his hands over his face, crying bitterly.

"What's the matter, darling?" said Sylvie, with her arms round his neck.

"Hurted mine self *welly* much!" sobbed the poor little fellow.

"I'm *so* sorry, darling! How ever *did* you manage to hurt yourself so?"

"Course I managed it!" said Bruno, laughing through his tears. "Doos oo think nobody else but *oo* ca'n't manage things?"

Matters were looking distinctly brighter, now Bruno had begun to argue. "Come, let's hear all about it!" I said.

"My foot took it into its head to slip——" Bruno began.

"A foot hasn't got a head!" Sylvie put in, but all in vain.

"I slipted down the bank. And I tripted over a stone. And the stone hurted my foot! And I trod on a Bee. And the Bee stinged my finger!" Poor Bruno sobbed again. The complete list of woes was too much for his feelings. "And it knewed I didn't *mean* to trod on it!" he added, as the climax.

"That Bee should be ashamed of itself!" I said severely, and Sylvie hugged and kissed the wounded hero till all tears were dried.

"My finger's quite unstung now!" said Bruno. "Why doos there be stones? Mister Sir, doos oo know?"

"They're good for *something*," I said: "even if we don't know *what*. What's the good of *dandelions*, now?"

"Dindledums?" said Bruno. "Oh, they're ever so pretty! And stones aren't pretty, one bit. Would oo like some dindledums, Mister Sir?"

"Bruno!" Sylvie murmured reproachfully. "You mustn't say 'Mister' and 'Sir,' both at once! Remember what I told you!"

"You telled me I were to say 'Mister' when I spoked *about* him, and I were to say 'Sir' when I spoked *to* him!"

"Well, you're not doing *both*, you know."

"Ah, but I *is* doing bofe, Miss Praticular!" Bruno exclaimed triumphantly. "I wishted to speak *about* the Gemplun——and I wishted to speak *to* the Gemplun. So a course I said 'Mister Sir'!"

"That's all right, Bruno," I said.

"*Course* it's all right!" said Bruno. "Sylvie just knows nuffin at all!"

"There never *was* an impertinenter boy!" said Sylvie, frowning till her bright eyes were nearly invisible.

"And there never was an ignoranter girl!" retorted Bruno. "Come along and pick some dindledums. *That's all she's fit for!*" he added in a very loud whisper to me.

"But why do you say 'Dindledums,' Bruno? *Dandelions* is the right word."

"It's because he jumps about so," Sylvie said, laughing.

"Yes, that's it," Bruno assented. "Sylvie tells me the words, and then, when I jump about, they get shooken up in my head——till they're all froth!"

I expressed myself as perfectly satisfied with this explanation. "But aren't you going to pick me any dindledums, after all?"

"Course we will!" cried Bruno. "Come along, Sylvie!" And the happy children raced away, bounding over the turf with the fleetness and grace of young antelopes.

"Then you didn't find your way back to Outland?" I said to the Professor.

"Oh yes, I did!" he replied, "We never got to Queer Street; but I found another way. I've been backwards and forwards several times since then. I had to be present at the Election, you know, as the author of the new Money-Act. The Emperor was so kind as to wish that *I* should have the credit of it. 'Let come what come may,' (I remember the very words of the Imperial Speech) 'if it *should* turn out that the Warden *is* alive, *you* will bear witness that the change in the coinage is the *Professor's* doing, not *mine!*' I never was so glorified in my life, before!" Tears trickled down his cheeks at the recollection, which apparently was not *wholly* a pleasant one.

"Is the Warden supposed to be *dead?*"

"Well, it's *supposed* so: but, mind you, *I* don't believe it! The evidence is *very* weak—mere hear-say. A wandering Jester, with a Dancing-Bear (they found their way into the Palace, one day) has been telling people he comes from Fairyland, and that the Warden died there. *I* wanted the Vice-Warden to question him, but, most unluckily, he and my Lady were always out walking when the Jester came round. Yes, the Warden's supposed to be dead!" And more tears trickled down the old man's cheeks.

"But what is the new Money-Act?"

The Professor brightened up again. "The Emperor started the thing," he said. "He wanted to make everybody in Outland twice as rich as he was before—just to make the new Government popular. Only there wasn't nearly enough money in the Treasury to do it. So *I* suggested that he might do it by doubling the value of every coin and bank-note in Outland. It's the simplest thing possible. I wonder nobody ever thought of it before! And you never saw such universal joy. The shops are full from morning to night. Everybody's buying everything!"

"And how was the glorifying done?"

A sudden gloom overcast the Professor's jolly face. "They did it as I went home after the Election," he mournfully replied. "It was kindly meant—but I didn't like it! They waved flags all round me till I was nearly blind: and they rang bells till I was nearly deaf: and they strewed the road so thick with flowers that I lost my way!" And the poor old man sighed deeply.

"How far is it to Outland?" I asked, to change the subject.

"About five days' march. But one *must* go back——occasionally. You see, as Court-Professor, I have to be *always* in attendance on Prince Uggug. The Empress would be *very* angry if I left him, even for an hour."

"But surely, every time you come here, you are absent ten days, at least?"

"Oh, more than that!" the Professor exclaimed. "A fortnight, sometimes. But of course I keep a memorandum of the exact time when I started, so that I can put the Court-time back to the very moment!"

"Excuse me," I said. "I don't understand."

Silently the Professor drew from his pocket a square gold watch, with six or eight hands, and held it out for my inspection. "This," he began, "is an Outlandish Watch——"

"So I should have thought."

"——which has the peculiar property that, instead of *its* going with the *time*, the *time* goes with *it*. I trust you understand me now?"

"Hardly," I said.

"Permit me to explain. So long as it is let alone, it takes its own course. Time has *no* effect upon it."

"I have known such watches," I remarked.

"It *goes*, of course, at the usual rate. Only the time has to go *with* it. Hence, if I move the hands, I change the time. To move them *forwards*, in *advance* of the true time, is impossible: but I can move them as much as a month *backwards*——that is the limit. And then you have the events all over again——with any alterations experience may suggest."

"*What* a blessing such a watch would be," I thought, "in real life! To be able to unsay some heedless word——to undo some reckless deed! Might I see the thing done?"

"With pleasure!" said the good natured Professor. "When I move *this* hand back to *here*," pointing out the place, "History goes back fifteen minutes!"

Trembling with excitement, I watched him push the hand round as he described.

"Hurted mine self *welly* much!"

Shrilly and suddenly the words rang in my ears, and, more startled than I cared to show, I turned to look for the speaker.

Yes! There was Bruno, standing with the tears running down his cheeks, just as I had seen him a quarter of an hour ago; and there was Sylvie with her arms round his neck!

I had not the heart to make the dear little fellow go through his troubles a second time, so hastily begged the Professor to push the hands round into their former position. In a moment Sylvie and Bruno were gone again, and I could just see them in the far distance, picking 'dindledums.'

"Wonderful, indeed!" I exclaimed.

"It has another property, yet more wonderful," said the Professor. "You see this little peg? That is called the 'Reversal Peg.' If you push it in, the events of the next hour happen in the reverse order. Do not try it now. I will lend you the Watch for a few days, and you can amuse yourself with experiments."

"Thank you very much!" I said as he gave me the Watch. "I'll take the greatest care of it——why, here are the children again!"

"We could only but find *six* dindledums," said Bruno, putting them into my hands, "'cause Sylvie said it were time to go back. And here's a big blackberry for *ooself!* We couldn't only find but *two!*"

"Thank you: it's *very* nice," I said. And I suppose *you* ate the other, Bruno?"

"No, I didn't," Bruno said, carelessly. "*Aren't* they pretty dindledums, Mister Sir?"

"Yes, very: but what makes you limp so, my child?"

"Mine foot's come *hurted* again!" Bruno mournfully replied. And he sat down on the ground, and began nursing it.

The Professor held his head between his hands—an attitude that I knew indicated distraction of mind. "Better rest a minute," he said. "It may be better then—or it may be worse. If only I had some of my medicines here! I'm Court-Physician, you know," he added, aside to me.

"Shall I go and get you some blackberries, darling?" Sylvie whispered, with her arms round his neck; and she kissed away a tear that was trickling down his cheek.

Bruno brightened up in a moment. "That *are* a good plan!" he exclaimed. "I thinks my foot would come *quite* unhurted, if I eated a blackberry—two or three blackberries—six or seven blackberries—"

Sylvie got up hastily. "I'd better go," she said, aside to me, "before he gets into the double figures!"

"Let me come and help you," I said. "I can reach higher up than you can."

"Yes, please," said Sylvie, putting her hand into mine: and we walked off together.

"Bruno *loves* blackberries," she said, as we paced slowly along by a tall hedge, that looked a promising place for them, "and it was so *sweet* of him to make me eat the only one!"

"Oh, it was *you* that ate it, then? Bruno didn't seem to like to tell me about it."

"No; I saw that," said Sylvie. "He's always afraid of being praised. But he *made* me eat it, really! I would much rather he—oh, what's that?" And she clung to my hand, half-frightened, as we came in sight of a hare, lying on its side with legs stretched out, just in the entrance to the wood.

"It's a *hare*, my child. Perhaps it's asleep."

"No, it isn't asleep," Sylvie said, timidly going nearer to look at it: "it's eyes are open. Is it—is it—" her voice dropped to an awe-struck whisper, "is it *dead*, do you think?"

"Yes, it's quite dead," I said, after stooping to examine it. "Poor thing! I think it's been hunted to death. I know the harriers were out yesterday. But they haven't touched it. Perhaps they caught sight of another, and left it to die of fright and exhaustion."

"Hunted to *death?*" Sylvie repeated to herself, very slowly and sadly. "I thought hunting was a thing they *played* at—like a game. Bruno and I hunt snails: but we never hurt them when we catch them!"

"Sweet angel!" I thought. "How am I to get the idea of *Sport* into your innocent mind?" And as we stood, hand-in-hand, looking down at the dead hare, I tried to put the thing into such words as she could understand. "You know what fierce wild-beasts lions and tigers are?" Sylvie nodded. "Well, in some countries men *have* to kill them, to save their own lives, you know."

"Yes," said Sylvie: "if one tried to kill *me*, Bruno would kill *it*—if he could."

"Well, and so the men—the hunters—get to enjoy it, you know: the running, and the fighting, and the shouting, and the danger."

"Yes," said Sylvie. "Bruno likes danger."

"Well, but, in *this* country, there aren't any lions and tigers, loose: so they hunt other creatures, you see." I hoped, but in vain, that this would satisfy her, and that she would ask no more questions.

"They hunt *foxes*," Sylvie said, thoughtfully. "And I think they *kill* them, too. Foxes are very fierce. I daresay men don't love them. Are hares fierce?"

"No," I said. "A hare is a sweet, gentle, timid animal—almost as gentle as a lamb."

"But, if men *love* hares, why—why—" her voice quivered, and her sweet eyes were brimming over with tears.

"I'm afraid they *don't* love them, dear child."

"All *children* love them," Sylvie said. "All *ladies* love them."

"I'm afraid even *ladies* go to hunt them, sometimes."

Sylvie shuddered. "Oh, no, not *ladies!*" she earnestly pleaded. "Not Lady Muriel!"

"No, *she* never does, I'm sure—but this is too sad a sight for *you*, dear. Let's try and find some—"

But Sylvie was not satisfied yet. In a hushed, solemn tone, with bowed head and clasped hands, she put her final question. "Does God love hares?"

"Yes!" I said. "I'm *sure* He does! He loves every living thing. Even sinful *men*. How much more the animals, that cannot sin!"

"I don't know what 'sin' means," said Sylvie. And I didn't try to explain it.

"Come, my child," I said, trying to lead her away. "Wish good-bye to the poor hare, and come and look for blackberries."

"Good-bye, poor hare!" Sylvie obediently repeated, looking over her shoulder at it as we turned away. And then, all in a moment, her self-command gave way. Pulling her hand out of mine, she ran back to where the dead hare was lying, and flung herself down at its side in such an agony of grief as I could hardly have believed possible in so young a child.

"Oh, my darling, my darling!" she moaned, over and over again. "And God meant your life to be so beautiful!"

Sometimes, but always keeping her face hidden on the ground, she would reach out one little hand, to stroke the poor dead thing, and then once more bury her face in her hands, and sob as if her heart would break.

I was afraid she would really make herself ill: still I thought it best to let her weep away the first sharp agony of grief: and, after a few minutes, the sobbing gradually ceased, and Sylvie rose to her feet, and looked calmly at me, though tears were still streaming down her cheeks.

I did not dare to speak again, just yet; but simply held out my hand to her, that we might quit the melancholy spot.

"Yes, I'll come now," she said. Very reverently she kneeled down, and kissed the dead hare; then rose and gave me her hand, and we moved on in silence.

A child's sorrow is violent, but short; and it was almost in her usual voice that she said, after a minute, "Oh stop, stop! Here are some *lovely* blackberries!"

We filled our hands with fruit, and returned in all haste to where the Professor and Bruno were seated on a bank, awaiting our return.

Just before we came within hearing-distance, Sylvie checked me. "Please don't tell *Bruno* about the hare!" she said.

"Very well, my child. But why not?"

Tears again glittered in those sweet eyes, and she turned her head away, so that I could scarcely hear her reply. "He's—he's very *fond* of gentle creatures, you know. And he'd—he'd be so sorry! I don't want him to be made sorry."

"And *your* agony of sorrow is to count for nothing, then, sweet unselfish child!" I thought to myself. But no more was said till we had reached our friends; and Bruno was far too much engrossed, in the feast we had brought him, to take any notice of Sylvie's unusually grave manner.

"I'm afraid it's getting rather late, Professor?" I said.

"Yes, indeed," said the Professor. "I must take you all through the Ivory Door again. You've stayed your full time."

"Mightn't we stay a *little* longer!" pleaded Sylvie.

"Just *one* minute!" added Bruno.

But the Professor was unyielding. "It's a great privilege, coming through at all," he said. "We must go now." And we followed him obediently to the Ivory Door, which he threw open, and signed to me to go through first.

"You're coming too, aren't you?" I said to Sylvie.

"Yes," she said: "but you won't see us after you've gone through."

"But suppose I wait for you outside?" I asked, as I stepped through the doorway.

"In that case," said Sylvie, "I think the potato would be *quite* justified in asking *your* weight. I can quite imagine a really *superior* kidney-potato declining to argue with any one under *fifteen stone!*"

With a great effort I recovered the thread of my thoughts. "We lapse very quickly into nonsense!" I said.

CHAPTER XXII.

CROSSING THE LINE.

"LET us lapse back again," said Lady Muriel. "Take another cup of tea? I hope *that's* sound common sense?"

"And all that strange adventure," I thought, "has occupied the space of a single comma in Lady Muriel's speech! A single comma, for which grammarians tell us to 'count *one*'*!*" (I felt no doubt that the Professor had kindly put back the time for me, to the exact point at which I had gone to sleep.)

When, a few minutes afterwards, we left the house, Arthur's first remark was certainly a strange one. "We've been there just *twenty minutes*," he said, "and I've done nothing but listen to you and Lady Muriel talking: and yet, somehow, I feel exactly as if *I* had been talking with her for an *hour* at least!"

And so he *had* been, I felt no doubt: only, as the time had been put back to the beginning of the tête-à-tête he referred to, the whole of it had passed into oblivion, if not into nothingness! But I valued my own reputation for sanity too highly to venture on explaining to *him* what had happened.

For some cause, which I could not at the moment divine, Arthur was unusually grave and silent during our walk home. It could not be connected with Eric Lindon, I thought, as he had for some days been away in London: so that, having Lady Muriel almost 'all to himself'—for *I* was only too glad to hear those two conversing, to have any wish to intrude any remarks of my own—he *ought*, theoretically, to have been specially radiant and contented with life. "Can he have heard any bad news?" I said to myself. And, almost as if he had read my thoughts, he spoke.

"He will be here by the last train," he said, in the tone of one who is continuing a conversation rather than beginning one.

"Captain Lindon, do you mean?"

"Yes—Captain Lindon," said Arthur: "I said 'he,' because I fancied we were talking about him. The Earl told me he comes to-night, though *to-morrow* is the day when he will know about the Commission that he's hoping for. I wonder he doesn't stay another day to hear the result, if he's really so anxious about it as the Earl believes he is."

"He can have a telegram sent after him," I said: "but it's not very soldier-like, running away from possible bad news!"

"He's a very good fellow," said Arthur: "but I confess it would be good news for *me*, if he got his Commission, and his Marching Orders, all at once! I wish him all happiness—with *one* exception. Good night!" (We had reached home by this time.) "I'm not good company to-night—better be alone."

It was much the same, next day. Arthur declared he wasn't fit for Society, and I had to set forth alone for an afternoon-stroll. I took the road to the Station, and, at the point where the road from the 'Hall' joined it, I paused, seeing my friends in the distance, seemingly bound for the same goal.

"Will you join us?" the Earl said, after I had exchanged greetings with him, and Lady Muriel, and Captain Lindon. "This restless young man is expecting a telegram, and we are going to the Station to meet it."

"There is also a restless young woman in the case," Lady Muriel added.

"That goes without saying, my child," said her father. "Women are *always* restless!"

"For generous appreciation of all one's *best* qualities," his daughter impressively remarked, "there's nothing to compare with a father, is there, Eric?"

"Cousins are not 'in it,'" said Eric: and then somehow the conversation lapsed into two duologues, the younger folk taking the lead, and the two old men following with less eager steps.

"And when are we to see your little friends again?" said the Earl. "They are singularly attractive children."

"I shall be delighted to bring them, when I can," I said. "But I don't know, myself, when I am likely to see them again."

"I'm not going to question you," said the Earl: "but there's no harm in mentioning that Muriel is simply tormented with curiosity! We know most of the people about here, and she has been vainly trying to guess what house they can possibly be staying at."

"Some day I may be able to enlighten her: but just at present——"

"Thanks. She must bear it as best she can. *I* tell her it's a grand opportunity for practising *patience*. But she hardly sees it from that point of view. Why, there *are* the children!"

So indeed they were: waiting (for *us*, apparently) at a stile, which they could not have climbed over more than a few moments, as Lady Muriel and her cousin had passed it without seeing them. On catching sight of us, Bruno ran to meet us, and to exhibit to us, with much pride, the handle of a clasp-knife—the blade having been broken off—which he had picked up in the road.

"And what shall you use it for, Bruno?" I said.

"Don't know," Bruno carelessly replied: "must think."

"A child's first view of life," the Earl remarked, with that sweet sad smile of his, "is that it is a period to be spent in accumulating portable property. That view gets modified as the years glide away." And he held out his hand to Sylvie, who had placed herself by me, looking a little shy of him.

But the gentle old man was not one with whom any child, human or fairy, could be shy for long; and she had very soon deserted my hand for his—Bruno alone remaining faithful to his first friend. We overtook the other couple just as they reached the Station, and both Lady Muriel and Eric greeted the children as old friends—the latter with the words "So you got to Babylon by candlelight, after all?"

"Yes, and back again!" cried Bruno.

Lady Muriel looked from one to the other in blank astonishment. "What, *you* know them, Eric?" she exclaimed. "This mystery grows deeper every day!"

"Then we must be somewhere in the Third Act," said Eric. "You don't expect the mystery to be cleared up till the Fifth Act, do you?"

"But it's such a *long* drama!" was the plaintive reply. "We *must* have got to the Fifth Act by this time!"

"*Third* Act, I assure you," said the young soldier mercilessly. "Scene, a railway-platform. Lights down. Enter Prince (in disguise, of course) and faithful Attendant. *This* is the Prince——" (taking Bruno's hand) "and here stands his humble Servant! What is your Royal Highness's next command?" And he made a most courtier-like low bow to his puzzled little friend.

"Oo're *not* a Servant!" Bruno scornfully exclaimed. "Oo're a *Gemplun!*"

"*Servant*, I assure your Royal Highness!" Eric respectfully insisted. "Allow me to mention to your Royal Highness my various situations——past, present, and future."

"What did oo begin wiz?" Bruno asked, beginning to enter into the jest. "Was oo a shoe-black?"

"Lower than that, your Royal Highness! Years ago, I offered myself as a *Slave*—as a '*Confidential* Slave,' I think it's called?" he asked, turning to Lady Muriel.

But Lady Muriel heard him not: something had gone wrong with her glove, which entirely engrossed her attention.

"Did oo get the place?" said Bruno.

"Sad to say, Your Royal Highness, I did *not!* So I had to take a situation as—as *Waiter*, which I have now held for some years—haven't I?" He again glanced at Lady Muriel.

"Sylvie dear, *do* help me to button this glove!" Lady Muriel whispered, hastily stooping down, and failing to hear the question.

"And what will oo be *next?*" said Bruno.

"My next place will, I hope, be that of *Groom*. And after that——"

"Don't puzzle the child so!" Lady Muriel interrupted. "What nonsense you talk!"

"—after that," Eric persisted, "I hope to obtain the situation of *Housekeeper*, which—*Fourth Act!*" he proclaimed, with a sudden change of tone. "Lights turned up. Red lights. Green lights. Distant rumble heard. Enter a passenger-train!"

And in another minute the train drew up alongside of the platform, and a stream of passengers began to flow out from the booking office and waiting-rooms.

"Did you ever make *real* life into a drama?" said the Earl. "Now just try. I've often amused myself that way. Consider this platform as our stage. Good entrances and exits on *both* sides, you see. Capital background scene: real engine moving up and down. All this bustle, and people passing to and fro, must have been most carefully rehearsed! How naturally they do it! With never a glance at the audience! And every grouping is quite fresh, you see. No repetition!"

It really was admirable, as soon as I began to enter into it from this point of view. Even a porter passing, with a barrow piled with luggage, seemed so realistic that one was tempted to applaud. He was followed by an angry mother, with hot red face, dragging along two screaming children, and calling, to some one behind, "John! Come on!" Enter John, very meek, very silent, and loaded with parcels. And he was followed, in his turn, by a frightened little nursemaid, carrying a fat baby, also screaming. All the children screamed.

"Capital byplay!" said the old man aside. "Did you notice the nursemaid's look of terror? It was simply *perfect!*"

"You have struck quite a new vein," I said. "To most of us Life and its pleasures seem like a mine that is nearly worked out."

"Worked out!" exclaimed the Earl. "For any one with true dramatic instincts, it is only the Overture that is ended! The real treat has yet to begin. You go to a theatre, and pay your ten shillings for a stall, and what do you get for your money? Perhaps it's a dialogue between a couple of farmers——unnatural in their overdone caricature of farmers' dress——more unnatural in their constrained attitudes and gestures——most unnatural in their attempts at ease and geniality in their talk. Go instead and take a seat in a third-class railway-carriage, and you'll get the same dialogue done *to the life!* Front-seats——no orchestra to block the view——and nothing to pay!"

"Which reminds me," said Eric. "There is nothing to pay on receiving a telegram! Shall we enquire for one?" And he and Lady Muriel strolled off in the direction of the Telegraph-Office.

"I wonder if Shakespeare had that thought in his mind," I said, "when he wrote 'All the world's a stage'?"

The old man sighed. "And so it is," he said, "look at it as you will. Life is indeed a drama; a drama with but few *encores*—and no *bouquets!*" he added dreamily. "We spend one half of it in regretting the things we did in the other half!"

"And the secret of *enjoying* it," he continued, resuming his cheerful tone, "is *intensity!*"

"But not in the modern æsthetic sense, I presume? Like the young lady, in Punch, who begins a conversation with 'Are you *intense?*'"

"By no means!" replied the Earl. "What I mean is intensity of *thought*—a concentrated *attention.* We lose half the pleasure we might have in Life, by not really *attending.* Take any instance you like: it doesn't matter *how* trivial the pleasure may be—the principle is the same. Suppose *A* and *B* are reading the same second-rate circulating-library novel. *A* never troubles himself to master the relationships of the characters, on which perhaps all the interest of the story depends: he 'skips' over all the descriptions of scenery, and every passage that looks rather dull: he doesn't half attend to the passages he does read: he goes on reading——merely from want of resolution to find another occupation——for hours after he ought to have put the book aside: and reaches the 'FINIS' in a state of utter weariness and depression! *B* puts his whole soul *into* the thing——on the principle that 'whatever is worth doing is worth doing *well*': he masters the genealogies: he calls up pictures before his 'mind's eye' as he reads about the scenery: best of all, he resolutely shuts the book at the end of some chapter, while his interest is yet at its keenest, and turns to other subjects; so that, when next he allows himself an hour at it, it is like a hungry man sitting down to dinner: and, when the book is finished, he returns to the work of his daily life like 'a giant refreshed'!"

"But suppose the book were really *rubbish*——nothing to repay attention?"

"Well, suppose it," said the Earl. "My theory meets *that* case, I assure you! *A* never finds out that it *is* rubbish, but maunders on to the end, trying to believe he's enjoying himself. *B* quietly shuts the book, when he's read a dozen pages, walks off to the Library, and changes it for a better! I have yet *another* theory for adding to the enjoyment of Life——that is, if I have not exhausted your patience? I'm afraid you find me a very garrulous old man."

"No indeed!" I exclaimed earnestly. And indeed I felt as if one *could* not easily tire of the sweet sadness of that gentle voice.

"It is, that we should learn to take our pleasures *quickly*, and our pains *slowly*."

"But why? I should have put it the other way, myself."

"By taking *artificial* pain——which can be as trivial as you please——*slowly*, the result is that, when *real* pain comes, however severe, all you need do is to let it go at its *ordinary* pace, and it's over in a moment!"

"Very true," I said, "but how about the *pleasure?*"

"Why, by taking it quick, you can get so much more into life. It takes *you* three hours and a half to hear and enjoy an opera. Suppose *I* can take it in, and enjoy it, in half-an-hour. Why, I can enjoy *seven* operas, while you are listening to *one!*"

"Always supposing you have an orchestra capable of *playing* them," I said. "And that orchestra has yet to be found!"

The old man smiled. "I have heard an air played," he said, "and by no means a short one—played right through, variations and all, in three seconds!"

"When? And how?" I asked eagerly, with a half-notion that I was dreaming again.

"It was done by a little musical-box," he quietly replied. "After it had been wound up, the regulator, or something, broke, and it ran down, as I said, in about three seconds. But it *must* have played all the notes, you know!"

"Did you *enjoy* it?" I asked, with all the severity of a cross-examining barrister.

"No, I didn't!" he candidly confessed. "But then, you know, I hadn't been trained to that kind of music!"

"I should much like to *try* your plan," I said, and, as Sylvie and Bruno happened to run up to us at the moment, I left them to keep the Earl company, and strolled along the platform, making each person and event play its part in an *extempore* drama for my especial benefit. "What, is the Earl tired of you already?" I said, as the children ran past me.

"No!" Sylvie replied with great emphasis. "He wants the evening-paper. So Bruno's going to be a little news-boy!"

"Mind you charge a good price for it!" I called after them.

Returning up the platform, I came upon Sylvie alone. "Well, child," I said, "where's your little news-boy? Couldn't he get you an evening-paper?"

"He went to get one at the book-stall at the other side," said Sylvie; "and he's coming across the line with it——oh, Bruno, you ought to cross by the bridge!" for the distant thud, thud, of the Express was already audible.

Suddenly a look of horror came over her face. "Oh, he's fallen down on the rails!" she cried, and darted past me at a speed that quite defied the hasty effort I made to stop her.

But the wheezy old Station-Master happened to be close behind me: he wasn't good for much, poor old man, but he was good for this; and, before I could turn round, he had the child clasped in his arms, saved from the certain death she was rushing to. So intent was I in watching this scene, that I hardly saw a flying figure in a light grey suit, who shot across from the back of the platform, and was on the line in another second. So far as one could take note of time in such a moment of horror, he had about ten clear seconds, before the Express would be upon him, in which to cross the rails and to pick up Bruno. Whether he did so or not it was quite impossible to guess: the next thing one knew was that the Express had passed, and that, whether for life or death, all was over. When the cloud of dust had cleared away, and the line was once more visible, we saw with thankful hearts that the child and his deliverer were safe.

"All right!" Eric called to us cheerfully, as he recrossed the line. "He's more frightened than hurt!"

He lifted the little fellow up into Lady Muriel's arms, and mounted the platform as gaily as if nothing had happened: but he was as pale as death, and leaned heavily on the arm I hastily offered him, fearing he was about to faint. "I'll just—sit down a moment—" he said dreamily: "—where's Sylvie?"

Sylvie ran to him, and flung her arms round his neck, sobbing as if her heart would break. "Don't do that, my darling!" Eric murmured, with a strange look in his eyes. "Nothing to cry about now, you know. But you very nearly got yourself killed for nothing!"

"For Bruno!" the little maiden sobbed. "And he would have done it for me. Wouldn't you, Bruno?"

"Course I would!" Bruno said, looking round with a bewildered air.

Lady Muriel kissed him in silence as she put him down out of her arms. Then she beckoned Sylvie to come and take his hand, and signed to the children to go back to where the Earl was seated. "Tell him," she whispered with quivering lips, "tell him——all is well!" Then she turned to the hero of the day. "I thought it was *death*," she said. "Thank God, you are safe! Did you see how near it was?"

"I saw there was just time," Eric said lightly. "A soldier must learn to carry his life in his hand, you know. I'm all right now. Shall we go to the telegraph-office again? I daresay it's come by this time."

I went to join the Earl and the children, and we waited—almost in silence, for no one seemed inclined to talk, and Bruno was half-asleep on Sylvie's lap—till the others joined us. No telegram had come.

"I'll take a stroll with the children," I said, feeling that we were a little *de trop*, "and I'll look in, in the course of the evening."

"We must go back into the wood, now," Sylvie said, as soon as we were out of hearing. "We ca'n't stay this size any longer."

"Then you will be quite tiny Fairies again, next time we meet?"

"Yes," said Sylvie: "but we'll be children again some day—if you'll let us. Bruno's very anxious to see Lady Muriel again."

"She are *welly* nice," said Bruno.

"I shall be very glad to take you to see her again," I said. "Hadn't I better give you back the Professor's Watch? It'll be too large for you to carry when you're Fairies, you know."

Bruno laughed merrily. I was glad to see he had quite recovered from the terrible scene he had gone through. "Oh no, it won't!" he said. "When *we* go small, *it'll* go small!"

"And then it'll go straight to the Professor," Sylvie added, "and you won't be able to use it any more: so you'd better use it all you can, *now.* We *must* go small when the sun sets. Good-bye!"

"Good-bye!" cried Bruno. But their voices sounded very far away, and, when I looked round, both children had disappeared.

"And it wants only two hours to sunset!" I said as I strolled on. "I must make the best of my time!"

CHAPTER XXIII.

AN OUTLANDISH WATCH.

As I entered the little town, I came upon two of the fishermen's wives interchanging that last word "which never was the last": and it occurred to me, as an experiment with the Magic Watch, to wait till the little scene was over, and then to 'encore' it.

"Well, good night t'ye! And ye winna forget to send us word when your Martha writes?"

"Nay, ah winna forget. An' if she isn't suited, she can but coom back. Good night t'ye!"

A casual observer might have thought "and there ends the dialogue!" That casual observer would have been mistaken.

"Ah, she'll like 'em, I war'n' ye! *They'll* not treat her bad, yer may depend. They're varry canny fowk. Good night!"

"Ay, they *are* that! Good night!"

"Good night! And ye'll send us word if she writes?"

"Aye, ah will, yer may depend! Good night t'ye!"

And at last they parted. I waited till they were some twenty yards apart, and then put the Watch a minute back. The instantaneous change was startling: the two figures seemed to flash back into their former places.

"——isn't suited, she can but coom back. Good night t'ye!" one of them was saying: and so the whole dialogue was repeated, and, when they had parted for the second time, I let them go their several ways, and strolled on through the town.

"But the real usefulness of this magic power," I thought, "would be to undo some harm, some painful event, some accident——"

I had not long to wait for an opportunity of testing *this* property also of the Magic Watch, for, even as the thought passed through my mind, the accident I was imagining occurred. A light cart was standing at the door of the 'Great Millinery Depôt' of Elveston, laden with card-board packing-cases, which the driver was carrying into the shop, one by one. One of the cases had fallen into the street, but it scarcely seemed worth while to step forward and pick it up, as the man would be back again in a moment. Yet, in that moment, a young man riding a bicycle came sharp round the corner of the street and, in trying to avoid running over the box, upset his machine, and was thrown headlong against the wheel of the spring-cart. The driver ran out to his assistance, and he and I together raised the unfortunate cyclist and carried him into the shop. His head was cut and bleeding; and one knee seemed to be badly injured; and it was speedily settled that he had better be conveyed at once to the only Surgery in the place. I helped them in emptying the cart, and placing in it some pillows for the wounded man to rest on;

and it was only when the driver had mounted to his place, and was starting for the Surgery, that I bethought me of the strange power I possessed of undoing all this harm.

"Now is my time!" I said to myself, as I moved back the hand of the Watch, and saw, almost without surprise this time, all things restored to the places they had occupied at the critical moment when I had first noticed the fallen packing-case.

Instantly I stepped out into the street, picked up the box, and replaced it in the cart: in the next moment the bicycle had spun round the corner, passed the cart without let or hindrance, and soon vanished in the distance, in a cloud of dust.

"Delightful power of magic!" I thought. "How much of human suffering I have—not only relieved, but actually annihilated!" And, in a glow of conscious virtue, I stood watching the unloading of the cart, still holding the Magic Watch open in my hand, as I was curious to see what would happen when we again reached the exact time at which I had put back the hand.

The result was one that, if only I had considered the thing carefully, I might have foreseen: as the hand of the Watch touched the mark, the spring-cart—which had driven off, and was by this time half-way down the street, was back again at the door, and in the act of starting, while—oh woe for the golden dream of world-wide benevolence that had dazzled my dreaming fancy!—the wounded youth was once more reclining on the heap of pillows, his pale face set rigidly in the hard lines that told of pain resolutely endured.

"Oh mocking Magic Watch!" I said to myself, as I passed out of the little town, and took the seaward road that led to my lodgings. "The good I fancied I could do is vanished like a dream: the evil of this troublesome world is the only abiding reality!"

And now I must record an experience so strange, that I think it only fair, before beginning to relate it, to release my much-enduring reader from any obligation he may feel to believe this part of my story. *I* would not have believed it, I freely confess, if I had not seen it with my own eyes: then why should I expect it of my reader, who, quite possibly, has never seen anything of the sort?

I was passing a pretty little villa, which stood rather back from the road, in its own grounds, with bright flower-beds in front—creepers wandering over the walls and hanging in festoons about the bow-windows—an easy-chair forgotten on the lawn, with a newspaper lying near it—a small pug-dog "couchant" before it, resolved to guard the treasure even at the sacrifice of life—and a front-door standing invitingly half-open. "Here is my chance," I thought, "for testing the reverse action of the Magic Watch!" I pressed the 'reversal-peg' and walked in. In *another* house, the entrance of a stranger might cause surprise—perhaps anger, even going so far as to expel the said stranger with violence: but *here*, I knew, nothing of the sort could happen. The *ordinary* course of events—first, to think nothing about me; then, hearing my footsteps to look up and see me; and then to wonder what business I had there—would be reversed by the action of my Watch. They would *first* wonder who I was, *then* see me, then look down, and think no more about me. And as to being expelled with violence, *that* event would necessarily come *first* in this case. "So, if I can once get *in*," I said to myself, "all risk of *expulsion* will be over!"

The pug-dog sat up, as a precautionary measure, as I passed; but, as I took no notice of the treasure he was guarding, he let me go by without even one remonstrant bark. "He that takes my life," he seemed to be saying, wheezily, to himself, "takes trash: But he that takes the *Daily Telegraph*——!" But this awful contingency I did not face.

The party in the drawing-room—I had walked straight in, you understand, without ringing the bell, or giving any notice of my approach—consisted of four laughing rosy children, of ages from about fourteen down to ten, who were, apparently, all coming towards the door (I found they were really walking *backwards*), while their mother, seated by the fire with some needlework on her lap, was saying, just as I entered the room, "Now, girls, you may get your things on for a walk."

To my utter astonishment—for I was not yet accustomed to the action of the Watch—"all smiles ceased" (as Browning says) on the four pretty faces, and they all got out pieces of needle-work, and sat down. No one noticed *me* in the least, as I quietly took a chair and sat down to watch them.

When the needle-work had been unfolded, and they were all ready to begin, their mother said "Come, *that's* done, at last! You may fold up your work, girls." But the children took no notice whatever of the remark; on the contrary, they set to work at once sewing—if that is the proper word to describe an operation such as *I* had never before witnessed. Each of them threaded her needle with a short end of thread attached to the work, which was instantly pulled by an invisible force through the stuff, dragging the needle after it: the nimble fingers of the little sempstress caught it at the other side, but only to lose it again the next moment. And so the work went on, steadily undoing itself, and the neatly-stitched little dresses, or whatever they were, steadily falling to pieces. Now and then one of the children would pause, as the recovered thread became inconveniently long, wind it on a bobbin, and start again with another short end.

At last all the work was picked to pieces and put away, and the lady led the way into the next room, walking backwards, and making the insane remark "Not yet, dear: we *must* get the sewing done first." After which, I was not surprised to see the children skipping backwards after her, exclaiming "Oh, mother, it *is* such a lovely day for a walk!"

In the dining-room, the table had only dirty plates and empty dishes on it. However the party——with the addition of a gentleman, as good-natured, and as rosy, as the children——seated themselves at it very contentedly.

You have seen people eating cherry-tart, and every now and then cautiously conveying a cherry-stone from their lips to their plates? Well, something like that went on all through this ghastly——or shall we say 'ghostly'?——banquet. An empty fork is raised to the lips: there it receives a neatly-cut piece of mutton, and swiftly conveys it to the plate, where it instantly attaches itself to the mutton already there. Soon one of the plates, furnished with a complete slice of mutton and two potatoes, was handed up to the presiding gentleman, who quietly replaced the slice on the joint, and the potatoes in the dish.

Their conversation was, if possible, more bewildering than their mode of dining. It began by the youngest girl suddenly, and without provocation, addressing her eldest sister. "Oh, you *wicked* story-teller!" she said.

I expected a sharp reply from the sister; but, instead of this, she turned laughingly to her father, and said, in a very loud stage-whisper, "To be a bride!"

The father, in order to do *his* part in a conversation that seemed only fit for lunatics, replied "Whisper it to me, dear."

But she *didn't* whisper (these children never did anything they were told): she said, quite loud, "Of course not! Everybody knows what *Dolly* wants!"

And little Dolly shrugged her shoulders, and said, with a pretty pettishness, "Now, Father, you're not to tease! You know I don't want to be bride's-maid to *anybody!*"

"And Dolly's to be the fourth," was her father's idiotic reply.

Here Number Three put in her oar. "Oh, it *is* settled, Mother dear, really and truly! Mary told us all about it. It's to be next Tuesday four weeks——and three of her cousins are coming to be bride's-maids——and——"

"*She* doesn't forget it, Minnie!" the Mother laughingly replied. "I do wish they'd get it settled! I don't like long engagements."

And Minnie wound up the conversation——if so chaotic a series of remarks deserves the name——with "Only think! We passed the Cedars this morning, just exactly as Mary

Davenant was standing at the gate, wishing good-bye to Mister——I forget his name. Of course we looked the other way."

By this time I was so hopelessly confused that I gave up listening, and followed the dinner down into the kitchen.

But to you, O hypercritical reader, resolute to believe no item of this weird adventure, what need to tell how the mutton was placed on the spit, and slowly unroasted——how the potatoes were wrapped in their skins, and handed over to the gardener to be buried——how, when the mutton had at length attained to rawness, the fire, which had gradually changed from red-heat to a mere blaze, died down so suddenly that the cook had only just time to catch its last flicker on the end of a match——or how the maid, having taken the mutton off the spit, carried it (backwards, of course) out of the house, to meet the butcher, who was coming (also backwards) down the road?

The longer I thought over this strange adventure, the more hopelessly tangled the mystery became: and it was a real relief to meet Arthur in the road, and get him to go with me up to the Hall, to learn what news the telegraph had brought. I told him, as we went, what had happened at the Station, but as to my further adventures I thought it best, for the present, to say nothing.

The Earl was sitting alone when we entered. "I am glad you are come in to keep me company," he said. "Muriel is gone to bed——the excitement of that terrible scene was too much for her——and Eric has gone to the hotel to pack his things, to start for London by the early train."

"Then the telegram has come?" I said.

"Did you not hear? Oh, I had forgotten: it came in after you left the Station. Yes, it's all right: Eric has got his commission; and, now that he has arranged matters with Muriel, he has business in town that must be seen to at once."

"What arrangement do you mean?" I asked with a sinking heart, as the thought of Arthur's crushed hopes came to my mind. "Do you mean that they are *engaged?*"

"They have been engaged——in a sense——for two years," the old man gently replied:

"that is, he has had my promise to consent to it, so soon as he could secure a permanent and settled line in life. I could never be happy with my child married to a man without an object to live for—without even an object to die for!"

"I hope they will be happy," a strange voice said. The speaker was evidently in the room, but I had not heard the door open, and I looked round in some astonishment. The Earl seemed to share my surprise. "Who spoke?" he exclaimed.

"It was I," said Arthur, looking at us with a worn, haggard face, and eyes from which the light of life seemed suddenly to have faded. "And let me wish *you* joy also, dear friend," he added, looking sadly at the Earl, and speaking in the same hollow tones that had startled us so much.

"Thank you," the old man said, simply and heartily.

A silence followed: then I rose, feeling sure that Arthur would wish to be alone, and bade our gentle host 'Good night': Arthur took his hand, but said nothing: nor did he speak again, as we went home, till we were in the house and had lit our bed-room candles. Then he said, more to himself than to me, "*The heart knoweth its own bitterness.* I never understood those words till now."

The next few days passed wearily enough. I felt no inclination to call again, by myself, at the Hall; still less to propose that Arthur should go with me: it seemed better to wait till Time—that gentle healer of our bitterest sorrows—should have helped him to recover from the first shock of the disappointment that had blighted his life.

Business, however, soon demanded my presence in town; and I had to announce to Arthur that I must leave him for a while. "But I hope to run down again in a month," I added. "I would stay now, if I could. I don't think it's good for you to be alone."

"No, I ca'n't face solitude, *here*, for long," said Arthur. "But don't think about *me*. I have made up my mind to accept a post in India, that has been offered me. Out there, I suppose I shall find something to live for; I ca'n't see *anything* at present. '*This life of mine I guard, as God's high gift, from scathe and wrong, Not greatly care to lose!'"*

"Yes," I said: "your name-sake bore as heavy a blow, and lived through it."

"A far heavier one than *mine*," said Arthur. "The woman *he* loved proved false. There is no such cloud as *that* on my memory of—— of——" He left the name unuttered, and went on hurriedly. "But *you* will return, will you not?"

"Yes, I shall come back for a short time."

"Do," said Arthur: "and you shall write and tell me of our friends. I'll send you my address when I'm settled down."

CHAPTER XXIV.

THE FROGS' BIRTHDAY-TREAT.

AND so it came to pass that, just a week after the day when my Fairy-friends first appeared as Children, I found myself taking a farewell-stroll through the wood, in the hope of meeting them once more. I had but to stretch myself on the smooth turf, and the 'eerie' feeling was on me in a moment.

"Put oor ear *welly* low down," said Bruno, "and I'll tell oo a secret! It's the Frogs' Birthday-Treat—and we've lost the Baby!"

"*What* Baby?" I said, quite bewildered by this complicated piece of news.

"The *Queen's* Baby, a course!" said Bruno. "Titania's Baby. And we's *welly* sorry. Sylvie, she's——oh so sorry!"

"*How* sorry is she?" I asked, mischievously.

"Three-quarters of a yard," Bruno replied with perfect solemnity. "And *I'm* a little sorry too," he added, shutting his eyes so as not to see that he was smiling.

"And what are you doing about the Baby?"

"Well, the *soldiers* are all looking for it——up and down——everywhere."

"The *soldiers?*" I exclaimed.

"Yes, a course!" said Bruno. "When there's no fighting to be done, the soldiers doos any little odd jobs, oo know."

I was amused at the idea of its being a 'little odd job' to find the Royal Baby. "But how did you come to lose it?" I asked.

"We put it in a flower," Sylvie, who had just joined us, explained with her eyes full of tears. "Only we ca'n't remember *which!*"

"She says *us* put it in a flower," Bruno interrupted, "'cause she doosn't want *I* to get punished. But it were really *me* what put it there. *Sylvie* were picking Dindledums."

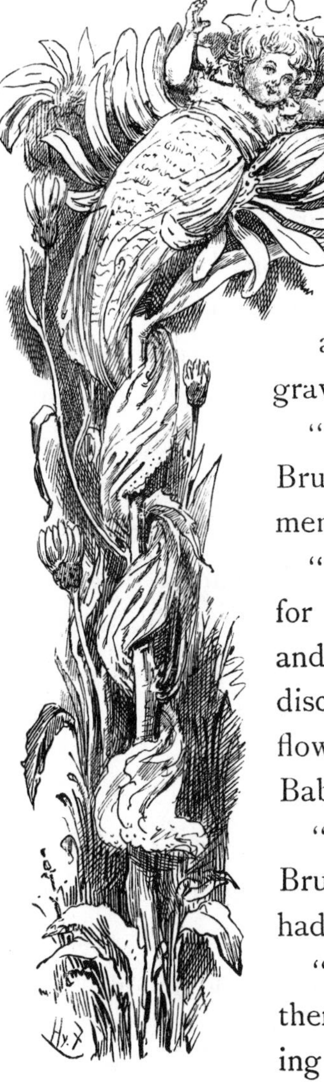

"You shouldn't say '*us* put it in a flower'," Sylvie very gravely remarked.

"Well, *hus*, then," said Bruno. "I never *can* remember those horrid H's!"

"Let me help you to look for it," I said. So Sylvie and I made a 'voyage of discovery' among all the flowers; but there was no Baby to be seen.

"What's become of Bruno?" I said, when we had completed our tour.

"He's down in the ditch there," said Sylvie, "amusing a young Frog."

I went down on my hands and knees to look for him, for I felt very curious to know how young Frogs *ought* to be amused. After a minute's search, I found him sitting at the edge of the ditch, by the side of the little Frog, and looking rather disconsolate.

"How are you getting on, Bruno?" I said, nodding to him as he looked up.

"Ca'n't amuse it no more," Bruno answered, very dolefully, "'cause it won't say what it would like to do next! I've showed it all the duck-weeds—and a live caddis-worm—but it won't say nuffin! What—would oo—like?' he shouted into the ear of the Frog: but the little creature sat quite still, and took no notice of him. "It's deaf, I think!" Bruno said, turning away with a sigh. "And it's time to get the Theatre ready."

"Who are the audience to be?"

"Only but Frogs," said Bruno. "But they haven't comed yet. They wants to be drove up, like sheep."

"Would it save time," I suggested, "if *I* were to walk round with Sylvie, to drive up the Frogs, while *you* get the Theatre ready?"

"That *are* a good plan!" cried Bruno. "But where *are* Sylvie?"

"I'm here!" said Sylvie, peeping over the edge of the bank. "I was just watching two Frogs that were having a race."

"Which won it?" Bruno eagerly inquired.

Sylvie was puzzled. "He *does* ask such hard questions!" she confided to me.

"And what's to happen in the Theatre?" I asked.

"First they have their Birthday-Feast," Sylvie said: "then Bruno does some Bits of Shakespeare; then he tells them a Story."

"I should think the Frogs like the Feast best. Don't they?"

"Well, there's generally very few of them that get any. They *will* keep their mouths shut so tight! And it's just as well they *do*," she added, "because Bruno likes to cook it himself: and he cooks *very* queerly. Now they're all in. Would you just help me to put them with their heads the right way?"

We soon managed this part of the business, though the Frogs kept up a most discontented croaking all the time.

"What *are* they saying?" I asked Sylvie.

"They're saying 'Fork! Fork!' It's very silly of them! You're not going to *have* forks!" she announced with some severity. "Those that want any Feast have just got to open their mouths, and Bruno 'll put some of it in!"

At this moment Bruno appeared, wearing a little white apron to show that he was a Cook, and carrying a tureen full of very queer-looking soup. I watched very carefully as he moved about among the Frogs; but I could not see that *any* of them opened their mouths to be fed—except one very young one, and I'm nearly sure it did it accidentally, in yawning. However Bruno instantly put a large spoonful of soup into its mouth, and the poor little thing coughed violently for some time.

So Sylvie and I had to share the soup between us, and to *pretend* to enjoy it, for it certainly was *very* queerly cooked.

I only ventured to take *one* spoonful of it ("Sylvie's Summer-Soup," Bruno said it was), and must candidly confess that it was not *at all* nice; and I could not feel surprised that so many of the guests had kept their mouths shut up tight.

"What's the soup *made* of, Bruno?" said Sylvie, who had put a spoonful of it to her lips, and was making a wry face over it.

And Bruno's answer was anything but encouraging. "Bits of things!"

The entertainment was to conclude with "Bits of Shakespeare," as Sylvie expressed it, which were all to be done by Bruno, Sylvie being fully engaged in making the Frogs keep their heads towards the stage: after which Bruno was to appear in his real character, and tell them a Story of his own invention.

"Will the Story have a Moral to it?" I asked Sylvie, while Bruno was away behind the hedge, dressing for the first 'Bit.'

"I *think* so," Sylvie replied doubtfully. "There generally *is* a Moral, only he puts it in too soon."

"And will he *say* all the Bits of Shakespeare?"

"No, he'll only *act* them," said Sylvie. "He knows hardly any of the words. When I see what he's dressed like, I've to tell the Frogs what character it is. They're always in such a hurry to guess! Don't you hear them all saying 'What? What?'" And so indeed they were: it had only sounded like croaking, till Sylvie explained it, but I could now make out the "Wawt? Wawt?" quite distinctly.

"But why do they try to guess it before they see it?"

"I don't know," Sylvie said: "but they always *do*. Sometimes they begin guessing weeks and weeks before the day!"

(So now, when you hear the Frogs croaking in a particularly melancholy way, you may be sure they're trying to guess Bruno's next Shakespeare 'Bit'. Isn't *that* interesting?)

However, the chorus of guessing was cut short by Bruno, who suddenly rushed on from behind the scenes, and took a flying leap down among the Frogs, to re-arrange them.

For the oldest and fattest Frog——who had never been properly arranged so that he could see the stage, and so had no idea what was going on——was getting restless, and had upset several of the Frogs, and turned others round with their heads the wrong way. And it was no good at all, Bruno said, to do a 'Bit' of Shakespeare when there was nobody to look at it (you see he didn't count *me* as anybody). So he set to work with a stick, stirring them up, very much as you would stir up tea in a cup, till most of them had at least *one* great stupid eye gazing at the stage.

"*Oo* must come and sit among them, Sylvie," he said in despair, "I've put these two side-by-side, with their noses the same way, ever so many times, but they *do* squarrel so!"

So Sylvie took her place as 'Mistress of the Ceremonies,' and Bruno vanished again behind the scenes, to dress for the first 'Bit.'

"Hamlet!" was suddenly proclaimed, in the clear sweet tones I knew so well. The croaking all ceased in a moment, and I turned to the stage, in some curiosity to see what Bruno's ideas were as to the behaviour of Shakespeare's greatest Character.

According to this eminent interpreter of the Drama, Hamlet wore a short black cloak (which he chiefly used for muffling up his face, as if he suffered a good deal from toothache), and turned out his toes very much as he walked. "To be or not to be!" Hamlet remarked in a cheerful tone, and then turned head-over-heels several times, his cloak dropping off in the performance.

I felt a little disappointed: Bruno's conception of the part seemed so wanting in dignity. "Won't he say any more of the speech?" I whispered to Sylvie.

"I *think* not," Sylvie whispered in reply. "He generally turns head-over-heels when he doesn't know any more words."

Bruno had meanwhile settled the question by disappearing from the stage; and the Frogs instantly began inquiring the name of the next Character.

"You'll know directly!" cried Sylvie, as she adjusted two or three young Frogs that had struggled round with their backs to the stage. "Macbeth!" she added, as Bruno re-appeared.

Macbeth had something twisted round him, that went over one shoulder and under the other arm, and was meant, I believe, for a Scotch plaid. He had a thorn in his hand, which he held out at arm's length, as if he were a little afraid of it. "Is this a *dagger?*" Macbeth inquired, in a puzzled sort of tone: and instantly a chorus of "Thorn! Thorn!" arose from the Frogs (I had quite learned to understand their croaking by this time).

"It's a *dagger!*" Sylvie proclaimed in a peremptory tone. "Hold your tongues!" And the croaking ceased at once.

Shakespeare has not told us, so far as I know, that Macbeth had any such eccentric habit as turning head-over-heels in private life: but Bruno evidently considered it quite an essential part of the character, and left the stage in a series of somersaults. However, he was back again in a few moments, having tucked under his chin the end of a tuft of wool (probably left on the thorn by a wandering sheep), which made a magnificent beard, that reached nearly down to his feet.

"Shylock!" Sylvie proclaimed. "No, I beg your pardon!" she hastily corrected herself, "King Lear! I hadn't noticed the crown." (Bruno had very cleverly provided one, which fitted him exactly, by cutting out the centre of a dandelion to make room for his head.)

King Lear folded his arms (to the imminent peril of his beard) and said, in a mild explanatory tone, "Ay, every *inch* a king!" and then paused, as if to consider how this could best be proved. And here, with all possible deference to Bruno as a Shakespearian critic, I *must* express my opinion that the poet did *not* mean his three great tragic heroes to be so strangely alike in their personal habits; nor do I believe that he would have accepted the faculty of turning head-over-heels as any proof at all of royal descent. Yet it appeared that King Lear, after deep meditation, could think of no other argument by which to prove his kingship: and, as this was the last of the 'Bits' of Shakespeare ("We never do more than *three*," Sylvie explained in a whisper), Bruno gave the audience quite a long series of somersaults before he finally retired, leaving the enraptured Frogs all crying out "More! More!" which I suppose was their way of encoring a performance. But Bruno wouldn't appear again, till the proper time came for telling the Story.

When he appeared at last in his *real* character, I noticed a remarkable change in his behaviour.

Harry Furniss

He tried no more somersaults. It was clearly his opinion that, however suitable the habit of turning head-over-heels might be to such petty individuals as Hamlet and King Lear, it would never do for *Bruno* to sacrifice his dignity to such an extent. But it was equally clear that he did not feel entirely at his ease, standing all alone on the stage, with no costume to disguise him: and though he began, several times, "There were a Mouse——," he kept glancing up and down, and on all sides, as if in search of more comfortable quarters from which to tell the Story. Standing on one side of the stage, and partly overshadowing it, was a tall fox-glove, which seemed, as the evening breeze gently swayed it hither and thither, to offer exactly the sort of accommodation that the orator desired. Having once decided on his quarters, it needed only a second or two for him to run up the stem like a tiny squirrel, and to seat himself astride on the topmost bend, where the fairy-bells clustered most closely, and from whence he could look down on his audience from such a height that all shyness vanished, and he began his Story merrily.

"Once there were a Mouse and a Crocodile and a Man and a Goat and a Lion." I had never heard the 'dramatis personæ' tumbled into a story with such profusion and in such reckless haste; and it fairly took my breath away. Even Sylvie gave a little gasp, and allowed three of the Frogs, who seemed to be getting tired of the entertainment, to hop away into the ditch, without attempting to stop them.

"And the Mouse found a Shoe, and it thought it were a Mouse-trap. So it got right in, and it stayed in ever so long."

"Why did it *stay* in?" said Sylvie. Her function seemed to be much the same as that of the Chorus in a Greek Play: she had to encourage the orator, and draw him out, by a series of intelligent questions.

"'Cause it thought it couldn't get out again," Bruno explained. "It were a clever mouse. It knew it couldn't get out of traps!"

"But why did it go in at all?" said Sylvie.

"—and it jamp, and it jamp," Bruno proceeded, ignoring this question, "and at last it got right out again. And it looked at the mark in the Shoe. And the Man's name were in it. So it knew it wasn't its own Shoe."

"Had it thought it *was?*" said Sylvie.

"Why, didn't I tell oo it thought it were a *Mouse-trap?*" the indignant orator replied. "Please, Mister Sir, will oo make Sylvie attend?" Sylvie was silenced, and was all attention: in fact, she and I were most of the audience now, as the Frogs kept hopping away, and there were very few of them left.

"So the Mouse gave the Man his Shoe. And the Man were welly glad, 'cause he hadn't got but one Shoe, and he were hopping to get the other."

Here I ventured on a question. "Do you mean 'hopping,' or 'hoping'?"

"Bofe," said Bruno. "And the Man took the Goat out of the Sack." ("We haven't heard of the *sack* before," I said. "Nor you won't hear of it again," said Bruno). "And he said to the Goat, 'Oo will walk about here till I comes back.' And he went and he tumbled into a deep hole. And the Goat walked round and round. And it walked under the Tree. And it wug its tail. And it looked up in the

Tree. And it sang a sad little Song. Oo never heard such a sad little Song!"

"Can you sing it, Bruno?" I asked.

"Iss, I can," Bruno readily replied. "And I sa'n't. It would make Sylvie cry——"

"It wouldn't!" Sylvie interrupted in great indignation. "And I don't believe the Goat sang it at all!"

"It did, though!" said Bruno. "It singed it right froo. I *sawed* it singing with its long beard——"

"It couldn't sing with its *beard*," I said, hoping to puzzle the little fellow: "a beard isn't a *voice*."

"Well then, *oo* couldn't walk with Sylvie!" Bruno cried triumphantly. "Sylvie isn't a *foot!*"

I thought I had better follow Sylvie's example, and be silent for a while. Bruno was too sharp for us.

"And when it had singed all the Song, it ran away——for to get along to look for the Man, oo know. And the Crocodile got along after it——for to bite it, oo know. And the Mouse got along after the Crocodile."

"Wasn't the Crocodile *running?*" Sylvie enquired. She appealed to me. "Crocodiles do run, don't they?"

I suggested "crawling" as the proper word.

"He wasn't running," said Bruno, "and he wasn't crawling. He went struggling along like a portmanteau. And he held his chin ever so high in the air——"

"What did he do *that* for?" said Sylvie.

"'cause he hadn't got a toofache!" said Bruno. "Ca'n't oo make out *nuffin* wizout I 'splain it? Why, if he'd had a toofache, a course he'd have held his head down——like this——and he'd have put a lot of warm blankets round it!"

"If he'd *had* any blankets," Sylvie argued.

"Course he *had* blankets!" retorted her brother. "Doos oo think Crocodiles goes walks wizout blankets? And he frowned with his eyebrows. And the Goat was welly flightened at his eyebrows!"

"I'd never be afraid of *eyebrows!*" exclaimed Sylvie.

"I should think oo *would*, though, if they'd got a Crocodile fastened to them, like these had! And so the Man jamp, and he jamp, and at last he got right out of the hole."

Sylvie gave another little gasp: this rapid dodging about among the characters of the Story had taken away her breath.

"And he runned away——for to look for the Goat, oo know. And he heard the Lion grunting——"

"Lions don't grunt," said Sylvie.

"This one did," said Bruno. "And its mouth were like a large cupboard. And it had plenty of room in its mouth. And the Lion runned after the Man——for to eat him, oo know. And the Mouse runned after the Lion."

"But the Mouse was running after the *Crocodile*," I said: "he couldn't run after *both!*"

Bruno sighed over the density of his audience, but explained very patiently. "He *did* runned after *bofe:* 'cause they went the same way! And first he caught the Crocodile, and then he didn't catch the Lion. And when he'd caught the Crocodile, what doos oo think he did——'cause he'd got pincers in his pocket?"

"I ca'n't guess," said Sylvie.

"Nobody couldn't guess it!" Bruno cried in high glee. "Why, he wrenched out that Crocodile's toof!"

"*Which* tooth?" I ventured to ask.

But Bruno was not to be puzzled. "The toof he were going to bite the Goat with, a course!"

"He couldn't be sure about that," I argued, "unless he wrenched out *all* its teeth."

Bruno laughed merrily, and half sang, as he swung himself backwards and forwards, "He did——wrenched——out——*all* its teef!"

"Why did the Crocodile wait to have them wrenched out?" said Sylvie.

"It had to wait," said Bruno.

I ventured on another question. "But what became of the Man who said 'You may wait here till I come back'?"

"He didn't say 'Oo *may*,'" Bruno explained. "He said, 'Oo *will*.' Just like Sylvie says to me 'Oo will do oor lessons till twelve o'clock.' Oh, I *wiss*," he added with a little sigh, "I *wiss* Sylvie would say 'Oo *may* do oor lessons'!"

This was a dangerous subject for discussion, Sylvie seemed to think. She returned to the Story. "But what became of the Man?"

"Well, the Lion springed at him. But it came so slow, it were three weeks in the air——"

"Did the Man wait for it all that time?" I said.

"Course he didn't!" Bruno replied, gliding head-first down the stem of the fox-glove, for the Story was evidently close to its end. "He sold his house, and he packed up his things, while the Lion were coming. And he went and he lived in another town. So the Lion ate the wrong man."

This was evidently the Moral: so Sylvie made her final proclamation to the Frogs. "The Story's finished! And whatever is to be *learned* from it," she added, aside to me, "I'm sure *I* don't know!"

I did not feel *quite* clear about it myself, so made no suggestion: but the Frogs seemed quite content, Moral or no Moral, and merely raised a husky chorus of "Off! Off!" as they hopped away.

CHAPTER XXV.

LOOKING EASTWARD.

"It's just a week," I said, three days later, to Arthur, "since we heard of Lady Muriel's engagement. I think *I* ought to call, at any rate, and offer my congratulations. Won't you come with me?"

A pained expression passed over his face. "When must you leave us?" he asked.

"By the first train on Monday."

"Well——yes, I *will* come with you. It would seem strange and unfriendly if I didn't. But this is only Friday. Give me till Sunday afternoon. I shall be stronger then."

Shading his eyes with one hand, as if half-ashamed of the tears that were coursing down his cheeks, he held the other out to me. It trembled as I clasped it.

I tried to frame some words of sympathy; but they seemed poor and cold, and I left them unspoken. "Good night!" was all I said.

"Good night, dear friend!" he replied. There was a manly vigour in his tone that convinced me he was wrestling with, and triumphing over, the great sorrow that had so nearly wrecked his life—and that, on the stepping-stone of his dead self, he would surely rise to higher things!

There was no chance, I was glad to think, as we set out on Sunday afternoon, of meeting *Eric* at the Hall, as he had returned to town the day after his engagement was announced. *His* presence might have disturbed the calm—the almost unnatural calm—with which Arthur met the woman who had won his heart, and murmured the few graceful words of sympathy that the occasion demanded.

Lady Muriel was perfectly radiant with happiness: sadness could not live in the light of such a smile: and even Arthur brightened under it, and, when she remarked "You see I'm watering my flowers, though it *is* the Sabbath-Day," his voice had almost its old ring of cheerfulness as he replied "Even on the Sabbath-Day works of mercy are allowed. But this *isn't* the Sabbath-Day. The Sabbath-Day has ceased to exist."

"I know it's not *Saturday*," Lady Muriel replied: "but isn't Sunday often called 'the Christian Sabbath'?"

"It is so called, I think, in recognition of the *spirit* of the Jewish institution, that one day in seven should be a day of *rest*. But I hold that Christians are freed from the *literal* observance of the Fourth Commandment."

"Then where is our *authority* for Sunday observance?"

"We have, first, the fact that the seventh day was 'sanctified', when God rested from the work of Creation. That is binding on us as *Theists*. Secondly, we have the fact that 'the Lord's Day' is a *Christian* institution. That is binding on us as *Christians*."

"And your practical rules would be——?"

"First, as Theists, to keep it *holy* in some special way, and to make it, so far as is reasonably possible, a day of *rest*. Secondly, as *Christians*, to attend public worship."

"And what of *amusements?*"

"I would say of them, as of all kinds of *work*, whatever is innocent on a week-day, is innocent on Sunday, provided it does not interfere with the duties of the day."

"Then you would allow children to *play* on Sunday?"

"Certainly I should. Why make the day irksome to their restless natures?"

"I have a letter somewhere," said Lady Muriel, "from an old friend, describing the way in which Sunday was kept in her younger days. I will fetch it for you."

"I had a similar description, *vivâ voce*, years ago," Arthur said when she had left us, "from a little girl. It was really touching to hear the melancholy tone in which she said 'On Sunday I mustn't play with my doll! On Sunday I mustn't run on the sands! On Sunday I mustn't dig in the garden!' Poor child! She had indeed abundant cause for hating Sunday!"

"Here is the letter," said Lady Muriel, returning. "Let me read you a piece of it."

"*When, as a child, I first opened my eyes on a Sunday-morning, a feeling of dismal anticipation, which began at least on the Friday, culminated. I knew what was before me, and my wish, if not my word, was 'Would God it were evening!' It was no day of rest, but a day of texts, of catechisms (Watts'), of tracts about converted swearers, godly charwomen, and edifying deaths of sinners saved.*

"*Up with the lark, hymns and portions of Scripture had to be learned by heart till* 8 *o'clock, when there were family-prayers, then breakfast, which I was never able to enjoy, partly from the fast already undergone, and partly from the outlook I dreaded.*

"*At* 9 *came Sunday-School; and it made me indignant to be put into the class with the village-children, as well as alarmed lest, by some mistake of mine, I should be put below them.*

"*The Church-Service was a veritable Wilderness of Zin. I wandered in it, pitching the tabernacle of my thoughts on the lining of the square family-pew, the fidgets of my small brothers, and the horror of knowing that, on the Monday, I should have to write out, from memory, jottings of the rambling disconnected extempore sermon, which might have had any text but its own, and to stand or fall by the result.*

"*This was followed by a cold dinner at* 1 (*servants to have* no *work*), *Sunday-School again from* 2 *to* 4, *and Evening-Service at* 6. *The intervals were perhaps the greatest trial of all, from the efforts I had to make, to be less than usually sinful, by reading books and sermons as barren as the Dead Sea. There was but one rosy spot, in the distance, all that day: and that was 'bed-time,' which never could come too early!*"

"Such teaching was well meant, no doubt," said Arthur; "but it must have driven many of its victims into deserting the Church-Services altogether."

"I'm afraid *I* was a deserter this morning," she gravely said. "I had to write to Eric. Would you—would you mind my telling you something he said about *prayer?* It had never struck me in that light before."

"In what light?" said Arthur.

"Why, that all Nature goes by fixed, regular laws——Science has proved *that.* So that asking God to *do* anything (except of course praying for *spiritual* blessings) is to expect a miracle: and we've no right to do *that.* I've not put it as well as *he* did: but that was the outcome of it, and it has confused me. Please tell me what you can say in answer to it."

"I don't propose to discuss *Captain Lindon's* difficulties," Arthur gravely replied; "specially as he is not present. But, if it is *your* difficulty," (his voice unconsciously took a tenderer tone) "then I will speak."

"It *is* my difficulty," she said anxiously.

"Then I will begin by asking 'Why did you except *spiritual* blessings?' Is not your mind a part of Nature?"

"Yes, but Free-Will comes in there—I can *choose* this or that; and God can influence my choice."

"Then you are not a Fatalist?"

"Oh, no!" she earnestly exclaimed.

"Thank God!" Arthur said to himself, but in so low a whisper that only *I* heard it. "You grant then that I can, by an act of free choice, move this cup," suiting the action to the word, "*this* way or *that* way?"

"Yes, I grant it."

"Well, let us see how far the result is produced by fixed laws. The *cup* moves because certain mechanical forces are impressed on it by my *hand.* My *hand* moves because certain forces—electric, magnetic, or whatever 'nerve-force' may prove to be—are impressed on it by my *brain.* This nerve-force, stored in the brain, would probably be traceable, if Science were complete, to chemical forces supplied to the brain by the blood, and ultimately derived from the food I eat and the air I breathe."

"But would not that be Fatalism? Where would Free-Will come in?"

"In *choice* of nerves," replied Arthur. "The nerve-force in the brain may flow just as naturally down one nerve as down another. We need something more than a fixed Law of Nature to settle *which* nerve shall carry it. That 'something' is Free-Will."

Her eyes sparkled." "I see what you mean!" she exclaimed. "Human Free-Will is an exception to the system of fixed Law. Eric said something like that. And then I think he pointed out that God can only influence Nature by influencing Human Wills. So that we *might* reasonably pray '*give us this day our daily bread*,' because many of the causes that produce bread are under Man's control. But to pray for rain, or fine weather, would be as unreasonable as——" she checked herself, as if fearful of saying something irreverent.

In a hushed, low tone, that trembled with emotion, and with the solemnity of one in the presence of death, Arthur slowly replied "*Shall he that contendeth with the Almighty instruct him?* Shall we, 'the swarm that in the noontide beam were born,' feeling in ourselves the power to direct, this way or that, the forces of Nature——of *Nature*, of which we form so trivial a part——shall we, in our boundless arrogance, in our pitiful conceit, *deny* that power to the Ancient of Days? Saying, to our Creator, 'Thus far and no further. Thou madest, but thou canst not rule!'?"

Lady Muriel had covered her face in her hands, and did not look up. She only murmured "Thanks, thanks!" again and again.

We rose to go. Arthur said, with evident effort, "One word more. If you would *know* the power of Prayer—in anything and everything that Man can need—*try* it. *Ask, and it shall be given you.* I—*have* tried it. I *know* that God answers prayer!"

Our walk home was a silent one, till we had nearly reached the lodgings: then Arthur murmured—and it was almost an echo of my own thoughts—"*What knowest thou, O wife, whether thou shalt save thy husband?*"

The subject was not touched on again. We sat on, talking, while hour after hour, of this our last night together, glided away unnoticed. He had much to tell me about India, and the new life he was going to, and the *work* he hoped to do. And his great generous soul seemed so filled with noble ambition as to have no space left for any vain regret or selfish repining.

"Come, it is nearly morning!" Arthur said at last, rising and leading the way upstairs.

"The sun will be rising in a few minutes: and, though I *have* basely defrauded you of your last chance of a night's rest here, I'm sure you'll forgive me: for I really *couldn't* bring myself to say 'Good night' sooner. And God knows whether you'll ever see me again, or hear of me!"

"*Hear* of you I am certain I shall!" I warmly responded, and quoted the concluding lines of that strange poem 'Waring':—

"Oh, never star
Was lost here, but it rose afar!
Look East, where whole new thousands are!
In Vishnu-land what Avatar?"

"Aye, look Eastward!" Arthur eagerly replied, pausing at the stair-case window, which commanded a fine view of the sea and the eastward horizon. "The West is the fitting tomb for all the sorrow and the sighing, all the errors and the follies of the Past: for all its withered Hopes and all its buried Loves! From the East comes new strength, new ambition, new Hope, new Life, new Love! Look Eastward! Aye, look Eastward!"

His last words were still ringing in my ears as I entered my room, and undrew the window-curtains, just in time to see the sun burst in glory from his ocean-prison, and clothe the world in the light of a new day.

"So may it be for him, and me, and all of us!" I mused. "All that is evil, and dead, and hopeless, fading with the Night that is past! All that is good, and living, and hopeful, rising with the dawn of Day!

"Fading, with the Night, the chilly mists, and the noxious vapours, and the heavy shadows, and the wailing gusts, and the owl's melancholy hootings: rising, with the Day, the darting shafts of light, and the wholesome morning breeze, and the warmth of a dawning life, and the mad music of the lark! Look Eastward!

"Fading, with the Night, the clouds of ignorance, and the deadly blight of sin, and the silent tears of sorrow: and ever rising, higher, higher, with the Day, the radiant dawn of knowledge, and the sweet breath of purity, and the throb of a world's ecstasy! Look Eastward!

"Fading, with the Night, the memory of a dead love, and the withered leaves of a blighted hope, and the sickly repinings and moody regrets that numb the best energies of the soul: and rising, broadening, rolling upward like a living flood, the manly resolve, and the dauntless will, and the heavenward gaze of faith——*the substance of things hoped for, the evidence of things not seen!*

"Look Eastward! Aye, look Eastward!"

THE END.

INDEX.

A CATALOG OF SELECTED

DOVER BOOKS

IN ALL FIELDS OF INTEREST

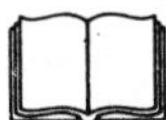

A CATALOG OF SELECTED DOVER BOOKS IN ALL FIELDS OF INTEREST

FRANK LLOYD WRIGHT'S HOLLYHOCK HOUSE, Donald Hoffmann. Lavishly illustrated, carefully documented study of one of Wright's most controversial residential designs. Over 120 photographs, floor plans, elevations, etc. Detailed perceptive text by noted Wright scholar. Index. 128pp. 9¼ × 10¾.
27133-1 Pa. $10.95

THE MALE AND FEMALE FIGURE IN MOTION: 60 Classic Photographic Sequences, Eadweard Muybridge. 60 true-action photographs of men and women walking, running, climbing, bending, turning, etc., reproduced from rare 19th-century masterpiece. vi + 121pp. 9 × 12. 24745-7 Pa. $10.95

1001 QUESTIONS ANSWERED ABOUT THE SEASHORE, N. J. Berrill and Jacquelyn Berrill. Queries answered about dolphins, sea snails, sponges, starfish, fishes, shore birds, many others. Covers appearance, breeding, growth, feeding, much more. 305pp. 5¼ × 8¼. 23366-9 Pa. $7.95

GUIDE TO OWL WATCHING IN NORTH AMERICA, Donald S. Heintzelman. Superb guide offers complete data and descriptions of 19 species: barn owl, screech owl, snowy owl, many more. Expert coverage of owl-watching equipment, conservation, migrations and invasions, etc. Guide to observing sites. 84 illustrations. xiii + 193pp. 5⅜ × 8½. 27344-X Pa. $7.95

MEDICINAL AND OTHER USES OF NORTH AMERICAN PLANTS: A Historical Survey with Special Reference to the Eastern Indian Tribes, Charlotte Erichsen-Brown. Chronological historical citations document 500 years of usage of plants, trees, shrubs native to eastern Canada, northeastern U.S. Also complete identifying information. 343 illustrations. 544pp. 6½ × 9¼. 25951-X Pa. $12.95

STORYBOOK MAZES, Dave Phillips. 23 stories and mazes on two-page spreads: Wizard of Oz, Treasure Island, Robin Hood, etc. Solutions. 64pp. 8¼ × 11.
23628-5 Pa. $2.95

NEGRO FOLK MUSIC, U.S.A., Harold Courlander. Noted folklorist's scholarly yet readable analysis of rich and varied musical tradition. Includes authentic versions of over 40 folk songs. Valuable bibliography and discography. xi + 324pp. 5⅜ × 8½. 27350-4 Pa. $7.95

MOVIE-STAR PORTRAITS OF THE FORTIES, John Kobal (ed.). 163 glamor, studio photos of 106 stars of the 1940s: Rita Hayworth, Ava Gardner, Marlon Brando, Clark Gable, many more. 176pp. 8⅜ × 11¼. 23546-7 Pa. $10.95

BENCHLEY LOST AND FOUND, Robert Benchley. Finest humor from early 30s, about pet peeves, child psychologists, post office and others. Mostly unavailable elsewhere. 73 illustrations by Peter Arno and others. 183pp. 5⅜ × 8½.
22410-4 Pa. $4.95

YEKL and THE IMPORTED BRIDEGROOM AND OTHER STORIES OF YIDDISH NEW YORK, Abraham Cahan. Film Hester Street based on Yekl (1896). Novel, other stories among first about Jewish immigrants on N.Y.'s East Side. 240pp. 5⅜ × 8½. 22427-9 Pa. $5.95

SELECTED POEMS, Walt Whitman. Generous sampling from *Leaves of Grass*. Twenty-four poems include "I Hear America Singing," "Song of the Open Road," "I Sing the Body Electric," "When Lilacs Last in the Dooryard Bloom'd," "O Captain! My Captain!"—all reprinted from an authoritative edition. Lists of titles and first lines. 128pp. 5³⁄₁₆ × 8¼. 26878-0 Pa. $1.00

THE BEST TALES OF HOFFMANN, E. T. A. Hoffmann. 10 of Hoffmann's most important stories: "Nutcracker and the King of Mice," "The Golden Flowerpot," etc. 458pp. 5⅜ × 8½. 21793-0 Pa. $8.95

FROM FETISH TO GOD IN ANCIENT EGYPT, E. A. Wallis Budge. Rich detailed survey of Egyptian conception of "God" and gods, magic, cult of animals, Osiris, more. Also, superb English translations of hymns and legends. 240 illustrations. 545pp. 5⅜ × 8½. 25803-3 Pa. $10.95

FRENCH STORIES/CONTES FRANÇAIS: A Dual-Language Book, Wallace Fowlie. Ten stories by French masters, Voltaire to Camus: "Micromegas" by Voltaire; "The Atheist's Mass" by Balzac; "Minuet" by de Maupassant; "The Guest" by Camus, six more. Excellent English translations on facing pages. Also French-English vocabulary list, exercises, more. 352pp. 5⅜ × 8½. 26443-2 Pa. $8.95

CHICAGO AT THE TURN OF THE CENTURY IN PHOTOGRAPHS: 122 Historic Views from the Collections of the Chicago Historical Society, Larry A. Viskochil. Rare large-format prints offer detailed views of City Hall, State Street, the Loop, Hull House, Union Station, many other landmarks, circa 1904-1913. Introduction. Captions. Maps. 144pp. 9⅜ × 12¼. 24656-6 Pa. $12.95

OLD BROOKLYN IN EARLY PHOTOGRAPHS, 1865-1929, William Lee Younger. Luna Park, Gravesend race track, construction of Grand Army Plaza, moving of Hotel Brighton, etc. 157 previously unpublished photographs. 165pp. 8⅞ × 11¾. 23587-4 Pa. $12.95

THE MYTHS OF THE NORTH AMERICAN INDIANS, Lewis Spence. Rich anthology of the myths and legends of the Algonquins, Iroquois, Pawnees and Sioux, prefaced by an extensive historical and ethnological commentary. 36 illustrations. 480pp. 5⅜ × 8½. 25967-6 Pa. $8.95

AN ENCYCLOPEDIA OF BATTLES: Accounts of Over 1,560 Battles from 1479 B.C. to the Present, David Eggenberger. Essential details of every major battle in recorded history from the first battle of Megiddo in 1479 B.C. to Grenada in 1984. List of Battle Maps. New Appendix covering the years 1967-1984. Index. 99 illustrations. 544pp. 6½ × 9¼. 24913-1 Pa. $14.95

SAILING ALONE AROUND THE WORLD, Captain Joshua Slocum. First man to sail around the world, alone, in small boat. One of great feats of seamanship told in delightful manner. 67 illustrations. 294pp. 5⅜ × 8½. 20326-3 Pa. $4.95

ANARCHISM AND OTHER ESSAYS, Emma Goldman. Powerful, penetrating, prophetic essays on direct action, role of minorities, prison reform, puritan hypocrisy, violence, etc. 271pp. 5⅜ × 8½. 22484-8 Pa. $5.95

MYTHS OF THE HINDUS AND BUDDHISTS, Ananda K. Coomaraswamy and Sister Nivedita. Great stories of the epics; deeds of Krishna, Shiva, taken from puranas, Vedas, folk tales; etc. 32 illustrations. 400pp. 5⅜ × 8½. 21759-0 Pa. $8.95

BEYOND PSYCHOLOGY, Otto Rank. Fear of death, desire of immortality, nature of sexuality, social organization, creativity, according to Rankian system. 291pp. 5⅜ × 8½. 20485-5 Pa. $7.95

A THEOLOGICO-POLITICAL TREATISE, Benedict Spinoza. Also contains unfinished Political Treatise. Great classic on religious liberty, theory of government on common consent. R. Elwes translation. Total of 421pp. 5⅜ × 8½. 20249-6 Pa. $7.95

EARLY NINETEENTH-CENTURY CRAFTS AND TRADES, Peter Stockham (ed.). Extremely rare 1807 volume describes to youngsters the crafts and trades of the day: brickmaker, weaver, dressmaker, bookbinder, ropemaker, saddler, many more. Quaint prose, charming illustrations for each craft. 20 black-and-white line illustrations. 192pp. 4⅝ × 6. 27293-1 Pa. $4.95

VICTORIAN FASHIONS AND COSTUMES FROM HARPER'S BAZAR, 1867–1898, Stella Blum (ed.). Day costumes, evening wear, sports clothes, shoes, hats, other accessories in over 1,000 detailed engravings. 320pp. 9⅜ × 12¼. 22990-4 Pa. $12.95

GUSTAV STICKLEY, THE CRAFTSMAN, Mary Ann Smith. Superb study surveys broad scope of Stickley's achievement, especially in architecture. Design philosophy, rise and fall of the Craftsman empire, descriptions and floor plans for many Craftsman houses, more. 86 black-and-white halftones. 31 line illustrations. Introduction. 208pp. 6½ × 9¼. 27210-9 Pa. $9.95

THE LONG ISLAND RAIL ROAD IN EARLY PHOTOGRAPHS, Ron Ziel. Over 220 rare photos, informative text document origin (1844) and development of rail service on Long Island. Vintage views of early trains, locomotives, stations, passengers, crews, much more. Captions. 8⅞ × 11¾. 26301-0 Pa. $13.95

THE BOOK OF OLD SHIPS: From Egyptian Galleys to Clipper Ships, Henry B. Culver. Superb, authoritative history of sailing vessels, with 80 magnificent line illustrations. Galley, bark, caravel, longship, whaler, many more. Detailed, informative text on each vessel by noted naval historian. Introduction. 256pp. 5⅜ × 8½. 27332-6 Pa. $6.95

TEN BOOKS ON ARCHITECTURE, Vitruvius. The most important book ever written on architecture. Early Roman aesthetics, technology, classical orders, site selection, all other aspects. Morgan translation. 331pp. 5⅜ × 8½. 20645-9 Pa. $8.95

THE HUMAN FIGURE IN MOTION, Eadweard Muybridge. More than 4,500 stopped-action photos, in action series, showing undraped men, women, children jumping, lying down, throwing, sitting, wrestling, carrying, etc. 390pp. 7⅞ × 10⅝. 20204-6 Clothbd. $24.95

TREES OF THE EASTERN AND CENTRAL UNITED STATES AND CANADA, William M. Harlow. Best one-volume guide to 140 trees. Full descriptions, woodlore, range, etc. Over 600 illustrations. Handy size. 288pp. 4½ × 6⅜. 20395-6 Pa. $4.95

SONGS OF WESTERN BIRDS, Dr. Donald J. Borror. Complete song and call repertoire of 60 western species, including flycatchers, juncoes, cactus wrens, many more—includes fully illustrated booklet. Cassette and manual 99913-0 $8.95

GROWING AND USING HERBS AND SPICES, Milo Miloradovich. Versatile handbook provides all the information needed for cultivation and use of all the herbs and spices available in North America. 4 illustrations. Index. Glossary. 236pp. 5⅜ × 8½. 25058-X Pa. $5.95

BIG BOOK OF MAZES AND LABYRINTHS, Walter Shepherd. 50 mazes and labyrinths in all—classical, solid, ripple, and more—in one great volume. Perfect inexpensive puzzler for clever youngsters. Full solutions. 112pp. 8⅛ × 11. 22951-3 Pa. $3.95

PIANO TUNING, J. Cree Fischer. Clearest, best book for beginner, amateur. Simple repairs, raising dropped notes, tuning by easy method of flattened fifths. No previous skills needed. 4 illustrations. 201pp. 5⅜ × 8½. 23267-0 Pa. $4.95

A SOURCE BOOK IN THEATRICAL HISTORY, A. M. Nagler. Contemporary observers on acting, directing, make-up, costuming, stage props, machinery, scene design, from Ancient Greece to Chekhov. 611pp. 5⅜ × 8½. 20515-0 Pa. $10.95

THE COMPLETE NONSENSE OF EDWARD LEAR, Edward Lear. All nonsense limericks, zany alphabets, Owl and Pussycat, songs, nonsense botany, etc., illustrated by Lear. Total of 320pp. 5⅜ × 8½. (USO) 20167-8 Pa. $5.95

VICTORIAN PARLOUR POETRY: An Annotated Anthology, Michael R. Turner. 117 gems by Longfellow, Tennyson, Browning, many lesser-known poets. "The Village Blacksmith," "Curfew Must Not Ring Tonight," "Only a Baby Small," dozens more, often difficult to find elsewhere. Index of poets, titles, first lines. xxiii + 325pp. 5⅝ × 8¼. 27044-0 Pa. $7.95

DUBLINERS, James Joyce. Fifteen stories offer vivid, tightly focused observations of the lives of Dublin's poorer classes. At least one, "The Dead," is considered a masterpiece. Reprinted complete and unabridged from standard edition. 160pp. 5³⁄₁₆ × 8¼. 26870-5 Pa. $1.00

THE HAUNTED MONASTERY and THE CHINESE MAZE MURDERS, Robert van Gulik. Two full novels by van Gulik, set in 7th-century China, continue adventures of Judge Dee and his companions. An evil Taoist monastery, seemingly supernatural events; overgrown topiary maze hides strange crimes. 27 illustrations. 328pp. 5⅜ × 8½. 23502-5 Pa. $7.95

THE BOOK OF THE SACRED MAGIC OF ABRAMELIN THE MAGE, translated by S. MacGregor Mathers. Medieval manuscript of ceremonial magic. Basic document in Aleister Crowley, Golden Dawn groups. 268pp. 5⅜ × 8½. 23211-5 Pa. $7.95

NEW RUSSIAN-ENGLISH AND ENGLISH-RUSSIAN DICTIONARY, M. A. O'Brien. This is a remarkably handy Russian dictionary, containing a surprising amount of information, including over 70,000 entries. 366pp. 4½ × 6⅛. 20208-9 Pa. $8.95

HISTORIC HOMES OF THE AMERICAN PRESIDENTS, Second, Revised Edition, Irvin Haas. A traveler's guide to American Presidential homes, most open to the public, depicting and describing homes occupied by every American President from George Washington to George Bush. With visiting hours, admission charges, travel routes. 175 photographs. Index. 160pp. 8¼ × 11. 26751-2 Pa. $10.95

NEW YORK IN THE FORTIES, Andreas Feininger. 162 brilliant photographs by the well-known photographer, formerly with *Life* magazine. Commuters, shoppers, Times Square at night, much else from city at its peak. Captions by John von Hartz. 181pp. 9¼ × 10¾. 23585-8 Pa. $12.95

INDIAN SIGN LANGUAGE, William Tomkins. Over 525 signs developed by Sioux and other tribes. Written instructions and diagrams. Also 290 pictographs. 111pp. 6⅛ × 9¼. 22029-X Pa. $3.50

ANATOMY: A Complete Guide for Artists, Joseph Sheppard. A master of figure drawing shows artists how to render human anatomy convincingly. Over 460 illustrations. 224pp. 8⅜ × 11¼. 27279-6 Pa. $9.95

MEDIEVAL CALLIGRAPHY: Its History and Technique, Marc Drogin. Spirited history, comprehensive instruction manual covers 13 styles (ca. 4th century thru 15th). Excellent photographs; directions for duplicating medieval techniques with modern tools. 224pp. 8⅜ × 11¼. 26142-5 Pa. $11.95

DRIED FLOWERS: How to Prepare Them, Sarah Whitlock and Martha Rankin. Complete instructions on how to use silica gel, meal and borax, perlite aggregate, sand and borax, glycerine and water to create attractive permanent flower arrangements. 12 illustrations. 32pp. 5⅜ × 8½. 21802-3 Pa. $1.00

EASY-TO-MAKE BIRD FEEDERS FOR WOODWORKERS, Scott D. Campbell. Detailed, simple-to-use guide for designing, constructing, caring for and using feeders. Text, illustrations for 12 classic and contemporary designs. 96pp. 5⅜ × 8½. 25847-5 Pa. $2.95

OLD-TIME CRAFTS AND TRADES, Peter Stockham. An 1807 book created to teach children about crafts and trades open to them as future careers. It describes in detailed, nontechnical terms 24 different occupations, among them coachmaker, gardener, hairdresser, lacemaker, shoemaker, wheelwright, copper-plate printer, milliner, trunkmaker, merchant and brewer. Finely detailed engravings illustrate each occupation. 192pp. 4⅝ × 6. 27398-9 Pa. $4.95

THE HISTORY OF UNDERCLOTHES, C. Willett Cunnington and Phyllis Cunnington. Fascinating, well-documented survey covering six centuries of English undergarments, enhanced with over 100 illustrations: 12th-century laced-up bodice, footed long drawers (1795), 19th-century bustles, 19th-century corsets for men, Victorian "bust improvers," much more. 272pp. 5⅝ × 8¼. 27124-2 Pa. $9.95

ARTS AND CRAFTS FURNITURE: The Complete Brooks Catalog of 1912, Brooks Manufacturing Co. Photos and detailed descriptions of more than 150 now very collectible furniture designs from the Arts and Crafts movement depict davenports, settees, buffets, desks, tables, chairs, bedsteads, dressers and more, all built of solid, quarter-sawed oak. Invaluable for students and enthusiasts of antiques, Americana and the decorative arts. 80pp. 6½ × 9¼. 27471-3 Pa. $7.95

HOW WE INVENTED THE AIRPLANE: An Illustrated History, Orville Wright. Fascinating firsthand account covers early experiments, construction of planes and motors, first flights, much more. Introduction and commentary by Fred C. Kelly. 76 photographs. 96pp. 8¼ × 11. 25662-6 Pa. $7.95

THE ARTS OF THE SAILOR: Knotting, Splicing and Ropework, Hervey Garrett Smith. Indispensable shipboard reference covers tools, basic knots and useful hitches; handsewing and canvas work, more. Over 100 illustrations. Delightful reading for sea lovers. 256pp. 5⅜ × 8½. 26440-8 Pa. $6.95

FRANK LLOYD WRIGHT'S FALLINGWATER: The House and Its History, Second, Revised Edition, Donald Hoffmann. A total revision—both in text and illustrations—of the standard document on Fallingwater, the boldest, most personal architectural statement of Wright's mature years, updated with valuable new material from the recently opened Frank Lloyd Wright Archives. "Fascinating"—*The New York Times*. 116 illustrations. 128pp. 9¼ × 10¾. 27430-6 Pa. $10.95

PHOTOGRAPHIC SKETCHBOOK OF THE CIVIL WAR, Alexander Gardner. 100 photos taken on field during the Civil War. Famous shots of Manassas, Harper's Ferry, Lincoln, Richmond, slave pens, etc. 244pp. 10⅝ × 8¼.
22731-6 Pa. $9.95

FIVE ACRES AND INDEPENDENCE, Maurice G. Kains. Great back-to-the-land classic explains basics of self-sufficient farming. The one book to get. 95 illustrations. 397pp. 5⅜ × 8½. 20974-1 Pa. $6.95

SONGS OF EASTERN BIRDS, Dr. Donald J. Borror. Songs and calls of 60 species most common to eastern U.S.: warblers, woodpeckers, flycatchers, thrushes, larks, many more in high-quality recording. Cassette and manual 99912-2 $8.95

A MODERN HERBAL, Margaret Grieve. Much the fullest, most exact, most useful compilation of herbal material. Gigantic alphabetical encyclopedia, from aconite to zedoary, gives botanical information, medical properties, folklore, economic uses, much else. Indispensable to serious reader. 161 illustrations. 888pp. 6½ × 9¼. 2-vol. set. (USO) Vol. I: 22798-7 Pa. $9.95
Vol. II: 22799-5 Pa. $9.95

HIDDEN TREASURE MAZE BOOK, Dave Phillips. Solve 34 challenging mazes accompanied by heroic tales of adventure. Evil dragons, people-eating plants, bloodthirsty giants, many more dangerous adversaries lurk at every twist and turn. 34 mazes, stories, solutions. 48pp. 8¼ × 11. 24566-7 Pa. $2.95

LETTERS OF W. A. MOZART, Wolfgang A. Mozart. Remarkable letters show bawdy wit, humor, imagination, musical insights, contemporary musical world; includes some letters from Leopold Mozart. 276pp. 5⅜ × 8½. 22859-2 Pa. $6.95

BASIC PRINCIPLES OF CLASSICAL BALLET, Agrippina Vaganova. Great Russian theoretician, teacher explains methods for teaching classical ballet. 118 illustrations. 175pp. 5⅜ × 8½. 22036-2 Pa. $3.95

THE JUMPING FROG, Mark Twain. Revenge edition. The original story of The Celebrated Jumping Frog of Calaveras County, a hapless French translation, and Twain's hilarious "retranslation" from the French. 12 illustrations. 66pp. 5⅜ × 8½.
22686-7 Pa. $3.50

BEST REMEMBERED POEMS, Martin Gardner (ed.). The 126 poems in this superb collection of 19th- and 20th-century British and American verse range from Shelley's "To a Skylark" to the impassioned "Renascence" of Edna St. Vincent Millay and to Edward Lear's whimsical "The Owl and the Pussycat." 224pp. 5⅜ × 8½.
27165-X Pa. $3.95

COMPLETE SONNETS, William Shakespeare. Over 150 exquisite poems deal with love, friendship, the tyranny of time, beauty's evanescence, death and other themes in language of remarkable power, precision and beauty. Glossary of archaic terms. 80pp. 5³⁄₁₆ × 8¼. 26686-9 Pa. $1.00

BODIES IN A BOOKSHOP, R. T. Campbell. Challenging mystery of blackmail and murder with ingenious plot and superbly drawn characters. In the best tradition of British suspense fiction. 192pp. 5⅜ × 8½. 24720-1 Pa. $5.95

THE WIT AND HUMOR OF OSCAR WILDE, Alvin Redman (ed.). More than 1,000 ripostes, paradoxes, wisecracks: Work is the curse of the drinking classes; I can resist everything except temptation; etc. 258pp. 5⅜ × 8½. 20602-5 Pa. $4.95

SHAKESPEARE LEXICON AND QUOTATION DICTIONARY, Alexander Schmidt. Full definitions, locations, shades of meaning in every word in plays and poems. More than 50,000 exact quotations. 1,485pp. 6½ × 9¼. 2-vol. set.
Vol. 1: 22726-X Pa. $15.95
Vol. 2: 22727-8 Pa. $15.95

SELECTED POEMS, Emily Dickinson. Over 100 best-known, best-loved poems by one of America's foremost poets, reprinted from authoritative early editions. No comparable edition at this price. Index of first lines. 64pp. $5\frac{3}{16} \times 8\frac{1}{4}$.
26466-1 Pa. $1.00

CELEBRATED CASES OF JUDGE DEE (DEE GOONG AN), translated by Robert van Gulik. Authentic 18th-century Chinese detective novel; Dee and associates solve three interlocked cases. Led to van Gulik's own stories with same characters. Extensive introduction. 9 illustrations. 237pp. 5⅜ × 8½.
23337-5 Pa. $5.95

THE MALLEUS MALEFICARUM OF KRAMER AND SPRENGER, translated by Montague Summers. Full text of most important witchhunter's "bible," used by both Catholics and Protestants. 278pp. 6⅝ × 10. 22802-9 Pa. $10.95

SPANISH STORIES/CUENTOS ESPAÑOLES: A Dual-Language Book, Angel Flores (ed.). Unique format offers 13 great stories in Spanish by Cervantes, Borges, others. Faithful English translations on facing pages. 352pp. 5⅜ × 8½.
25399-6 Pa. $7.95

THE CHICAGO WORLD'S FAIR OF 1893: A Photographic Record, Stanley Appelbaum (ed.). 128 rare photos show 200 buildings, Beaux-Arts architecture, Midway, original Ferris Wheel, Edison's kinetoscope, more. Architectural emphasis; full text. 116pp. 8¼ × 11. 23990-X Pa. $9.95

OLD QUEENS, N.Y., IN EARLY PHOTOGRAPHS, Vincent F. Seyfried and William Asadorian. Over 160 rare photographs of Maspeth, Jamaica, Jackson Heights, and other areas. Vintage views of DeWitt Clinton mansion, 1939 World's Fair and more. Captions. 192pp. 8⅞ × 11. 26358-4 Pa. $12.95

CAPTURED BY THE INDIANS: 15 Firsthand Accounts, 1750–1870, Frederick Drimmer. Astounding true historical accounts of grisly torture, bloody conflicts, relentless pursuits, miraculous escapes and more, by people who lived to tell the tale. 384pp. 5⅜ × 8½. 24901-8 Pa. $7.95

THE WORLD'S GREAT SPEECHES, Lewis Copeland and Lawrence W. Lamm (eds.). Vast collection of 278 speeches of Greeks to 1970. Powerful and effective models; unique look at history. 842pp. 5⅜ × 8½. 20468-5 Pa. $12.95

THE BOOK OF THE SWORD, Sir Richard F. Burton. Great Victorian scholar/adventurer's eloquent, erudite history of the "queen of weapons"—from prehistory to early Roman Empire. Evolution and development of early swords, variations (sabre, broadsword, cutlass, scimitar, etc.), much more. 336pp. 6⅛ × 9¼. 25434-8 Pa. $8.95

AUTOBIOGRAPHY: The Story of My Experiments with Truth, Mohandas K. Gandhi. Boyhood, legal studies, purification, the growth of the Satyagraha (nonviolent protest) movement. Critical, inspiring work of the man responsible for the freedom of India. 480pp. 5⅜ × 8½. (USO) 24593-4 Pa. $6.95

CELTIC MYTHS AND LEGENDS, T. W. Rolleston. Masterful retelling of Irish and Welsh stories and tales. Cuchulain, King Arthur, Deirdre, the Grail, many more. First paperback edition. 58 full-page illustrations. 512pp. 5⅜ × 8½. 26507-2 Pa. $9.95

THE PRINCIPLES OF PSYCHOLOGY, William James. Famous long course complete, unabridged. Stream of thought, time perception, memory, experimental methods; great work decades ahead of its time. 94 figures. 1,391pp. 5⅜ × 8½. 2-vol. set.
Vol. I: 20381-6 Pa. $12.95
Vol. II: 20382-4 Pa. $12.95

THE WORLD AS WILL AND REPRESENTATION, Arthur Schopenhauer. Definitive English translation of Schopenhauer's life work, correcting more than 1,000 errors, omissions in earlier translations. Translated by E. F. J. Payne. Total of 1,269pp. 5⅜ × 8½. 2-vol. set. Vol. 1: 21761-2 Pa. $10.95
Vol. 2: 21762-0 Pa. $11.95

MAGIC AND MYSTERY IN TIBET, Madame Alexandra David-Neel. Experiences among lamas, magicians, sages, sorcerers, Bonpa wizards. A true psychic discovery. 32 illustrations. 321pp. 5⅜ × 8½. (USO) 22682-4 Pa. $7.95

THE EGYPTIAN BOOK OF THE DEAD, E. A. Wallis Budge. Complete reproduction of Ani's papyrus, finest ever found. Full hieroglyphic text, interlinear transliteration, word-for-word translation, smooth translation. 533pp. 6½ × 9¼. 21866-X Pa. $9.95

MATHEMATICS FOR THE NONMATHEMATICIAN, Morris Kline. Detailed, college-level treatment of mathematics in cultural and historical context, with numerous exercises. Recommended Reading Lists. Tables. Numerous figures. 641pp. 5⅜ × 8½. 24823-2 Pa. $11.95

THEORY OF WING SECTIONS: Including a Summary of Airfoil Data, Ira H. Abbott and A. E. von Doenhoff. Concise compilation of subsonic aerodynamic characteristics of NACA wing sections, plus description of theory. 350pp. of tables. 693pp. 5⅜ × 8½. 60586-8 Pa. $13.95

THE RIME OF THE ANCIENT MARINER, Gustave Doré, S. T. Coleridge. Doré's finest work; 34 plates capture moods, subtleties of poem. Flawless full-size reproductions printed on facing pages with authoritative text of poem. "Beautiful. Simply beautiful."—*Publisher's Weekly*. 77pp. 9¼ × 12. 22305-1 Pa. $5.95

NORTH AMERICAN INDIAN DESIGNS FOR ARTISTS AND CRAFTSPEOPLE, Eva Wilson. Over 360 authentic copyright-free designs adapted from Navajo blankets, Hopi pottery, Sioux buffalo hides, more. Geometrics, symbolic figures, plant and animal motifs, etc. 128pp. 8⅜ × 11. (EUK) 25341-4 Pa. $6.95

SCULPTURE: Principles and Practice, Louis Slobodkin. Step-by-step approach to clay, plaster, metals, stone; classical and modern. 253 drawings, photos. 255pp. 8⅛ × 11. 22960-2 Pa. $9.95

THE INFLUENCE OF SEA POWER UPON HISTORY, 1660–1783, A. T. Mahan. Influential classic of naval history and tactics still used as text in war colleges. First paperback edition. 4 maps. 24 battle plans. 640pp. 5⅜ × 8½.
25509-3 Pa. $12.95

THE STORY OF THE TITANIC AS TOLD BY ITS SURVIVORS, Jack Winocour (ed.). What it was really like. Panic, despair, shocking inefficiency, and a little heroism. More thrilling than any fictional account. 26 illustrations. 320pp. 5⅜ × 8½.
20610-6 Pa. $7.95

FAIRY AND FOLK TALES OF THE IRISH PEASANTRY, William Butler Yeats (ed.). Treasury of 64 tales from the twilight world of Celtic myth and legend: "The Soul Cages," "The Kildare Pooka," "King O'Toole and his Goose," many more. Introduction and Notes by W. B. Yeats. 352pp. 5⅜ × 8½. 26941-8 Pa. $7.95

BUDDHIST MAHAYANA TEXTS, E. B. Cowell and Others (eds.). Superb, accurate translations of basic documents in Mahayana Buddhism, highly important in history of religions. The Buddha-karita of Asvaghosha, Larger Sukhavativyuha, more. 448pp. 5⅜ × 8½.
25552-2 Pa. $9.95

ONE TWO THREE . . . INFINITY: Facts and Speculations of Science, George Gamow. Great physicist's fascinating, readable overview of contemporary science: number theory, relativity, fourth dimension, entropy, genes, atomic structure, much more. 128 illustrations. Index. 352pp. 5⅜ × 8½. 25664-2 Pa. $7.95

ENGINEERING IN HISTORY, Richard Shelton Kirby, et al. Broad, nontechnical survey of history's major technological advances: birth of Greek science, industrial revolution, electricity and applied science, 20th-century automation, much more. 181 illustrations. ". . . excellent . . ."—Isis. Bibliography. vii + 530pp. 5⅜ × 8¼.
26412-2 Pa. $13.95

Prices subject to change without notice.

Available at your book dealer or write for free catalog to Dept. GI, Dover Publications, Inc., 31 East 2nd St., Mineola, N.Y. 11501. Dover publishes more than 500 books each year on science, elementary and advanced mathematics, biology, music, art, literary history, social sciences and other areas.